# THE
# SABOTEUR

## TRUE ADVENTURES OF THE GENTLEMAN
## COMMANDO WHO TOOK ON THE NAZIS

# PAUL KIX

WILLIAM
COLLINS

William Collins
An imprint of HarperCollins*Publishers*
1 London Bridge Street
London
SE1 9GF

www.WilliamCollinsBooks.com

First published in Great Britain by William Collins in 2017
First published in the United States by Harper, an imprint of HarperCollins in 2017

1

A catalogue record for this book is available from the British Library

HB ISBN 978-0-00-755380-8
TPB ISBN 978-0-00-755382-2

Designed by William Ruoto

Set in Dante MT

Printed and bound in Great Britain by CPI Group (UK) Ltd, Croydon CR0 4YY

MIX
Paper from
responsible sources

FSC
www.fsc.org

FSC® C007454

*For Sonya, as always*

# AUTHOR'S NOTE

This is a work of narrative nonfiction, meant to relay what it was like for Robert de La Rochefoucauld to fight the Nazis from occupied France as a special operative and *résistant*. I relied on a few primary sources to tell this story, most notably La Rochefoucauld's memoir, *La Liberté, C'est Mon Plaisir: 1940–1946*, published in 2002, a decade before his death. La Rochefoucauld's family, ever gracious, also gave me a copy of the audio recording in which Robert recounted his war and life for his children and grandchildren. This was great source material, as was a DVD I received, which was directed, edited, and produced by one of Robert's nephews, and which tells the tale of his storied family, specifically his parents, his nine brothers and sisters, and the courage that Robert himself needed to fight his war. The DVD, like the audio recording, was made for the La Rochefoucauld family to share with successive generations, but Robert's daughter Constance was kind enough to make me a copy.

I spoke with her and her three siblings at length about their father—in person, over Skype, on the telephone, and by email. I kept contacting them long after I said I would, and kept apologizing for it. But Astrid, Constance, Hortense, and Jean were always amenable and happy to share what they knew. I'm eternally grateful.

This narrative is the result of four years of work, with research and reporting conducted in five countries. I talked with dozens of people, read roughly fifty books, in English and French, and parsed thousands of pages of military and historical documents, in four languages. Despite all this, and no doubt because of the secret nature of La Rochefoucauld's work, there are certain instances where Robert's account of what happened is the best and sometimes only account of what happened. Thankfully, in those spots, Robert's recollections are vivid and reflect the larger historical record of the region and time.

**PAUL KIX, JANUARY 2017**

# THE
# SABOTEUR

# PROLOGUE

H is family kept asking him *why*. Why would a hero of the war align himself with one of its alleged traitors? Why would Robert de La Rochefoucauld, a man who had been knighted in France's Legion of Honor, risk sullying his name to defend someone like Maurice Papon, who had been charged, these many decades after World War II, with helping the Germans during the Occupation?

The question trailed La Rochefoucauld all the way to the witness stand, on a February afternoon in 1998, four months into a criminal trial that would last six, and become the longest in French history.

When he entered the courtroom, La Rochefoucauld looked debonair. His silver hair had just begun to recede, and he still swept it straight back. At seventy-four, he carried the dignified air of middle age. He had brown eyes that took in the world with an ironic slant, the mark of his aristocratic forebears, and a Roman, ruling-class nose. His posture was tall and upright as he walked to the stand and gave his oath and, lowering himself to his seat at the center of international attention, he appeared remarkably relaxed—his complexion even had a bronze tint, despite the bleak French winter. He remained a handsome man, nearly as handsome as he'd been in those first postwar years, when he'd moved from one girl to the next, until he'd met Bernadette de Marcieu de Gontaut-Biron, his wife and mother of his four children.

On the stand, La Rochefoucauld wore a green tweed check jacket over a light blue shirt and a patterned brown tie. The outfit suited the country squire, who'd traveled to Bordeaux today from Pont Chevron, his thirty-room chateau overlooking sixty-six acres in the Loiret department of north-central France. He radiated a charisma that burned all the brighter when set against the gray sobriety of the courthouse. La Rochefoucauld looked better than anyone in the room.

A reputation for bravery preceded him, and almost out of curiosity for why someone like La Rochefoucauld would defend someone like Papon, the court allowed him an opening statement. La Rochefoucauld nodded at the defendant, who sat in a dark suit behind bulletproof glass. The makings of wry exasperation curled La Rochefoucauld's lips as he recalled events from fifty years earlier.

"First, I would like to say that in 1940, although I was very young, I was against the Germans, against Pétain and against Vichy. I was in favor of the continuation of the war in the South of France and in North Africa." He was sixteen then, and came from a family that despised the Germans. His father, Olivier, a decorated World War I officer who'd re-enlisted in 1939, was arrested by the Nazis five days after the Armistice in part because he'd tried to fight beyond the agreed-to peace. His mother, Consuelo, who ran a local chapter of the Red Cross, was known to German officers as the Terrible Countess. On the stand, La Rochefoucauld skipped over almost all of what happened after 1940, the acts of bravery that had earned him four war medals and a knighthood. He instead focused his testimony on one episode in the summer of 1944 and experiences that greatly compromised the allegations against Papon.

Maurice Papon had been an administrator within the German-collaborating Vichy government. He rose to a position of authority in the Gironde department of southwestern France, whose jurisdiction included Bordeaux. The charge against Papon was that from his post as general secretary of the Gironde prefecture, overseeing Jewish affairs, he signed deportation papers for eight of the ten convoys of Jewish civilians that left for internment camps in France, and ultimately the concentration camps of Eastern Europe. In total, Vichy officials in the Gironde shipped out 1,690 Jews, 223 of them children. Papon had been indicted for crimes against humanity.

The reality of Papon's service was far messier than the picture the prosecutors depicted. Despite Papon's lofty title, he was a local administrator within Vichy and so removed from authority that he later claimed he didn't know the final destination of the cattle cars or the fate that awaited Jews there. Furthermore, Vichy's national police chief, René Bousquet, was the person who had actually issued the deportations. Papon claimed that he had merely done as he was told, that he was a bureaucrat with the misfortune of literally signing off on orders. When the trial opened in the fall of 1997, the historian who first unearthed the papers that held Papon's signatures, Michel Bergès, told the court he no longer believed the documents proved Papon's guilt. Even two attorneys for the victims' families felt "queasiness" about prosecuting the man.

Robert de La Rochefoucauld (pronounced *Roash-foo-coe*) knew something that would further undercut the state's case against Papon. As he told the court, in the summer of 1944, he joined a band of Resistance fighters who called their group Charly. "There was a Jewish community there," La Rochefoucauld testified, "and when I saw how many of them there were, I asked them what was the reason for them being part of this [group]. The commander's answer was very simple: . . . 'They had been warned by the prefecture that there would be a rounding up.'" In other words, these Jewish men were grateful they had been tipped off and happy to fight in the Resistance.

In the 1960s, La Rochefoucauld met and grew friendly with Papon, who was by then Paris' prefect of police. "I learned he was at the [Gironde] prefecture during the war," Robert testified. "It was then that I told him the story of the Jews of [Charly]. He smiled and said, 'We were very well organized at the prefecture.'" Despite La

Rochefoucauld's own heroics, he said on the stand it took "monstrous reserves of personal courage" to work for the Resistance within Vichy. "I consider Mr. Papon one of those brave men."

His testimony lasted fifteen minutes, and following it one of the judges read written statements from four other *résistants*, whose sentiments echoed La Rochefoucauld's: If Papon had signed the deportation documents, he had also helped Jews elude imprisonment. Roger-Samuel Bloch, a Jewish *résistant* from Bordeaux, wrote that from November 1943 to June 1944, Papon hid and lodged him several times, at considerable risk to his career and life.

The court recessed until the next morning. La Rochefoucauld walked outside and took in a Bordeaux that was so very different from 1944, where no swastika flags swayed in the breeze, where no people wondered who would betray them, where no one listened for the hard tap of Gestapo boots coming up behind. How to relay in fifteen minutes the anxiety and fear that once clung to a man as surely as the wisps of cigarette smoke in a crowded café? How to explain the complexity of life under Occupation to generations of free people who would never experience the war's exhausting calculations and would therefore view it in simple terms of good and evil? La Rochefoucauld was beyond the gated entryway of the courthouse when he saw Papon protesters move toward him. One of them got very close, and spit on him. La Rochefoucauld stared at the young man, furious, but kept walking.

What people younger than him could not understand—and this included his adult children and nieces and nephews—was that his motivation for testifying wasn't really even about Papon, a man he hadn't known during the war. La Rochefoucauld took the stand instead out of a fealty for the brotherhood, the tiny bands of *résistants* who had fought the mighty Nazi Occupation. They knew the personal deprivations, and they saw the extremes of barbarity. A silent understanding still passed between these rebels who had endured and prevailed as La Rochefoucauld had. A shared loyalty still bound them. And no allegation, not even one as grave as crimes against humanity, could sever that tie.

La Rochefoucauld hadn't said any of this, of course, because he seldom said anything about his service. Even when other veterans had alluded to his exploits at commemorative parties over the years, he'd stayed quiet. He was humble, but it also pained him to dredge it all up again. So his four children and nieces and nephews gathered the snippets they'd overheard of La Rochefoucauld's famous war, and they'd discussed them throughout their childhood and well into adulthood: *Had he really met Hitler once, only to later slink across German lines dressed as a nun? Had he really escaped a firing squad or killed a man with his bare hands? Had he really trained with a secret force of British agents that changed the course of the war?* For most of his adult life, La Rochefoucauld remained, even to family, a man unknown.

Now, La Rochefoucauld got in his Citroën and began the five-hour drive back to Pont Chevron. Maybe one day he would tell the whole story of why he had defended someone like Papon, which was really a story of what he'd seen during the war and why he'd fought when so few had.

Maybe one day, he told himself. But not today.

# CHAPTER 1

One cannot answer for his courage if he has never been in danger.

—François de La Rochefoucauld, *Maxims*

On May 16, 1940, a strange sound came from the east. Robert de La Rochefoucauld was at home with his siblings when he heard it: a low buzz that grew louder by the moment until it was a persistent and menacing drone. He moved to one of the floor-to-ceiling windows of the family chateau, called Villeneuve, set on thirty-five acres just outside Soissons, an hour and a half northeast of Paris. On the horizon, Robert saw what he had long dreaded.

It was a fleet of aircraft, ominous and unending. The planes already shadowed Soissons' town square, and the smaller ones now broke from the formation. These were the German Stukas, the two-seater single-engine planes with arched wings that looked to Robert as predatory as they in fact were. They dove out of the sky, the sirens underneath them whining a high-pitched wail. The sight and sound paralyzed the family, which gathered round the windows. Then the bombs dropped: indiscriminately and catastrophically, over Soissons and ever closer to the chateau. Huge plumes of dirt and sod and splintered wood shot up wherever the bombs touched down, followed by cavernous reports that were just as frightening; Robert could feel them thump against his chest. The world outside his window was suddenly loud and on fire. And amid the cacophony, he heard his mother scream: "We must go, we must go, we must go!"

World War II had come to Soissons. Though it had been declared eight months earlier, the fight had truly begun five days ago, when the Germans feinted a movement of troops in Belgium, and then broke through the Allied lines south of there, in the Ardennes, a heavily forested collection of hills in France. The Allies had thought that terrain too treacherous for a Nazi offensive—which is of course why the Germans had chosen it.

Three columns of German tanks stretching back for more than one hundred miles had emerged from the forest. And for the past few days, the French and Belgian soldiers who defended the line, many of them reservists, had lived a nightmare if they'd lived at all: attacked from the sky by Stukas and from the ground by ghastly panzers too numerous to be counted. In response, Britain's Royal Air Force had sent out seventy-one bombers, but they were overwhelmed, and thirty-nine of the aircraft had not returned, the greatest rate of loss in any operation of comparable size in British aviation history. On the ground, the Germans soon raced through a hole thirty miles wide and fifteen miles deep. They did not head southwest to Paris, as the French military expected, but northwest to the English Channel, where they could cut off elite French and British soldiers stuck in Belgium and effectively take all of France.

Soissons stood in that northwestern trajectory. Robert and his six siblings rushed outside, where the scream of a Stuka dive was even more horrifying. Bombs fell on Soissons' factories and the children ran to the family sedan, their mother, Consuelo, ushering them into the car. Consuelo told her eldest, Henri, then seventeen, one year older than Robert, to go to the castle at Châteaneuf-sur-Cher, the home of Consuelo's mother, the Duchess of Maillé, some 230 miles south. Consuelo would stay behind; as the local head of the Red Cross, she had to oversee its response in the Aisne department. She would catch up with them later, she shouted at Henri and Robert. Her stony look told her eldest sons that there was no point in arguing. She was not about to lose her children, who ranged in age from seventeen to four, to the same fiery blitzkrieg that had perhaps already consumed her husband, Olivier, who—at fifty— was serving as a liaison officer for the RAF on the Franco-German border.

"Go!" she told Henri.

So the children set out, the bombs falling around them, largely unchecked by Allied planes. Though history would dub these days the Battle for France, France's fleet was spread throughout its worldwide empire, with only 25 percent stationed in country and only one-quarter of that in operational formations. This left Soissons with minimal protection. The ceaseless screaming whine of a Stuka and deep reverberating echo of its bombs drove the La Rochefoucaulds to the roads in something like a mindless panic.

But the roads were almost at a standstill. The Germans bombed the train stations and many of the bridges in Soissons and the surrounding towns. The occasional Stuka strafed the flow of humanity, and the younger children in the La Rochefoucaulds' car screamed with each report, but the gunfire always landed behind them.

As they inched out of the Nazis' northwestern trajectory that afternoon, more and more Frenchmen joined the procession. Already cars were breaking down around them. Some families led horses or donkeys that carried whatever possessions they could gather and load. It was a surreal scene for Robert and the other La Rochefoucauld children, pressing their faces against the windows, a movement unlike any modern France had witnessed. The French reconnaissance pilot Antoine de Saint-Exupéry saw the exodus from the sky, and as he would later write in his book, *Flight to Arras*, "German bombers bearing down upon the villages squeezed out a whole people and sent it flowing down the highways like a black syrup . . . I can see from my plane the long swarming highways, that interminable syrup flowing endless to the horizon."

Hours passed, the road stretched ahead, and though the occasional

Stuka whined above, the La Rochefoucaulds were not harmed by them—these planes' main concern was joining the formation heading to the Channel. News was sparse. Local officials had sometimes been the first to flee. The La Rochefoucauld children saw around them cars with mattresses tied to their roofs as protection from errant bombs. But Robert watched as those mattresses served a more natural purpose when the traffic forced people to camp on that first night, somewhere in the high plains of central France.

Makeshift shelters rose around them just off the road, and though no one heard the echo of bombs, Henri ordered his siblings to stay together as they climbed, stiff-legged, out of the car. Henri was serious and studious, the firstborn child who was also the favorite. Robert, with high cheekbones and a countenance that rounded itself into a slight pout, as if his lips were forever holding a cigarette, was the more handsome of the two, passing for something like Cary Grant's French cousin. But he was also the wild one. He managed to attend a different boarding school nearly every year. The brothers understood that they were to watch over their younger siblings now as surrogate parents, but it was really Henri who was in charge. Robert, after all, had been the one immature enough to dangle from the parapet of the family chateau, fifty feet above the ground, or to once say *shit* in front of Grandmother La Rochefoucauld, for the thrill it gave his siblings.

The children gathered together, Henri and Robert, Artus and Pierre Louis, fifteen and thirteen, and their sister Yolaine, twelve. The youngest ones, Carmen and Aimery, seven and four, naturally weren't part of their older siblings' clique. They were not invited to play soccer with their brothers and Yolaine, and only occasionally did they swim with them in the Aisne river, which flowed around the family estate. They were already their own unit, unaware of the idiosyncrasies and dynamics of the older crew: the way Artus favored the company of his younger brother Pierre Louis to Henri and Robert's, or the way all the boys tended to gang up on Yolaine, the lone girl, until Robert defended her, sometimes with his fists, the bad brother with the good heart.

Years later Robert would not recall how they spent that first night—on blankets that Consuelo had quickly stored into the trunk or with grass as their bedding and the night stars to comfort them. But he would remember walking among the great anxious swarm of humanity, who settled in clusters on a field that, under the moonlight, seemed to stretch to the horizon. Robert was as scared as the travelers around him. But, in the jokes the refugees told or even in their silent resolve, he felt a sense of fraternity spreading, tangible and real. He had often lived his life at a remove from this kind of experience: He was landed gentry, his lineage running through one thousand years of French history. When Robert and his family vacationed at exclusive resorts in Nice or Saint Tropez, they avoided mass transit, traveling aboard Grandmother La Rochefoucauld's private rail car—with four sleeper cabs, a lounge and dining room. But the night air and communion of his countrymen stirred something in Robert, something similar to what his father, Olivier, had experienced twenty years earlier in the trenches of the Great War. There, among soldiers of all classes, Olivier had dropped his vestigial ties to monarchy and become, he said, a committed Republican. Tonight, looking out at the campfires and the families who laid down wherever they could, with whatever they had, Robert felt the urge to honor *La France*, and to defend it, even if the military couldn't.

The children were on the road for four days. As many as eight million people fled their homes during the Battle for France, or one-fifth of the country's population. The highways became so congested during this exodus that bicycles were the best mode of travel, as if the streets of Bombay had moved to the French countryside. Abandoning their car and walking would have been quicker for the La Rochefoucaulds, but Henri would have none of it. Thousands of parents lost track of their children during the movement south, and newspapers would fill their pages for months afterward with advertisements from families in search of the missing. The La Rochefoucaulds stayed in the car, always together, nudging ahead, taking hours just to cross the Loire River on the outskirts of southern France, on one of the few bridges the Germans hadn't bombed.

The skies were clear of Stukas now, yet the roads remained as crowded as ever. This was a full-on panic, Robert thought, and though he wasn't the best of students he understood its cause. It wasn't just the invasion people saw that forced them out of their homes. It was the invasion they'd replayed for twenty years, the invasion they'd remembered.

World War I had killed 1.7 million Frenchmen, or 18 percent of those who fought, a higher proportion than any other developed country. Many battles were waged in France, and the fighting was so horrific, its damage so ubiquitous, it was as if the war had never ended. The La Rochefoucaulds' own estate, Villeneuve, had been a battle site, captured and recaptured seventeen times, the French defending the chateau, the Germans across the Aisne river, firing. The fighting left Villeneuve in rubble, and the neighboring town of Soissons didn't fare much better: 80 percent of it was destroyed. Even after the La Rochefoucaulds rebuilt, the foundation of the estate showed the classic pockmarks of heavy shells. The soil of Villeneuve's thirty-five acres smoldered for seven years from all the mortar rounds. Steam rose from the earth, too hot to till. Well into the 1930s, Robert would watch as a plow stopped and a farmhand dug out a buried artillery round or hand grenade.

The 1,600-year-old cathedral in Soissons, where the La Rochefoucaulds occasionally went for Mass, carried the indentations of bullet and artillery fire, clustering here and boring into the edifice there, from its stone foundation to its mighty Gothic peaks. Storefronts all around them wore similar marks, while veterans

like Robert's father hobbled home after service. For Olivier, an ankle wound incurred in 1915 limited his ability to walk unassisted.
His injury intruded into his pastimes: When he hunted game, he
brought his wife, and Consuelo carried the gun until Olivier spotted the prey, which allowed him to momentarily ditch his cane and
hoist the rifle to his shoulder. Olivier was lucky. Other veterans
were so disfigured, they didn't appear in public.

"Throughout my childhood, I heard people talk mostly about
the Great War: my parents, my grandparents, my uncles," Robert
later said. But even as it remained a constant topic, Olivier seldom
discussed its basic facts: his four years at the front, as an officer
whose job was to watch artillery shells land on German positions
and relay back whether the next round should be aimed higher
or lower. Nor did Olivier discuss the more intimate details of the
fighting, as other veterans did in memoirs: stepping on the "meat"
of dead comrades in an offensive or the madness the trenches induced. Instead Olivier walked the halls of Villeneuve, in some
sort of private and almost unceasing conversation with the ghosts
of his past. He was a distant father, telling his children that they
"must not cry—ever," and finding solace in nature's beauty. He had
earned a law degree after the war, but spent Robert's childhood
as Villeneuve's gentleman farmer. Olivier felt most at ease talking
about the dahlias he planted. Consuelo, who'd lost two brothers
to the trenches, was far more outspoken. She instructed her children that they were never to buy German-made goods and told
her daughters they could not learn such an indelicate tongue. Even
her job moored her to the past: As chair of the Aisne chapter of the
Red Cross, Consuelo spent most of her time helping families whose
lives had been upended by the war.

The La Rochefoucaulds were not unique: No one in France
could look beyond his disfigured memories. The French military
was itself so scarred that it did nothing in the face of Hitler's mount-
ing power. In 1936, the führer's army reoccupied the Rhineland (the

areas around the Rhine River in Belgium), in violation of World War I treaties, without a fight, even though France had one hundred divisions, and the Third Reich's crippled army could send only three battalions to the Rhine. As Gen. Alfred Jodl, head of the German armed forces operational staff, later testified: "Considering the situation we were in, the French covering army could have blown us to pieces." But despite overwhelming numerical strength, the French did nothing, and Germany retook the Rhine. Hitler never feared France again.

German military might grew, and as a new war seemed imminent, the French kept forestalling its reality, traumatized by what they'd already endured. In 1938, the French Parliament voted 537 to 75 for the Munich Agreement, which gave Hitler portions of Czechoslovakia. Meanwhile, the World War I veteran and novelist Jean Giono wrote that war was pointless, and if it broke out again soldiers should desert. "There is no glory in being French," Giono wrote. "There is only one glory: To be alive." Léon Emery, a primary school teacher, wrote a newspaper column that may as well have been a refrain for people in the late 1930s: "Rather servitude than war."

This frightened pacifism reigned even after the new war began. In the fall of 1939, after Britain and France declared war on Germany, William Shirer, an American journalist, took a train along a hundred-mile stretch of the Franco-German border: "The train crew told me not a shot had been fired on this front . . . The troops . . . went about their business [building fortifications] in full sight and range of each other . . . The Germans were hauling up guns and supplies on the railroad line, but the French did not disturb them. Queer kind of war."

So at last, in May 1940, when the German planes screamed overhead, many Frenchmen saw not just a new style of warfare but the nightmares of the last twenty years superimposed on the wings of those Stukas. That's why it took four days for the La Rochefoucauld children to reach their grandmother's house: Memory heightened the terror of Hitler's blitzkrieg. "We were lucky we weren't on the road longer," Robert's younger sister Yolaine later said.

Grandmother Maillé's estate sat high above Châteauneuf-sur-Cher, a three-winged castle whose sprawling acreage served as the town's eponymous centerpiece. It was a stunning, almost absurdly grand home, spread across six floors and sixty rooms, featuring some thirty bedrooms, three salons, and an art gallery. The La Rochefoucauld children, accustomed to the liveried lifestyle, never tired of coming here. But on this spring day, the bliss of the reunion gave way rather quickly to a hollowed-out exhaustion. The anxious travel had depleted the children—and the grandmother who'd awaited them. Making matters worse, the radio kept reporting German gains, alarming everyone anew.

That very night, the Second Panzer Division reached Abbeville, at the mouth of the Somme river and the English Channel. The Allies' best soldiers, still in Belgium, were trapped. A note of panic rose in the broadcasters' voices. The Nazis now had a stronghold within the country—never in the four years of the Great War had the Germans gained such a position. And now they had done it in just ten days.

Consuelo rejoined the family a few nights later. She told her children how she had barely escaped death. Her car, provided by the Red Cross, was bombed by the Germans. She was not in it at the time, she said, but it quickened her departure. She got another car from a local politician and stuffed family heirlooms into it, certain that the German bombardment would continue and the Villeneuve estate would be destroyed again. Her Red Cross office was already in shambles. "This is it. No more windows, almost no more doors," Consuelo had written in her diary on May 18, from her desk at the local headquarters. "Two bombings during the day. The rail station is barely functional. We have to close [this diary] . . . until times get better."

But after reuniting with her children, times did not get better. The radio blared constantly in the chateau, and the reports were grim. On June 3, three hundred German aircraft bombed the Citroën and Renault factories on the southwestern border of Paris, killing 254, 195 of them civilians. Parisians left the city in such droves that cows wandered some of its richest streets, mooing. Trains on the packed railway platforms departed without destination; they just left. The government evacuated on June 10 to the south of France, where everyone else had already headed, and the city was declared open—the French military would not defend it. The Nazis marched in at noon on June 14.

Robert and his family bunched round the radio in their grandmother's salon that day, their faces ashen. The reporters said that roughly two million people had fled and the city was silent. Then came the news flashes: the Nazis cutting through the west end and down the Champs-Elysées; a quiet procession of tanks, armored cars, and motorized infantry; only a few Frenchmen watching them from the boulevards or storefronts that had not been boarded up; and suddenly, high above the Eiffel Tower, a swastika flag whipping in the breeze.

And still, no one had heard from Olivier, who had been stationed somewhere on the Franco-German border. Consuelo, a brash and strong woman who rolled her own cigarettes from corn husks, appeared anxious now before her children, a frailty they rarely saw, as she openly fretted about her country and husband. The news turned still worse. Marshal Philippe Pétain, who had assumed control of France's government, took to the radio June 17. "It is with a heavy heart that I tell you today that we must try to cease hostilities," he said.

Robert drew back when he heard the words. Was Pétain, a nearly mythical figure, the hero of the Great War's Battle of Verdun, asking for an armistice? Was the man who'd once beaten the Germans now surrendering to them?

The war itself never reached Grandmother Maillé's chateau, roughly 170 miles south of Paris, but in the days ahead the family heard fewer grim reports from the front, which was unsettling in its own way. It meant soldiers were following Pétain's orders. June 22 formalized the surrender: The governments of both countries agreed to sign an armistice. On that day, the La Rochefoucaulds gathered round the radio once again, unsure how their lives would change.

Hitler wanted this armistice signed on the same spot as the last—in a railway car in the forest of Compiègne. It seemed the Great War had not ended for him either. At 3:15 on an otherwise beautiful summer afternoon, Hitler arrived in his Mercedes, accompanied by his top generals, and walked to an opening in the forest. There, he stepped on a great granite block, about three feet above the ground with engraving in French that read: HERE ON THE ELEVENTH OF NOVEMBER 1918 SUCCUMBED THE CRIMINAL PRIDE OF THE GERMAN EMPIRE—VANQUISHED BY THE FREE PEOPLES WHICH IT TRIED TO ENSLAVE.

William Shirer stood some fifty yards from the führer. "I look for the expression in Hitler's face," Shirer later wrote. "It is afire with scorn, anger, hate, revenge, triumph. He steps off the monument and contrives to make even this gesture a masterpiece of contempt . . . He swiftly snaps his hands on his hips, arches his shoulders, plants his feet wide part. It is a magnificent gesture . . . of burning contempt for this place now and all that it has stood for in the twenty-two years since it witnessed the humbling of the German Empire."

Then the French delegation arrived, the officers led by Gen. Charles Huntziger, commander of the Second Army at Sedan. The onlookers could see that signing the armistice on this site humiliated the Frenchmen.

Hitler left as soon as Gen. Wilhelm Keitel, his senior military advisor, read the preamble. The terms of the armistice were numerous and harsh. They called for the French navy to be demobilized and disarmed and the ships returned to port, to ensure that renegade French boats did not align themselves with the British fleet; the army and nascent air force were to be disposed of; guns and weapons of any kind would be surrendered to the Germans; the Nazis would oversee the country but the French would be allowed to govern it in the southern zone, the unoccupied and so-called Free Zone, in which France's fledgling provisional government resided; Paris and all of northern France would fall under the occupied, or Unfree Zone, where travel would be limited and life, due to rations and other restrictions, would be much harder.

Breaking the country in two and allowing the French to govern half of it would later be viewed as one of Hitler's brilliant political moves. To give the French sovereignty in the south would keep political and military leaders from fleeing the country and establishing a central government in the French colonies of Africa, countries that Hitler had not yet defeated and where the French could continue to fight German forces.

But that afternoon on the radio, the La Rochefoucaulds heard only about the severing of a country their forebears had helped build. Worse still, all of Paris and the Villeneuve estate to the north of it fell within the Germans' occupied zone. The family would be prisoners in their own home. Listening to the terms broadcast over the airwaves, the otherwise proud Consuelo made no attempt to hide her sobbing. "It was the first time I saw my mother cry over the fate of our poor France," Robert later wrote. This led his sisters and some of his brothers to cry. Robert, however, burned with shame. "I was against it, absolutely against it," he wrote, the resolve he'd felt under the stars amid other refugees building within him. In his idealistic and proud sixteen-year-old mind, to surrender was traitorous, and for a French marshal like Pétain to do it, a hero who had defeated the Germans at Verdun twenty-four years ago? "Monstrous," La Rochefoucauld wrote.

In the days after the armistice, Robert gravitated to another voice on the radio. The man was Charles de Gaulle, the most junior general in France, who had left the country for London on June 17, the day Pétain suggested a cease-fire. However difficult the decision—de Gaulle had fought under Pétain in World War I and even ghostwritten one of his books—he had left quickly, departing with only a pair of trousers, four clean shirts, and a family photo in his personal luggage. Once situated in London, de Gaulle began to appeal to his countrymen on the BBC French radio service. These soon became notorious broadcasts, for their criticisms of French political and military leadership and for de Gaulle's insistence that the war go on despite the armistice. "I, General de Gaulle . . . call upon the French officers or soldiers who may find themselves on British soil, with or without their weapons, to join me," de Gaulle said in his first broadcast. "Whatever happens, the flame of French Resistance must not and shall not die."

De Gaulle called his resistance movement the Free French. It would be based in London but operate throughout France. Robert de La Rochefoucauld listened to de Gaulle day after day, and though he had been an aimless student, he began to see how he might define his young life.

He could go to London, and join the Free French.

# CHAPTER 2

The family drove back to a Soissons they did not recognize. German bombs had leveled some storefronts and German soldiers had pillaged others. Out the car window Robert saw half-collapsed homes and the detritus of shattered livelihoods littering the sidewalks and spilling onto the streets. The damage was not total—some houses and shops still stood—but this capriciousness made the wreckage all the more harrowing.

Approaching the Rochefoucaulds' home, the car turned onto the familiar secluded avenue just outside Soissons; Robert saw the lines of chestnut trees and the small brick-covered path that cut through them. The car slowed and made the left, bouncing along. Groves of oak and basswood crowded the view and the car kept jostling as the path curved to the right, then the left, and back again. At last they saw the clearing.

The chateau of Villeneuve still rose from the earth, with its neo-classical design, brick façade, and white-stone trim, a stately home that the La Rochefoucauld family had purchased from the daughter of one of Napoléon's generals in 1861. Beams of sunlight still winked from the windows of the northern wing, a welcoming light that bathed the interior, and all the chateau's forty-seven rooms, with an incandescent glow. But at the circular driveway at the side of the home, something strange came into view.

German military vehicles.

A cadre of German soldiers seemed to have made the La Rochefoucauld house their own, judging from the armored cars and trucks parked at odd angles. But this wasn't even the worst news:

On closer inspection, the family saw that the chateau's roof was missing.

*My God*, Robert thought, trying to absorb it all.

The children clustered together in the driveway, gawking. Then, unsure what else to do, the family made its way to the front door.

When they opened it, Consuelo and her children saw the same stone staircase rising from the entryway to the front hall. But passing above them were German officers, who barely acknowledged their arrival. The Nazis had indeed requisitioned Villeneuve, just as they would other homes and municipal buildings, hoping that the houses and schools and offices might serve as command posts for the French Occupation, or as forward bases for Germany's upcoming battle with Britain. From the Germans' apathetic looks, the family saw that the chateau was no longer theirs. "There was absolutely nothing we could do against it," Robert later said.

Consuelo told her children not to acknowledge the officers, to show them that they were impermanent and therefore unremarkable: Robert would not sketch in any journal who these Germans were, what they looked like, or which one led them. But he and his siblings did record the broad outlines of the arrangement. The Nazis begrudgingly made room for the family. They soon redistributed themselves across one half of the house, so the La Rochefoucaulds could have the other. On the first floor, the officers chose the great room, whose floor-to-ceiling windows looked out on the magnificent manicured gardens, and the dining room, which seated twenty. The family took the salon—where they had once entertained visiting dignitaries and had debated Hitler's rise to power—and the living room, cozy with chairs, rows of books, and, above the fireplace, the family crest, which depicted a beautiful woman with a witch's tail—which in earlier times instructed La Rochefoucauld to live fully and enjoy all of life's delights. The second and third floors—the bedrooms and playrooms for the children, and utility rooms for the staff of twelve—were divided similarly: Nazis on one side, the family on the other. Robert still had his own room, a grand chamber with fifteen-foot ceilings, a private bathroom, and fireplace. But he couldn't stand the heavy clacking echo of German boots going up and down the second and third floors' stone staircase. The noise seemed to almost taunt him.

The family and Germans did not eat together. The La Rochefoucaulds set up a new dining room in the salon. They shared the grand spiral staircase because they had to, but the family and its staff never spoke to the Germans, and the Germans only spoke to Consuelo, once they learned she was the matriarch and local head of the Red Cross.

Consuelo's relationship with these occupying officers was, to put it mildly, difficult. In little time they settled on a nickname for her: the Terrible Countess.

It is easy to understand why. First, Consuelo had built this house. When she and Olivier were married after the Great War, a plump girl who was more confident than pretty, she looked at the ruins of what remained of the La Rochefoucauld estate and told her husband she would prefer it if the rebuilt chateau no longer faced east-west, as it had for centuries, but north-south. That way the windows could take in more sunlight. Olivier obeyed his young wife's wishes and brick by brick a neoclassical marvel emerged, one that indeed glowed with natural light. Now, twenty years later, the Germans were sullying the chateau, German soldiers who played to type, too, always loud, always shouting *Ja!*, parking up to seven bulky tanks in her yard and then endlessly cleaning them, meeting in her house, meeting in a tent they set up outside her house, their decorum gauche regardless of where they went, the sort of people who literally found it appropriate to *write on her walls*.

Then there was the damage to the roof. And though Consuelo learned that a British bomb, and not a German one, had missed the bridge it aimed for a half mile distant during the fight for France and instead flattened the fourth floor of the chateau, she resented that the Nazis hadn't offered to close the gaping hole above them, especially as the summer became late fall and the temperature turned cold. The Villeneuve staff had to put a tarp over the roof's remnants, but that did little good. When it rained, water still flowed down the stairwell. Winter nights chilled everyone, brutal hours that required multiple layers of clothing. The bomb had set off a fire that momentarily spread on the second floor, which destroyed the central heating system. Now, before the children went to bed, they had to warm a brick over a wood-fired oven and then rub the brick over their sheets, which heated their beds just enough so they might fall asleep.

Finally, there was Olivier. The family found out that he had been arrested by German forces near Saint-Dié-des-Vosges, a commune in Lorraine in northeastern France, on June 27, five days after the armistice. He was now imprisoned in the sinister-sounding Oflag XVII-A, a POW camp for French officers in eastern Austria known as "little Siberia." He was allowed to write two letters home every month, which had been censored by guards. What little Consuelo gleaned of her husband's true experience at the camp infuriated her further.

Given all this, it wasn't really a surprise to see Consuelo act out against the Germans. On one occasion, a Nazi officer, who was a member of the German cavalry and an aristocrat, wanted to pay his respects to Madame La Rochefoucauld, whose name traveled far in noble circles. When he arrived at Villeneuve, he walked up the steps, took off his gloves, and approached Consuelo, who waited at the entry, all stocky frame and suspicious gaze. He gripped her hand in his and kissed it, but before he could tell her it was a pleasure to stay in this grand home, she slapped him across the face. The Terrible Countess would not be wooed by any German. For a moment, no one knew how to respond. Then the officers, only half joking, told Consuelo a welcome like that put her at risk of deportation.

obert was his mother's son. The fact that the Nazi officers were a few rooms away only increased his talk about how much he hated them, those *Boche*. He was brash enough, would say these epithets just loud enough, that even Consuelo had to shush him. But Robert seemed not to care. His olive complexion reddened with indignant righteousness when he listened to Charles de Gaulle's speeches, and even after the German high command in Paris banned the French from turning on the BBC, Robert did it in secret. He never wanted to miss the general's daily message. Oftentimes, to evangelize, he would travel across Soissons to the estate of his cousin, Guy de Pennart, who was his age and shared, roughly, his temperament. Guy and Robert talked about how they were going to join the British and fight on. "I was convinced that we had to continue the war at all costs," Robert later said.

He was seventeen by the fall of 1940 and had graduated from high school. He wanted to join de Gaulle but wasn't sure how. One didn't "enlist" in the Resistance. Even a well-connected young man like Robert didn't know the underground routes that could get him to London. So he enrolled at an agricultural college in Paris, ostensibly to become a gentleman farmer like his father, but, more likely, he went to meet people who might help him reach de Gaulle.

These individuals, though, were not easy to find. There was little reason to be a *résistant* in 1940. The Germans had disbanded the army and all weapons, all the way down to hunting knives, had been handed in or taken by Nazi authorities. The "resistance" amounted to little more than underground newspapers that were often snuffed out, their editors imprisoned or sentenced to death by German judges presiding in France.

So Robert and a small number of new friends, all of them more boys than men, turned to one another with refrains about how much they despised the Germans, and despised Vichy, a spa town in the south of France where Pétain and his collaborating government resided. The boys talked about how France had lost her honor. "I didn't have much good sense," Robert said, "but honor—that's all my friends and I could talk about."

Its vestiges were all around him. Villeneuve was not just a home but also a monument to the family's history, replete with portraits and busts of significant men. The La Rochefoucauld line dated back to 900 AD and the family had shaped France for nearly as long. Robert had learned from his parents about François Alexandre Frédéric de La Rochefoucauld-Liancourt, a duke in Louis XVI's court. He awoke the king during the storming of the Bastille in 1789. King Louis asked La Rochefoucauld-Liancourt if it was a revolt. "No, sire," he answered. "It is a revolution." And indeed it was. Then there was François VI, Duc de La Rochefoucauld, a seventeenth-century duke who published a book of aphoristic maxims, whose style and substance influenced writers as diverse as Bernard Mandeville, Nietzsche, and Voltaire. Another La Rochefoucauld, a friend of Benjamin Franklin's, helped found the Society of the Friends of the Blacks, which abolished slavery some seventy years before it could be done in the United States. Two La Rochefoucauld brothers, both priests, were martyred during the Reign of Terror and later beatified by Rome. One La Rochefoucauld was *directeur des Beaux Arts* during the Bourbon Restoration. Others appeared in the pages of Proust. Many were lionized within the military—fighting in the Crusades, the Hundred Years' War, against the Prussians. The city of Paris named a street after the La Rochefoucaulds.

For Robert, the family's legacy had followed him everywhere throughout his childhood, inescapable: He was baptized beneath a stained-glass mural of the brother priests' martyrdom; taught in school about the aphorisms in François VI's *Maxims*; raised by a father who'd received the Legion of Honor, France's highest military commendation. Greatness was expected of him, and the expectation shadowed his days. Now, with the Germans living in the chateau, it was as if the portraits that hung on the walls darkened when Robert passed them, judging him and asking what he would do to rid the country of its occupiers and write his own chapter in the family history. To reclaim the France that his family had helped mold—that's what mattered. "I firmly believed that . . . honor commanded us to continue the fight," he said.

But Robert felt something beyond familial pressure. In his travels around Paris or on frequent stops home—he split his weeks between the city and Villeneuve—he grew genuinely angry at his defeated countrymen. He felt cheated. His life, his limitless young life, was suddenly defined by terms he did not set and did not approve of.

What galled him was that few people seemed to think as he did. He found that a lot of people in Paris and in Soissons were relieved the war was over, even if it meant the country was no longer theirs. The prewar pacifism had gelled into a postwar defeatism. Fractured France was experiencing an "intellectual and moral anesthesia," in the words of one prefect. It was bizarre. Robert had the sense that the ubiquitous German soldiers who hopped onto the Métro or sipped coffee in a café were already part of a passé scenery for the natives.

Other people got the same sense. In a surprisingly short amount of time, the hatred of the Germans and the grudges held against them "assumed a rather abstract air" for the vast majority of French, philosopher Jean-Paul Sartre wrote, because "the occupation was a *daily* affair." The Germans were everywhere, after all, asking for directions or eating dinner. And even if Parisians hated them as much as Robert de La Rochefoucauld did, calling them dirty names beneath their breath, Sartre argued that "a kind of shameful, indefinable solidarity [soon] established itself between the Parisians and these troopers who were, in the end, so similar to the French soldiers . . .

"The concept of enemy," Sartre continued, "is only entirely firm and clear when the enemy is separated from us by a wall of fire."

Even at Villeneuve, Robert witnessed the ease with which the perception of the Germans could be colored in warmer hues. Robert's younger sister, Yolaine, returned from boarding school for a holiday, and sat in the salon one afternoon listening to a German officer play the piano in the next room. He was an excellent pianist. Yolaine dared not smile as she sat there, for fear of what her mother or older brother might say if they walked past, but her serene young face showed how much she enjoyed the German's performance. "He was playing very, very well," she admitted years later.

It was no easy task to hate your neighbor all the time. That was the simple truth of 1940. And the Germans made their embrace all the more inviting because they'd been ordered to treat the French with dignity. Hitler didn't want another Poland, a country he had torched whose people he had either killed or more or less enslaved. Such tactics took a lot of bureaucratic upkeep, and Germany still had Britain to defeat. So every Nazi in France was commanded to show a stiff disciplined courteousness to the natives. Robert saw this at Villeneuve, where the German officers treated the Terrible Countess with a respect she did not reciprocate. (In fact, that they never deported his mother can be read to a certain extent as an exercise in decorous patience.) One saw this treatment extended to other families as they resettled after the exodus: PUT YOUR TRUST IN THE GERMAN SOLDIER, signs read. The Nazis gave French communities beef to eat, even if it was sometimes meat that the Germans had looted during the summer. Parisians like Robert saw Nazis offering their seats to elderly *madames* on the Métro, and on the street watched as these officers tipped their caps to the French police. In August, one German army report on public opinion in thirteen French departments noted the "exemplary, amiable and helpful behavior of the German soldiers . . ."

Some French, like Robert, remained wary: That same report said German kindness had "aroused little sympathy" among certain natives; and young women in Chartres, who had heard terrible stories from the First World War, had taken to smearing their vaginas with Dijon mustard, "to sting the Germans when they rape," one Frenchwoman noted in her diary. But on the whole, the German Occupation went over relatively seamlessly for Christian France. By October 1940, it seemed not at all strange for Marshal Pétain, the eighty-four-year-old president of France's provisional government and hero of the Great War, to meet with Hitler in Montoire, about eighty miles southwest of Paris. There, the two agreed to formalize their alliance, shaking hands before a waiting press corps while Pétain later announced in a radio broadcast: "It is in the spirit of honor, and to maintain the unity of France . . . that I enter today upon the path of collaboration."

Though Pétain refused to join the side of the Germans in their slog of a fight against the British, he did agree to the Nazis' administrative and civil aims. The country, in short, would begin to turn Fascist. "The Armistice . . . is not peace, and France is held by many obligations with respect to the winner," Pétain said. To strengthen itself, France must "extinguish" all divergent opinions.

Pétain's collaboration speech outraged Robert even as it silenced him. He thought it was "the war's biggest catastrophe," but his mother quieted him. With that threat about divergent opinions, "There could be consequences," she said. She had lost her husband and wasn't about to lose a son to a German prison. So Robert traveled back to Paris for school, careful but resolved to live a life in opposition to what he saw around him.

# CHAPTER 3

H e was still a boy, only seventeen, not even of military age, but he understood better than most the darkening afternoon that foretold France's particularly long night. Robert saw a country that was falling apart.

He saw it first in the newspapers. Many new dailies and weeklies emerged with a collaborationist viewpoint, sometimes even more extreme than what Pétain promoted. Some Paris editors considered Hitler a man who would unite all of Europe; others likened the Nazis to French Revolutionaries, using war to impose a new ideology on the continent. There were political differences among the collaborators; some were socialists, and others pacifists who saw fascism as a way to keep the peace. One paper began publishing nothing but denunciations of Communists, Freemasons, and Jews. Another editor, Robert Brasillach, of the Fascist *Je Suis Partout* (I Am Everywhere), praised "Germany's spirit of eternal youth" while calling the French Republic "a syphilitic strumpet, smelling of cheap perfume and vaginal discharge." But even august publications with long histories changed with the times: The *Nouvelle Revue Française*, or *NRF* (a literary magazine much like *The New Yorker*), received a new editor in December 1940, Pierre Drieu La Rochelle, an acclaimed novelist and World War I veteran who had become a Fascist. Otto Abetz, the German ambassador, could not believe his good fortune. "There are three great powers in France: Communism, the big banks and the *NRF*," he said. The magazine veered hard right.

At the same time, Robert also noticed the Germans begin to bombard the radio and newsreels with propaganda. Hitler was portrayed as the strong man, a more beneficent Napoléon even, with the people he ruled laughing over their improved lives. Robert found it disgusting, in no small part because he had witnessed this warped reality before, in Austria in 1938 at boarding school. He had even met Hitler there.

It was in the Bavarian Alps, hiking with a priest and some boys from the Marist boarding school he attended outside Salzburg. The priests had introduced their pupils to the German youth organizations Hitler favored and, at the time, Robert loved them, because they promoted hiking at the expense of algebra. He didn't know much about the German chancellor then, aside from the fact that everyone talked about him, but he knew it was a big deal for the priest to take the boys to Berghof, Hitler's Alpine retreat, perched high above the market town of Berchtesgaden. When they reached it they saw a gently sloping hill on which sat a massive compound: a main residence as large as a French chateau and, to the right, a smaller guest house. The estate was the first home Hitler called his own and where he spent "the finest hours of my life," he once said. "It was there that all my great projects were conceived and ripened."

The students stood lightly panting before it when a convoy of black cars wended down the long driveway and turned out onto the road. The path cut right in front of the boys, and one sedan stopped in front of them. Out stepped Adolf Hitler. The priest, stunned, began explaining that he and his group had just come to look—but Hitler was in a playful mood, not suspicious in the least, and began questioning the boys, many of whom were Austrian, about their backgrounds. When Hitler got to Robert, the priest said that this boy was French. Robert tried to make an impression, and began speaking to Hitler in the German he'd acquired living in Austria. But the phrases emerged with an unmistakable accent, and when Robert finished, Hitler just patted him on the cheek. "Franzose," he responded. ("Frenchman.") And then he moved on.

In a moment, the führer was back in the car and out of view. The encounter was as brief as it was shocking: The boys had seen, had even been touched by, the most famous man in Europe, the shaper of history himself. They looked at each other, and Robert couldn't help but feel giddy.

The bliss wouldn't last, however. Austria was quickly losing whatever independence it had, and when Chancellor Kurt Schuschnigg said in a radio address in February that he could make no more concessions to the Nazis, a frenzied, yelling mob of twenty thousand Fascists invaded the city of Graz, ripped out the loudspeakers that had broadcast Schuschnigg's address, then pulled down the Austrian flag and replaced it with a swastika banner. A month later Hitler invaded, and within days the Anschluss was complete.

Robert saw a demonstration in Salzburg a few days later, where everyone shouted, "Heil Hitler! Long live Hitler!" He felt the threat of violence begin to cloud the interactions of everyday life. The Nazis occupied the buildings next to the Marist school and one day Robert looked in a window and suddenly a man stormed from the building, insulting and threatening him, simply for peering inside. Robert began to second-guess a führer who would champion these bullies. By the end of the school year, he was happy to leave Austria for good.

Now, at the beginning of the Occupation, he saw a similar malice embedded within the French newsreels: Everyone smiling too hard and striving to look the same. With each passing day, the Frenchmen he encountered seemed to follow in the Austrians' footsteps, embracing a fascism they were either too scared or ignorant of to oppose. One exhibition defaming Freemasonry attracted 900,000 Parisians, nearly half the city's population. Another, called "European France," with Hitler as the pan-national leader, drew 635,000. Meanwhile, the German Institute's language courses flourished to the point that they had to turn away applicants. For

90 percent of France, La Rochefoucauld later mused, Pétain and Hitler's alliance represented the second coming of Joan of Arc. The historical record would show that collaborators, those who subscribed to newspapers committed to the cause and joined special interest groups, were never actually a majority, but Robert could be forgiven for thinking this because all around him people declared themselves friends of Hitler. The founder of the cosmetics firm L'Oréal turned out to be a collaborator. So was the director of Paris' Opéra-Comique, the curator of the Rodin Museum, even the rector of the Catholic University of Paris. By the end of 1940, in fact, the country's assembly of cardinals and archbishops demanded in a letter that laity give a "complete and sincere loyalty . . . to the established order." One Catholic priest finished Sunday Mass with a loud "Heil Hitler."

It was all so disorienting. Robert felt like he no longer recognized *La France*. He was eighteen and impetuous and London and de Gaulle called to him—but couldn't he do something here, now? He wanted to show the Germans that they could control his country, his faith, his *house*, but they could not control him.

One day he met in secret with his cousin, Guy, and they launched a plan to steal a train loaded with ammunition that stopped in Soissons. Maybe they would blow it up, maybe they would just abscond with it. The point was: The Germans would *know* they didn't rule everything. Guy and Robert talked about how wonderful it would be, and ultimately Robert approached a man of their fathers' generation, whom Robert blindly suspected of being in the fledgling Resistance, and asked for help.

The man stared hard at Robert. He told him that he and his cousin could not carry out their mission. Even if they stole this train, what would they do with it? And how would it defeat the Germans? And did they realize that their act risked more lives than their own? German reprisals for "terrorism" sometimes demanded dozens of executions.

Already, an amateur rebellion had cost the community lives. A Resistance group in Soissons called La Vérité Française had affiliated itself with one in Paris that formed in the Musée de l'Homme. It was a brave but naive group, unaware of the double agents within its ranks as it published underground newspapers and organized escape routes for French prisoners of war. The German secret police raided the Musée and Vérité groups. One museum *résistant* was deported, three sentenced to prison and seven to death. In Soissons, two members of Vérité Française were beheaded, six shot, and six more died in concentration camps. The Nazi agents who organized the Soissons raid worked in an elegant gray-stone building—across the street from the cathedral where the La Rochefoucaulds occasionally attended Mass.

So their plan was foolish, the man said, and Robert and his cousin were lucky to be stopped before the brutal secret police or, for that matter, the army officers billeting in Robert's house could get to them.

The scolding shamed La Rochefoucauld, and stilled his intent. But the situation in France continued to worsen. The French government was responsible for the upkeep of the German army in France, which cost a stunning 400 million francs a day, after the Nazis rigged the math and overvalued the German mark by 60 percent. Soon, it was enough money to actually buy France from the French, one German economist noted. Oil grew scarce. Robert began biking everywhere. The German-backed government in Vichy imposed rations, and Robert soon saw long lines of people at seemingly every bakery and grocery store he passed. The Germans set a shifting curfew for Paris, as early as 9 p.m. or as late as midnight, depending on the Nazis' whims. This would have annoyed any college-aged man, but the German capriciousness carried a sinister edge, too: After dark, Parisians heard the echo of the patrolling secret police's boots and might wake the next day to find a neighbor or acquaintance missing and everyone too frightened to ask questions. In 1941, the terror spilled out into the open. Small cliques of Communist *résistants* in Nantes and Bordeaux assassinated two high-ranking Nazi officers, and, in response, Hitler ordered the execution of ninety-eight people, some of them teenagers, who had at most nominal ties to Communism. One by one they were sent to the firing squad, some of them singing the French national anthem. As news of the executions spread—ninety-eight people dead—a police report noted: "The German authorities have sown consternation everywhere."

The urge to fight rose again in Robert and his college friends. Pétain seemed to be speaking directly to young men like Robert when he warned in a broadcast: "Frenchmen . . . I appeal to you in a broken voice: Do not allow any more harm to be done to France." But that proved difficult as 1941 became 1942, and the Occupation entered its third year. Travel to certain areas was allowed only by permit, thirteen thousand Jews were rounded up in Paris and sent to Auschwitz, and the United States entered the war. The Germans, to feed their fighting machine, gave the French even less to eat, forcing mothers to wait all morning for butter and urban families to beg their rural cousins for overripened vegetables. Robert now heard of sabotages of German equipment and materiel carried out by people very much like himself. He no doubt heard of the people who feared the growing Resistance as well, who wanted to keep the peace whatever the cost, who called *résistants* "bandits" or even "terrorists," adopting the language of the occupier. In 1942, denunciations were common. Radio Paris had a show, *Répétez-le* (Repeat It), in which listeners named their neighbors, business associates, or sometimes family members as enemies of the state. The Sicherheitsdienst (SD), the feared agency colloquially known as the Gestapo, read at least three million denunciatory letters during the war, many of them signed by Frenchmen.

This self-policing—which can be read as an attempt to curry favor with the Germans or to divert attention from oneself or simply to spite a disliked neighbor—oppressed the populace more than the SD could have. As the historian Henry Charles Lea said of the culture of denunciation: "No more ingenious device has been invented to subjugate a whole population, to paralyze its intellect and to reduce it to blind obedience." Even children understood the terror behind the collective censorship. As Robert de La Rochefoucauld's younger sister, Yolaine, who was thirteen years old in 1942, put it: "I remember silence, silence, silence."

Robert, though, couldn't live like that. "Every time I met with friends," Robert would later say, "we always endlessly talked about how to kick the Germans out, how to resolve the situation, how to fight." By the summer of that year, Robert was about to turn nineteen. The German officers had moved on, as quickly as they'd come, leaving the chateau without explanation for another destination. This only emboldened La Rochefoucauld, who still listened to Charles de Gaulle and cheered when he said things like, "It is completely normal and completely justified that Germans should be killed by French men and French women. If the Germans did not wish to be killed by our hands, they should have stayed home and not waged war on us."

One day a Soissons postman knocked on the door of the chateau and asked to see Robert's mother, Consuelo. The conversation they had greatly upset her. When he left, she immediately sought out Robert.

She told him that she'd just met with a mail carrier who set aside letters addressed to the secret police. This postman took the letters home with him and steamed open the envelopes to see who in the correspondence was being denounced. If the carrier didn't know the accused, he burned the letter. But if he did, well, and here Consuelo produced a piece of paper with writing scrawled across it. If the postman did know the accused, Consuelo said, he warned the family. She passed the letter to her son. It had been sent anonymously, but in it the writer denounced Robert as being a supporter of de Gaulle's, against collaboration, and above all a terrorist.

Anger and fear shot through him. Who might have done this? Why? But to fixate on that obscured the larger point: Robert was no longer safe in Soissons. If someone out there had been angry enough to see him arrested, might not a second person also feel this way? Might not another letter appear and, in the hands of a less courageous postal worker, be sent right along to the Nazis? Robert and his mother discussed it at length, but both knew instinctively.

He had to leave.

# CHAPTER 4

He went first to Paris, in search of someone who could at long last get him to de Gaulle and his Free French forces. After asking around, Robert met with a man who worked in the Resistance, and Robert told him about his hope to head to London, join de Gaulle, and fight the Nazis. Could the Parisian help?

The man paused for a moment. "Come back in fifteen days," he said, "and I'll tell you what I can do."

Two weeks later, Robert and the *résistant* met again. The Germans patrolled the coast between France and England, so a Frenchman's best bet to reach the UK was to head south, to Spain, which had stayed out of the war and was a neutral country. If La Rochefoucauld could get there and then to the British embassy in, say, Madrid, he might find a way to London.

Robert was grateful, even joyous, but he had a question. Before he could cross into another country, he'd have to cross France's demarcation line, separating the occupied from unoccupied zones. How was he to do that under his own name? The Parisian said he could help arrange a travel permit and false papers for La Rochefoucauld. But this in turn only raised more questions. If lots of Frenchmen got to London by way of Spain—if that passage was a *résistant*'s best bet—wouldn't the Germans know that, too?

Probably, the man said. Everything in war is a risk. But the Parisian had a friend in Vichy with a government posting who secretly worked for the Resistance. If the Parisian placed a call, the Vichy friend could help guide Robert to a lesser-known southern route. Robert asked the man to phone his friend.

The Parisian and Robert also discussed false IDs. Maybe Robert needed two aliases. With two names it would be even harder to trace him as he traveled south. Of course, if the Germans found out about either, Robert would almost certainly be imprisoned. La Rochefoucauld seemed to accept this risk because French military files show him settling on two names: Robert Jean Renaud and René Lallier. The first was a take on his given name: Robert Jean-Marie. The second he just thought up, "a nom de guerre I'd found who knows where," he later wrote. Both had the mnemonic advantage of carrying some of his real name's initials.

He used René Lallier for the journey south to Vichy. The photo in his false identity card depicted La Rochefoucauld in a three-piece suit, with his wavy black hair parted to the right in a pompadour, the corner of his lips curling into a smile, as if he couldn't keep from laughing at the deception. At the demarcation line, the Nazi auxiliaries in the gray uniforms who checked papers, and whom the French called "the gray mice," studied La Rochefoucauld's ID, the name René Lallier in big block type, the black-and-white photo beneath. The date of birth was given as August 28, 1925, almost two years after La Rochefoucauld's real birthday. The residence was listed in the Oise department, which was to the immediate west of La Rochefoucauld's actual home in the Aisne. The gray mouse pored over the form, and then handed it back to La Rochefoucauld. He could proceed.

He took the train to Vichy, but when he got off, a wave of panic swelled within him. He wondered if it had been idiotic to come here, to the epicenter of German collaboration. Everyone seemed to eye him suspiciously; even cars and buildings looked "hostile," he later wrote. He tried to push down the fear rising up his throat and appear casual, as if he belonged. But that was a difficult act. In the end, "I made an effort to be seen as little as possible," he wrote, walking in the shadows of the streets, avoiding eye contact. He settled into a hotel that his Paris friend had arranged for him. The plan was to meet the man from the Vichy government in the lobby, but now that he was in his room, the whole affair seemed absurd: To meet with an actual Vichy official? In a Vichy hotel? Was this madness? "I was wary of everything and everyone," he wrote.

Still, at the appointed time, he found the strength to walk to the lobby. He saw the government official the Parisian had described. The two greeted each other; Robert tried to ignore any gooseflesh pimpling his neck. They sat down, the official opening the conversation lightly, with banal questions and asides. He was trying to feel Robert out, which began to put him at ease—the official was "extremely nice," La Rochefoucauld later said. The two could only playact for so long, though. The Vichy man told La Rochefoucauld that a group was about to leave for Perpignan, a city in southeastern France near the border with Spain. The official had a friend there, someone Robert would meet and who would help him cross over.

The official gave La Rochefoucauld an address for the man in Perpignan—and then stopped Robert before he could write it down. He said La Rochefoucauld had to commit the address to memory. "I began to soak up this code of conduct," Robert later wrote, "which was so necessary to what I was undertaking but previously not really in my nature." The Vichy man said once Robert arrived, the Perpignan friend would in turn put him in contact with smugglers who moved other clandestine agents or downed British pilots into Spain. How La Rochefoucauld got to the safety of, say, a British embassy would be at the discretion of the smugglers. The Vichy official and La Rochefoucauld then wished each other well and Robert watched him leave the lobby.

The meeting apparently made him feel better because Robert later described the trip to Perpignan as "very pleasant," free of the paranoia of Vichy. At the given address in Perpignan, a man in his thirties answered La Rochefoucauld's knock on the door, greeting Robert formally and aware of his plans. The Perpignan man was, like the one from Vichy, also a civil servant secretly awaiting the fall of Pétain's government, and insisted La Rochefoucauld make himself comfortable. It could be a while before the next trip across the border, he said. So Robert stayed that night, and then seven more: The man and his smuggler friends planned to take a few clandestine fighters at a time and were rounding them up, he said. On the eighth night the Perpignan man told Robert that the smugglers would traffic two British pilots desperate to make it to Spain. Robert would travel with these Englishmen across the border.

One day soon thereafter Robert and the man from Perpignan set out to meet the Brits and the smugglers who would guide them across. The Occupation and scarcity of oil in France—the Nazis demanded more of it from the French than Germany produced annually—had forced many of the French by 1942 to abandon their vehicles and live as if it were the nineteenth century. "Distances," one observer wrote, were suddenly "measured in paces—of man or horse." The people who kept a vehicle often retrofitted the engine so that a pump placed near the rear of the car, resembling the cylinder jutting up above a steam-engine train, could convert coal or wood chips into fuel in lieu of oil. That was what the man from Perpignan had: A rickety bus with what was known as a gasified tank grafted onto it, its cylinder rising high above the rest of the bus's body. He and La Rochefoucauld traveled along the small roads snaking through the outskirts of the Pyrenees mountains, stopping at a modest village a dozen miles from Perpignan. They parked the bus and the man, pointing to the heavy forest around them, said they would walk from here. They set off through the woods and the sloping mountainside until they saw it, about three miles into their hike: the makeshift camp of a dozen mountain men. They were large, hairy, and not particularly clean, but after introductions they promised they knew the routes to Spain better than anyone. Before trafficking Resistance fighters, they'd moved a lot of alcohol and cigarettes across the border. La Rochefoucauld snorted his approval.

The French and sympathetic Spaniards had their preferred escape routes, and the British government even sanctioned one, through an offshoot of MI6, called the VIC line. But many border crossings shared a common starting point in Perpignan, in part because the city lay at the foot of the Pyrenees that divided France from Spain. A crossing through the range there, though arduous, wasn't as demanding as in the high mountains, more than two hundred miles to the west. The problem, of course, was that the Nazis knew this too, and Spain was "honeycombed with German agents," one official wrote. So if the Pyrenees themselves didn't endanger lives, a *résistant*'s run to freedom might.

The British pilots arrived, noticeably older than La Rochefoucauld and not speaking a word of French. Robert's childhood with English nannies suddenly came in handy. He said hello, and soon found that they were career soldiers, a pilot and a radioman, who'd been shot down over central France during a mission, but parachuted out and escaped the German patrols. They had hiked for days to get here. La Rochefoucauld translated all this and the group decided to let the exhausted English rest. They would set out the next night.

In the end, seven left for Spain: La Rochefoucauld, the Brits, and four guides—two advance scouts and two pacing the refugees. They took paths only the smugglers knew, guided by their intuition and a faint moon. The narrow passages and ever-steepening incline meant the men walked single file. "The hike was particularly difficult," La Rochefoucauld later wrote. Vineyards gave way to terraced vineyards until the vegetation disappeared, the mountain rising higher before them, loose rubble and stone at their feet. As the night deepened, Robert could see little of the person in front of him. The people who scaled these mountains often misjudged distances, stubbing their toes on the boulders or twisting their ankles on uneven earth or, when the night was at its darkest, flailing their arms when they expected a jut in the mountain's face that was nothing more than open air. This last was the most terrifying. Germans posted observation decks on the crests of certain peaks, which discouraged strongly lit torches and slowed or, conversely, sometimes quickened the pace, depending on whether and when the guides believed the Germans to be peering through their telescopes. The peaks at this part of the Pyrenees were roughly four thousand feet, and the descent was as limb- and life-threatening as the climb. The passage exhausted everyone. "Every two hours, we took a quarter of an hour's rest," La Rochefoucauld wrote. At dawn the group closed in on a stretch of the range that straddled the two countries, but didn't want to risk a crossing during the day. So they hid out and waited for nightfall. When they resumed their hike, the going proved "just as hard, and increasingly dangerous," Robert later recalled. The group nearly stumbled into view of a German post, etched into the night's skyline. They detoured quietly around it, but then, having rejoined the route, saw another Nazi lookout, rising amid the shadows. So once more they redirected themselves, trying to be safe but also trying to take advantage of the darkness; they needed to cross into Spain before dawn. These were tense moments, moving quickly and silently and almost blindly, and all while listening for footsteps behind them. Eventually they made it to the Perthus Pass, a mountainous area right on the border. Nazi patrols were known to roam the grounds at all hours here. The group's advance scouts went ahead and came back in the last small minutes before daylight. "The road is clear!" they said. With a rush of adrenaline and fear, everyone scurried across, into Spain.

Robert and the airmen laughed, euphoric. They were hundreds of miles south, but so much closer to London.

The guides said they needed to head back; smugglers out after dawn risked imprisonment. Everyone shook hands. The guides pointed to the road. "This will take you to a town," one of them said.

Robert and the Brits set out, with a plan to get to the village, clean up somewhere, and take a train to Madrid without raising suspicion. Once there, they would cautiously make their way to the British embassy.

Though they had slept little and eaten sparingly, they walked at a good pace, full of life. They reached a thriving market town that morning; it was likely Figueres, the first municipality of any note across the Spanish border. They immediately discovered that it was crawling with police and customs agents. They were three men who had just climbed through the Pyrenees over two sleepless nights—"We looked more like highway robbers than peaceful citizens," La Rochefoucauld wrote—and before they could find a hiding spot or a public washroom, two Spanish agents approached them on the street. The Spaniards were kind and one of them spoke French. Given their appearance and the toll the trek had taken on them, they felt that any story they might concoct wouldn't sync with reality. So La Rochefoucauld tried an honest tack, to appeal to the officers' intelligence. He said he had escaped from France with these British pilots, who had been shot down and fled to the border. The Spanish agents' faces didn't harden; they seemed to appreciate the honesty. But the lead officer told the men they had no choice but "to take you with us to the station." In the days ahead, with Spanish bureaucracy in wartime Europe being what it was, La Rochefoucauld and the Brits went from one law-enforcement agency to another, and ended up at Campdevànol in Girona, twenty-five miles south of Figueres.

Robert Jean Renaud, La Rochefoucauld's twenty-two-year-old French-Canadian alias, was booked in the Girona prison on December 17, 1942. The Girona authorities found Renaud's case beyond their jurisdiction and on December 23, they transferred him and, according to La Rochefoucauld, the British pilots to a place even less accommodating: the prisoner of war camp in Miranda de Ebro.

**B**uilt in 1937 during the Spanish Civil War, the concentration camp near the Ebro River in the homely flatness of northern Spain first housed Republican soldiers and political dissidents who defied Franco's fascism. Its watchtowers, barbed-wire fences, and barracks in parallel lines across 103 acres of Castilian soil were designed with the help of Paul Winzer, a Nazi member of both the SS and Gestapo, then working in Madrid. Franco's men understood cruelty as well as any budding Nazi. They shipped the Republican prisoners to Miranda in cattle cars, starved them, humiliated them, exposed them to weather conditions and savage guards and all the diseases that thrive in overly populated spaces. The twenty-two barracks, made to hold two thousand men, held 18,406 prisoners at one point in 1938. All told, an estimated ten thousand people died there during the Spanish Civil War.

With Franco's victory in 1939 and the outbreak of World War II, the camp was converted into a prison for refugees fleeing Hitler's Europe. Its political allegiances shifted and baffled both the Allied and Axis powers. One would think a Nazi supporter as fierce as Franco would listen to the Germans and allow them sway within the camp, considering an SS man built the place. But Spanish officials informed the Nazis that because they'd overseen the prison since 1937, they didn't need any outside guidance. No German helped to direct it during World War II. And because of Franco's friendliness toward Great Britain and the diplomatic dexterity of British ambassador Samuel Hoare, to whom the general listened, British prisoners at Miranda served shorter stints than nationals from any other European country.

But that didn't endear the remaining Allied prisoners to the Miranda staff. It routinely complied with the German embassy in Madrid, which issued exit visas and repatriation documents for its "subjects," the Czechs, Poles, and French who had fled the German occupation of their home countries.

In short, it was a bad time to be a Frenchman entering Miranda—

which is why French-Canadian seemed such an inspired nationality for La Rochefoucauld's nom de guerre Robert Jean Renaud. To say he was a Canadian freed La Rochefoucauld from a forced return to Vichy France, or from the more barbaric treatment the Miranda staff imposed on certain French nationals: the beatings and the exhausting, morally degrading forced labor.

None of this meant, however, that Robert's stay in Miranda was enjoyable. After his and the Brits' booking, the guards shoved all three in the same cell, which other political prisoners described as "cattle stalls" or "windowless huts." It was little better outside their unit. Miranda was well beyond its capacity of 2,000 prisoners, holding 3,500 by the end of 1942. Everyone risked whippings or smaller humiliations from taunting guards. In January 1943, some prisoners began a hunger strike.

Every day the two British pilots wrote letters to their embassy in Madrid, begging for release. While they awaited a response, food was scarce and the three subsisted on little more than the morning's slice of bread and conversation. The winter wind whipped through the airy barracks and inmates froze in their thin uniforms. Medical care was inconsistent, and when doctors did perform rounds they often asked that hot irons be pressed onto inmates' dirty clothes, to kill off the lice. Scabies and diarrheic diseases, which prisoners called "mirandite," were rampant. Rats attacked the camp dogs in broad daylight. To visit the latrines at night "necessitated a good deal of courage," the British spy and Miranda survivor George Langelaan wrote, because there the same great rats "fought and squealed furiously, regardless and unafraid of men." Sleep came fleetingly. The guards on night patrol sporadically shouted *Alerta!*, either to make sure other guards were awake or to torture dozing inmates. In the morning, everyone stood outside for roll call and on Sundays they marched by the commandant and his officers who were clustered around a Nationalist flag on a miniature grandstand. The Miranda staff, dressed in their Sunday best of white belts, white epaulets, and white gloves, formed a band, and the prisoners walked behind it in time to music. This amused the elderly officers in their large silk sashes. Inevitably, one of the band members fell out of step or grew confused by the complicated formations, and the prisoners snickered under their breath at the band.

Every week, two large trucks from the British embassy arrived, dropping off cigarettes and other provisions and picking up whichever Brits the Spanish authorities had agreed to release. Ambassador Hoare had a keen interest in freeing pilots; the Allies increased their air missions over France in 1942 and '43, dangerous missions in which the Germans often shot the planes down. If the pilots survived the crash and ended up in Miranda, getting them back to London and back in the air took less time than training new men.

In late February 1943, after roughly three months in prison, the British pilots with La Rochefoucauld heard that a man from His Majesty's Government awaited them in the visitors' room. The three inmates smiled. Quickly, the British men gathered themselves and made for their meeting, with Robert calling after them, *Don't forget me*, and begging them to mention that he wanted to meet de Gaulle and join the Free French. A short while later, the pilots returned to the cell, smirking, and Robert soon found out why.

He was called to meet with the British representative. This was likely a military attaché, Major Haslam, who made frequent trips to the camp in 1943. Once La Rochefoucauld reached the visitors' room, the Brit profusely thanked him "for all you've done to help my countrymen." Robert was dumbfounded: What had he done? He'd served as the pilots' interpreter, little more. But the representative went on and Robert figured the pilots had "grossly embellished my role." He tried to set the man straight, explaining that though he was happy to know the pilots, and even befriend them, his passage through Spain had no purpose other than getting to de Gaulle and joining the Free French.

The Brit stared at him, not upset that he had been misled, but seemingly working something out in his mind. At last, he said he would do his best to grant La Rochefoucauld's wish. "I thanked him with all my heart," La Rochefoucauld wrote, "and once back in the cell, fell into the arms of the pilots." A few days later, he got on a truck with the airmen and departed for Madrid and the British embassy.

They arrived at night, the Spanish capital so brilliantly lit it shocked them; it had been months since they'd seen such iridescence. At the embassy they ate a "top-notch dinner," La Rochefoucauld wrote, "then we were brought to our rooms, the dimensions and comfort of which seemed incredible." An embassy staffer told them they would meet with Ambassador Hoare himself in the morning.

After a proper English breakfast, each man had his meeting. Hoare was aging and short, with the look of upper-class British severity about him: his gray hair trimmed and parted crisply to the right, his dress fastidious, and his manners formal. Hoare was ambitious and competitive; his taut frame reflected the tournament-level tennis he still played. He had been part of Prime Minister Neville Chamberlain's cabinet, the secretary of the Home Office, and one of the key advisors to Chamberlain when he appeased Hitler in the Munich Agreement in 1938. Churchill dismissed Hoare when he became prime minister in 1940, offering Hoare the ambassadorship in Madrid that many in London saw as the old man's proper banishment. Hoare seemed to wear this rejection in his delicate facial features and his searching, almost wounded eyes. Still, his mission in Madrid had been to keep the pro-German Franco out of the war, and he had done his job with aplomb. Spain remained neutral, even after the Allies' North African landings in November 1942, and Franco continued to allow the release of British troops and Resistance fighters from Miranda.

Because of his ease with the French language, Hoare had been the man in Chamberlain's cabinet to sit next to French Prime Minister Léon Blum at a state luncheon, the two talking literature, and now in Madrid he opened the conversation with La Rochefoucauld in similarly "perfect French," the fledgling *résistant* later wrote. "He was indeed aware of my plans to join up with the Free French forces in London but, without rushing, without ever opposing my determination, he revealed to me a sort of counter project." During the First World War, Hoare had headed the British Secret Intelligence Service in Petrograd, Russia—he may have even originated a plot to kill Rasputin—and still relished the dark arts of espionage. What would you say, Hoare asked Robert, to enlisting in a branch of the British special services that carried out missions in France?

La Rochefoucauld wasn't sure what that implied, and so Hoare continued, revealing his proposition slowly.

"The British agents have competence and courage that are beyond reproach," Hoare said. But their French, even if passable, was heavily accented. German agents found them out. So Great Britain had formed a new secret service, the likes of which the world had never before seen, training foreign nationals in London and then parachuting them back into their home countries where they fought the Nazis with—well, Hoare stressed that he could not disclose too much. But if the Frenchman agreed to join this new secret service, and if he passed its very demanding training procedures, all would be revealed.

The mystery intrigued Robert. It also tore at him. He had listened to de Gaulle for close to two years and lived by the general's defiant statements to battle on. It had seemed at times that only de Gaulle spoke sanely about France and its future. But though he'd wished to be a soldier in the general's army, what Robert really wanted, now that he thought about it, was simply to fight the Nazis. If the British could train and arm him as well if not better than de Gaulle—if the Brits had the staff and the money and the weapons—why not join the British? If Robert wanted to liberate France, did it really matter in whose name he did it?

Hoare could see the young man considering his options and asked, "How old are you?"

"Twenty-one," La Rochefoucauld answered, which was not only a lie—he was nineteen—but revealed which way he was leaning. He wanted Hoare to think he was older and more experienced.

At last, Robert said he was honored by the offer, and he might like to join the new British agency. He wanted, however, when he arrived in London, to first ask de Gaulle what he thought. It was a presumptuous request, but Hoare nonetheless said such a thing could be arranged.

The next week, La Rochefoucauld flew to England.

# CHAPTER 5

**W**hen he landed, military police shuttled him to southwest London, to an ornately Gothic building at Fitzhugh Grove euphemistically known as the London Reception Center, whose real name, the Royal Victoria Patriotic Building, still didn't describe what actually happened there: namely, the harsh interrogation of incoming foreign nationals by MI6 officers. The hope was to flush out German spies who, once identified, were either quarantined in windowless concrete cells or flipped into double agents—sending them back into the field with a supposed allegiance to the Nazis but a true fealty to Great Britain.

La Rochefoucauld's interrogation opened with him giving the Brits a fake name—which may very well be why Robert Jean Renaud appeared in the Royal Victoria Patriotic files in March 1943. He also said he was twenty-one. He would come to regret these statements as the interrogation stretched from one day to two, and then beyond. Though he eventually admitted to the officers his real identity, that only prolonged the questioning, because now the agents wanted to know why he had lied in the first place. And the answer seemed to be: because he was a nineteen-year-old who still acted like a boy, creating mischief amid authority figures. In some sense, deceiving the British was the same as climbing a lycée's homeroom curtains. It was a fun thing to do.

The British officers in the Patriotic Building would later claim they didn't rely on torture but used numerous "techniques" to get people to talk: forcing them to stand for hours and recount in mind-numbing detail how they had arrived or to sit in a painfully hard-backed chair and do the same; or filling up refugees with English tea and forbidding them to leave, seeing if their stories changed as their bladders cried for relief; or questioning applicants from sunup to sundown, or from sundown to sunup; or tag-teaming a refugee and playing good cop, bad cop. Robert remembered emerging from marathon sessions and talking to the "twenty or so fugitives there, in a situation similar to mine, who had come from various European countries." The people he saw were some of the thirty thousand or so who ultimately filtered through the Patriotic Building during the war: men and women who in other lands were politicians or military personnel or just flat-out adventurers, washing ashore in England, sleeping in barracks, and awaiting their next interrogation slumped over on small benches, remnants of the building's former life as a school for orphans.

La Rochefoucauld was there for eight days. In the end, an interrogating officer who spoke French knew of Robert's family and its lineage, and soon he and the officer were chatting about the La Rochefoucaulds like old friends. Because the British espionage services brimmed with upper-class Englishmen, the spies identified with a Frenchman from the "right" sort of family, and it soon became evident that this nobleman was not a German agent. Robert was free to go.

A man waited for him as he left the grounds. He had a boy's way of smiling, turning up his lips without revealing his teeth, an attempt to give his slender build a tough veneer. His name was Eric Piquet-Wicks, and he helped oversee a branch of the new secret service that Ambassador Hoare had mentioned to La Rochefoucauld. His features had an almost ethereal fineness to them, but his personality was much hardier, all seafaring wanderlust. He was aging gracefully, the thin creases around his eyes and cheeks granting him the gravitas his smile did not. He wore a suit well.

Piquet-Wicks and La Rochefoucauld walked around the neighborhood, Robert taking in the spring air, free of the paranoid thoughts of the last months, while Piquet-Wicks discussed his own life and how Robert might be able to help him.

Piquet-Wicks's mother was French. The name that many Brits pronounced *Pick-it* Wicks was in fact *Pi-kay* Wicks, after his mother, Alice Mercier-Piquet, of the port city of Calais. He was born in Colchester and split his formative education between England and France, earning his college degree, in Spanish, at a university in Barcelona and making him trilingual when he graduated in the middle of the 1930s. He found work, of all places, in the Philippines, on the island of Cebù, where he became the French consular agent. From there he moved to the Paris office of a multinational firm called Borax, which extracted mineral deposits from sites around the world. In Paris, Piquet-Wicks was the managing director of Borax Français, but he longed to be a spy.

After Britain declared war on Germany, Piquet-Wicks received a commission with the Royal Inniskilling Fusiliers, an infantry regiment. He was stationed in Northern Ireland and woefully bored. He seems to have approached MI5, Britain's security service, which oversaw domestic threats, to inquire about how he could best serve the agency, because it had a report on him. The agency described him as an "adventurer" who had once used his military permit at the Alexandra Hotel in Hyde Park as the means to gain whiskey; he'd told the barman it wouldn't be long before he worked for MI5. The report also said that before the war Piquet-Wicks had had pro-Nazi leanings, but that wasn't the reason the agency stayed away from hiring him. "We considered him unsuitable for employment on Intelligence duties, in view of his indiscreet behavior," the report stated.

MI6, the famed spy agency, then began asking about Piquet-Wicks in July 1940, the idea being that he was an intelligent if unstable man whose dexterity with languages—he also knew some Portuguese and Italian—might still benefit Britain. But again a concern over indiscretion surfaced, and MI6 kept its distance, with one agent even saying Piquet-Wicks didn't have "enough guts to be an adventurer."

He may have stayed in Northern Ireland, living in a former brewery where "it was difficult to feel embarked in a war of . . . consequence," he later wrote, were it not for a new security service that was in need of qualified agents.

Piquet-Wicks's new life began one day in April 1941 at 3 a.m., pulling night duty in Belfast as a punishment for marching too far ahead of his company in drills. The phone rang. He didn't think to answer it, but the ringing wouldn't stop and so he picked up.

"Have you a Second Lieutenant Piquet-Wicks?" a man said. Piquet-Wicks thought this had to be someone in the mess pulling his leg.

"I am the poor bastard," he said.

The shocked splutterings on the other end made Piquet-Wicks realize this was someone official. Startled, he hung up.

The phone rang again.

"Inniskilling," Piquet-Wicks said, trying another tactic.

"Have you a Second Lieutenant Piquet-Wicks with the battalion?" the same voice said, but angrier.

"Yes, sir."

"Where is he? A few minutes ago I had someone on this line. I thought—"

Piquet-Wicks broke in, saying this was the night duty officer speaking. "The officer you are calling is undoubtedly asleep," he said. "Shall I wake him for you, sir?"

"Of course not, at this hour," said the caller, who was a colonel from the Northern Ireland district. "Take note that he should report to the War Office . . . at 1500 hours on Friday the fourth."

The War Office was in London, and the fourth was the next day.

In the morning, Piquet-Wicks went to his superior, to see what to make of the message. "I'm afraid you won't be able to continue your disciplinary training as night duty officer," the superior said, his eyes twinkling. "However, good luck and good-bye."

If Piquet-Wicks were to make it to London, he would have to catch the next boat, which departed before he could properly gather all his things, or comprehend why he needed to rush to the capital.

When he arrived at the given room inside the War Office, he met with a general, who said the British were establishing a new department—unlike MI5 and MI6, and unlike anything seen before. "I was to be seconded to a secret organization," Piquet-Wicks later wrote, "to become involved in events whose existence I had never suspected."

On his walk now with La Rochefoucauld, almost two years later, Piquet-Wicks implied he would like Robert to work under him, as an agent in his branch of this secret organization, which he had built up almost single-handedly. More details and the particulars of missions would be disclosed if and when La Rochefoucauld made it through training.

"Here is my address," Piquet-Wicks said.

He was "surprisingly close to each prospective agent," he later admitted, and La Rochefoucauld sensed the humanity behind the spy's implacable eyes. Like virtually every French agent whose life was to be guided and ultimately transformed by Eric Piquet-Wicks, Robert liked the man with the goofy smile immensely. So he thought it best to level with him. He said he had to seek out de Gaulle and ask the general's advice on joining a British agency out to save France.

Robert didn't know how closely Piquet-Wicks worked with the Free French forces. He was taken aback when Piquet-Wicks not only agreed to the sensibility of the meeting but offered him directions to Carlton Gardens, de Gaulle's headquarters in London.

"If you get to meet him," Piquet-Wicks said, "ask him what you need to ask him, then come meet me." The display of camaraderie eased La Rochefoucauld's mind and pushed him ever closer to joining the British.

N o. 4 Carlton Gardens sat amid two blocks of impeccable terraced apartments, their white-stone façades overlooking St. James Park, the oldest of London's eight Royal Parks. Built on the order of King George IV in the early 1800s and designed by architect John Nash, the rows of four-story buildings collectively called Carlton House Terrace had been home to many a proper Londoner over the years—earls and lords and even Louis-Napoléon in 1839. The German embassy occupied 7–9 Carlton Gardens until the outbreak of World War II. In 1941, during an air raid, a bomb fell on No. 2 Carlton House Terrace, leaving its roof open and exposed for the rest of the fighting. No. 4 Carlton Gardens housed de Gaulle's Free French forces, and one didn't need to look for the address to know who worked there. A French soldier in full military fatigues, rifle at his side and a helmet on his head, stood guard outside the entrance, itself marked by the Cross of Lorraine, which the Knights Templar had once carried during the Crusades but which was now the symbol of the Free French movement.

Robert kept his appointment, arranged by the Brits, with an aide of de Gaulle's. La Rochefoucauld mentioned his family name, "which may have possibly facilitated things," he wrote, and because de Gaulle's daily schedule allowed for fugitive Frenchmen who wanted to see him, Robert was told he would meet with the general that afternoon. He gulped.

The interior was all dark wood and high Gothic ceilings—an airy space with lots of natural light but poor insulation. In the winter, the Free French, across four floors, each nearly three thousand square feet, shivered in their huge rooms.

When the hour came, the secretary asked La Rochefoucauld if he was ready, and they climbed an ornate stairwell to a landing where doors led first to the offices of De Gaulle's aide-de-camp, and then past those to the general's own quarters. La Rochefoucauld's heart thrummed in his chest.

Then the door opened and there he was. The man whose voice

over the last few years Robert had heard scores of times, *The soul of Free France*, La Rochefoucauld thought. He sat behind his desk, peering over his glasses, with a look that asked, *Now what might this one want?* His presence filled the room. Everyone in London called him Le Grand Charles, due only in part to his towering height. Robert took in the office, uncluttered and organized, befitting a general, with a map of the world pinned to the wall behind de Gaulle and one of France hanging to his right. Out of his large French windows, the general had a view of St. James Park.

He rose to greet La Rochefoucauld, unbending his immense frame and straightening to his full six feet five inches, a half-foot taller than the nineteen-year-old. He had an odd body, "a head like a pineapple and hips like a woman's," as Alexander Cadogan, Britain's permanent under-secretary at the Foreign Office, once put it. His trimmed half mustache, a hairy square on his upper lip, was not a good look for a man with such a long face. The severed patch of facial hair only drew attention to his high forehead, and rather than shave the mustache, de Gaulle had taken to wearing military caps in many photographs and official portraits. He was aware of his ungainliness. "We people are never quite at ease," he once told a colleague. "I mean—giants. The chairs are always too small, the tables too low, the impression one makes too strong." Perhaps because of this, the general had welcomed solitude in London, taken on few friends, and worked in Carlton Gardens most days from 9 a.m. until evening, which allowed him to see people like La Rochefoucauld but returned him home only in time to talk with his wife and perhaps kiss his two daughters good night.

Visitors did not mistake his remoteness for timidity though. He came from a bourgeois family and his Jesuit education and elite military training at Saint-Cyr had instilled in him a kind of moral absolutism. Because he alone had cried out to continue the fight among his military brethren, because he alone had established an exile government of sorts in London, he alone spoke for the true France, he felt, and he alone could return it to grandeur.

"You are not France," Churchill had once barked at him during a wartime negotiation. "I do not recognize you as France."

To which the general replied: "Why are you [negotiating] with me if I am not France?"

Indeed, part of the reason no one else could claim to speak for France was because no one else had the bully pulpit of the BBC. By 1943 his name had become a political position, *Gaullism*, in the same way that his former mentor, Pétain, now stood for collaboration (*Pétainism*). And where he had once bluffed about his prowess—his initial Council of Defense consisted of himself and one other man—by 1943 the Free French fought alongside Allied troops throughout the world, and acolytes like La Rochefoucauld fled France almost daily to meet de Gaulle.

Still, he had a habit of treating impressionable Resistance fighters with such incuriosity or outright derision that they came away heartbroken. One described his rudeness as being like that of an "authoritarian prelate." Another man, a courageous Resistance leader, said upon leaving a meeting with the general: "I have . . . witnessed ingratitude in my life, but never on this scale." Walking now across the room and shaking La Rochefoucauld's hand, de Gaulle's greeting was characteristically "simple" but also "cordial," La Rochefoucauld would later write, proving what Alain Peyrefette, a spokesman, once said of his boss: "To each his own de Gaulle. He was different with each new person he met."

La Rochefoucauld explained how he'd gotten to London, and "de Gaulle first complimented me on wanting to join the Free French forces," Robert wrote. La Rochefoucauld then said that the British had intervened and asked him to join its clandestine service; he wasn't yet clear on the details, but that's why he had come to see de Gaulle. He had only wanted to work under the general, but now he wondered: Should he join this secret British organization?

De Gaulle had a complicated and contentious relationship with the Brits. He demanded autonomy and yet relied on Britain financially to train and equip his troops. He needed to be diplomatic with London to achieve his ends but, to appeal to Frenchmen as the true voice of France, needed to undercut his diplomacy, too. "He had to be rude to the British to prove to French eyes that he was not a British puppet," Churchill wrote. "He certainly carried out this policy with perseverance." Churchill loved and loathed him. The romantic in Churchill saw a rebel and great adventurer in de Gaulle, "the man of destiny." But the general's incorrigible rudeness and unending demands on behalf of a sovereign nation that was, in truth, occupied by the Nazis, drove Churchill mad. Over the course of the war the prime minister went from wondering if de Gaulle had "gone off his head," to calling him a "monster," to saying he should be kept "in chains." Franklin Roosevelt didn't like him any better. The United States president gave de Gaulle all of three hours' notice before the Allies' massive 1942 landings in French-controlled Algeria and Morocco.

De Gaulle didn't get along well with the British intelligence services, either. His Free French staff initially believed Piquet-Wicks and other Brits were poaching would-be French agents. Some Free French staffers thought of the British as a "rival organization," Piquet-Wicks wrote. But in time certain spies in London saw the benefit of working with de Gaulle—nearly every Frenchman who came to the city wanted to meet him—and so Piquet-Wicks's division began sharing information, and then missions, with the intelligence bureau of the Free French. Loyalties blurred, and many secret agents Piquet-Wicks oversaw considered themselves to be working first for de Gaulle, and the operatives' success in France drew more people to London, which in turn strengthened the general, militarily as well as politically.

Now, weighing La Rochefoucauld's question of joining the British, de Gaulle peered again at the young man, until he reached a conclusion that Robert would remember for the rest of his life: "It's still for France," de Gaulle said, "even if it's allied with the Devil. Go!"

# CHAPTER 6

The idea had come in the spring of 1938. Hitler had annexed his native Austria and was now eying other countries, and a few people in the British government began to consider something called "clandestine warfare" to combat the threat. The government secretly established three authorities. The first, overseen by the Foreign Office and ultimately called the Political Warfare Executive, developed propaganda to influence German opinion. The second, an outgrowth of MI6 called Section D, considered German targets vulnerable to sabotage and the sort of people who might do the work. The third was little more in the beginning than two officers and a typist, but it became MI(R), which studied how guerrilla fighting—light equipment, evasive tactics, high mobility—might shape future wars.

Section D worked on time fuses for explosives and helped convince senior civil servants that there really should be a secret agency dealing in sabotage overseas. This was a concept "until that time unheard-of," as one author noted. MI(R) helped form an understanding of what it would mean to train foreign soldiers in guerrilla tactics. This was equally novel and just as fascinating, because a superpower like Britain had historically defended itself against such threats.

For as long as there had been war, in fact, there had been guerrilla warfare. The Jews in the bushes above the narrow mountain paths outside Beth Horon had "covered the Roman army with their darts" in AD 66, in the words of the historian Josephus, forcing the empire to retreat from its advance to the Mediterranean coast. The "fast moving and light armed" natives of northwestern Greece had destroyed the armored Athenians. The Spanish resistance of the Peninsular War (1807–14)—from which the modern-day term *guerrilla* derives—repelled Napoléon's army. The British lost first to a Revolutionary American militia composed in part of farmers who blended into the population, then to Pashtun tribes whose "pin-pricking hit-and-run tactics" didn't really cease until India's independence, and nearly lost to the elusive Boers in South Africa at the turn of the twentieth century.

Asymmetrical fighting was in fact so well established that the first counterinsurgency manual emerged in 600 AD, while the most famous guerrilla tract was T. E. Lawrence's *The Seven Pillars of Wisdom*, the book based on his experiences in World War I helping disparate bands of Bedouin tribesman push the mighty Turks out of Arabia. But by the outset of World War II, even though Lawrence's colleagues had survived, the agencies that had supported them had not. So, in May of 1940, with the situation in France worsening, the British chiefs of staff looked to the fledgling Section D and MI(R), and recommended to the war cabinet a new and "special organization" that could create "widespread revolt in [Germany's] conquered territories."

By July 2, with the armistice in France signed and Britain standing alone against a continent of Nazis, Minister of Economic Warfare Hugh Dalton wrote a letter to Britain's foreign secretary, Lord Halifax, continuing the theme of the earlier recommendation:

> We have got to organize movements in enemy-occupied territory . . . This "democratic international" must use many different methods, including industrial and military sabotage, labour agitation and strikes, continuous propaganda, terrorist acts against traitors and German leaders, boycotts and riots . . . What is needed is a new organization to coordinate, inspire, control and assist the nationals of the oppressed countries who must themselves be the direct participants. We need absolute secrecy,

a certain fanatical enthusiasm, willingness to work with people of different nationalities, complete political reliability . . . The organization should, in my view, be entirely independent of the War Office machine.

For two weeks the cabinet debated this secret organization. At last the outgoing prime minister, Neville Chamberlain, who had appeased Hitler in 1938 by giving him Czechoslovakia without a fight, signed a "most secret paper," one of the last of his life, and one that would have begun to redeem his reputation had anyone known of it. Chamberlain said that, on the authority of the prime minister, "a new organization shall be established forthwith to co-ordinate all action, by way of subversion and sabotage, against the enemy overseas . . . This organization will be known as Special Operations Executive."

The document became SOE's founding charter, and its passages—explicitly stated or implied—charged the agency with many responsibilities. First, SOE would train the foreign nation-als flooding England's shores in accepted and many unaccepted styles of war, and then parachute these fighters back to their oc-cupied countries, where they would assassinate high-ranking Ger-mans, sabotage the factories that made Nazi weaponry and the trains that transported it, and recruit other like-minded natives to the cause of liberation. Furthermore, inside enemy lines, SOE would drop tons of firearms, ammunition, explosives, and money near the camps of known Resistance groups, so that they might continue their anarchic efforts and draw out the men and women who wanted to fight but by dint of circumstance couldn't get to London.

Really, the world had seen nothing like SOE. Yes, guerrilla warfare had been around for millennia, but it had been exercised locally, by small and often subjected bands of people, not adminis-tered by a foreign superpower that first trained and equipped and then sent back the rebel fighters who might free their countries from Nazi subjugation. For that reason alone, SOE was remarkable. But the agency had even greater ambitions, and here it's important to return to T. E. Lawrence. While Lawrence served as SOE's spiritual father, his actions in the Arabian desert in 1917 and '18 were often of his own devising. Sometimes superiors had no idea what he was doing. SOE, by contrast, would develop and closely monitor the actions of thousands of Lawrences as they spread their ill-will across an entire nation—across an entire continent.

The scope of it was breathtaking. And Winston Churchill, who had become prime minister on the very day of the German blitzkrieg into France, loved it. It drew on his own history with irregular warfare.

Churchill lived to regale people with how, in 1895, under contract for London's *Daily Graphic*, he'd traveled to Cuba and watched revolutionaries usurp their Spanish overlords, sabotaging train tracks that the Spanish general staff frequented, and raiding the Spaniards' forts when they least expected it. The guerrillas, one Spanish officer told Churchill, with a quivering breath, were "everywhere and nowhere." Churchill had seen the same thing in India, as a second lieutenant in the cavalry, fighting the rebels who'd revolted against Britain's control of the Malakand Pass, and then again in Cape Town, South Africa, in 1899, where he'd gone to cover the Second Boer War for London's *Morning Post*. At one point, the Boers derailed the train on which Churchill was traveling, and then opened fire. Churchill narrowly escaped, but was ultimately taken prisoner along with fifty other men in an officers' camp in Pretoria. His subsequent tale, of fleeing the camp and trekking to the border of Portuguese East Africa some three hundred miles away, without a compass, food, or knowledge of Afrikaans, made his name back in London. But his conviction that greater military flexibility would be needed against Britain's future enemies clung to him as closely as his political fame, and so over the next twenty years he traveled with T. E. Lawrence to Cairo, funneled millions of pounds to a tsarist morphine addict out to topple Lenin's Communism, and even dined with Michael Collins, the guerrilla who led the fight for Irish independence.

Across all those years, he never lost his admiration for the saboteur. And by 1940, facing an enemy that threatened to overwhelm his tiny island, the newly sworn prime minister, who had spent three decades among insurgents from five countries, set out to create a force worthy of them to defend his own land. "And now, set Europe ablaze," he said of SOE's founding. SOE was more for Churchill than a last resort to repel Hitler's domination. It was the lessons of his wars incarnate. It was his proof that any army, even one as great as Germany's, could be defeated in part by small bands of rebels, trained like British commandos, striking hard against the Nazi underbelly, and blending back into the population. *Everywhere and nowhere.*

In his busy wartime schedule, Churchill would meet with visiting SOE agents. But like the codebreakers at Bletchley Park who intercepted German intelligence, Churchill could say nothing publicly of SOE or its ambition. When the war cabinet approved the organization, it insisted that no record of its formation appear on the "order paper" of the House of Commons. Secret funds covered some of SOE's costs, and Parliament had no control over them.

It was an "eccentrically English organization . . . The sort of thing that looks odd at the time, and eminently sensible later," wrote SOE historian M. R. D. Foot. First, agency oversight fell to a little-known bureaucracy, the Ministry of Economic Warfare. Any other leader would have placed it under his purview, as Franklin Roosevelt did when the Office of Strategic Services (OSS), the predecessor to the CIA, formed in World War II. But Churchill wanted SOE free of the pressures to hew to a prime minister's political necessities. So he wouldn't oversee it, which also began to explain why the Ministry of Defense wouldn't either. Churchill wanted nothing smelling of conventional warfare near SOE. In theory, one of the existing intelligence services could have provided support, but Churchill was unhappy with MI6's oversight of a bungled Section D mission in Stockholm. Churchill held the affair as proof that existing intelligence services shouldn't be allowed to manage the newly christened Special Operations Executive.

As a result, SOE wasn't exactly beloved by other intelligence branches. Churchill created a coordinating committee between the groups, which met twice then never again, due to hostilities against SOE. Some of this was to be expected. MI6 depended on the discreet collection of foreign intelligence; SOE used some of that same intelligence to literally bomb its way across Europe. MI6 officers wondered if what Britain was really sabotaging was its own efforts. Still, some of the animus seemed little more than petty jealousy, rising from the belief that Churchill saw SOE as a favorite child. The discarded boys of MI6 grew petulant, celebrating any bad news. "SOE's in the shit," the assistant chief of the agency, Claude Dansey, gleefully told another agent after the Gestapo's infiltration of a massive SOE-funded Resistance network. "The Germans are mopping them up all over the place." MI6 tried to convince Churchill to disband SOE. But, as always, the prime minister stood by it.

This infuriated the air force, too. The RAF said throughout the war that it could spare few planes for SOE missions, which some RAF officers saw as inefficient if not pointless. "Your work is a gamble which may give us a valuable dividend or may produce nothing," one RAF commander told an SOE staffer. "My bombing offensive is not a gamble." But Desmond Morton, the MI6 officer who gave Churchill raw intelligence through the 1930s, said the prime minister always loved the great risk and greater reward of "funny operations." Churchill drew constantly from his past, and let the softly lit sepia of his memory—the cosmopolitan saboteurs and fevered adventurers—inform his present-day decisions, sure that in the small corners of occupied Europe ideologues like those from his youth lived on.

# CHAPTER 7

R obert de La Rochefoucauld was enchanted by the little he'd
learned of SOE, and the agency's asymmetrical battlefields—a
new kind of war—played to his youthful arrogance. He could make
his mark as no La Rochefoucauld had, and have fun doing it. By the
time Robert left his meeting at Carlton Gardens with de Gaulle,
he had a sense that SOE carried a reputation the Free French could
never equal—that no fighting force could. The agency, in fact, had
already engineered two of the Allies' biggest victories in the European theater. The first was the assassination of Reinhard Heydrich, the architect of the Nazis' plan to rid Europe of Jews, by two
Czech agents who threw a contact-sensitive bomb onto Heydrich's
Mercedes as it took a hairpin turn on a Prague street. The second
feat was the sabotage of the Norsk Hydro facility in Norway, where
the Germans made heavy water, a key substance in the production
of nuclear weapons. There, nine Norwegian SOE agents raided the
heretofore impenetrable grounds high atop a mountain, found the
heavy-water cells in the basement of one building, and set their
timed bombs against them. The agents then took with them the
Norwegian scientist who monitored the room, backtracked across
the grounds they'd trespassed, and watched the explosion in awe—
all without firing their weapons.

When Robert de La Rochefoucauld met again with Eric Piquet-
Wicks, he said he wanted to join this secret organization, whose
members had the temerity to go where no one dared. Piquet-
Wicks smiled. Robert was a nobleman with an adventurous streak,
and though all sorts of people joined SOE—its thirteen thousand
worldwide agents ranged "from pimps to princesses," wrote one

historian—Piquet-Wicks said his agency required a certain type of commando in 1943. More important than Robert's class, in fact, or even his sense of daring, was his nationality. SOE needed Frenchmen.

France's geographic proximity, and its strategic, military, and political importance to Britain outweighed the considerations of other nations. SOE's organizational chart reflected this: Most occupied countries were overseen by a single section of SOE. The agency's brass thought France required six sections.

Two of these did the majority of the work in country and left the deepest impressions. The first was F Section. It launched in 1940, with bilingual British agents on the ground who organized French subversion. Some of SOE's best people came from F Section, but the agency expanded beyond it because, early in the war, F Section made a mistake. It had the hubris to refuse to work with de Gaulle's Free French forces in London. In fact, SOE called F Section the "independent French" section, and de Gaulle's Free French staff were told it didn't exist. When the Free French found out otherwise, they were furious, and this gave rise to another French section within SOE: R/F Section.

R/F worked closely with the Free French. SOE created it in May of 1941 out of political necessity—someone had to play nice with de Gaulle—but as the worldwide battle wore on, R/F arguably passed F Section in importance, especially as Frenchmen made their way to London and asked to meet with the general. De Gaulle melded the oversight of R/F with his own intelligence agency, the Bureau central de renseignements et d'action, or BCRA.

Eric Piquet-Wicks, with his goofy smile, was put in charge of R/F in the summer of 1941, his headquarters at 1 Dorset Square being a short walk from de Gaulle's Free French headquarters at Carlton Gardens. Piquet-Wicks's R/F and De Gaulle's intelligence bureau worked so closely that many missions were shaded by Free

French imperatives. Even Piquet-Wicks had a hard time separating the overlap.

R/F started "woefully small," Piquet-Wicks wrote, but grew to perhaps five hundred agents; an exact figure is difficult to ascertain because of the porous loyalties of the men and women who worked within it. But it was R/F that convinced Churchill to provide massive arms and aircraft to the French Resistance; R/F that handled four times the number of parachute drops of F Section; and R/F that first interviewed and recruited Jean Moulin, the French *résistant* who built massive networks throughout the country, and the saboteur who, above all, the Germans wanted captured and killed.

Eric Piquet-Wicks blew life onto the kindling of his section until its flames billowed and clouded the sky. The effort exhausted the man. By the time Robert de La Rochefoucauld met him, Piquet-Wicks had developed tuberculosis. He had ceded his post and was on doctor's orders to keep to a normal eight-hour schedule, but he loved the work too much, which was why he saw La Rochefoucauld now after the young's *résistant*'s meeting with de Gaulle.

Piquet-Wicks told Robert he wanted the young man to work for the "action" division, the clandestine operations unit that the Free French oversaw in conjunction with the R/F Section. La Rochefoucauld would be a British agent, but because of the byzantine bureaucracy of R/F, Robert could also call himself a proper French saboteur, a *résistant nonpareil*.

If, the agency man stressed, Robert could make it through the training.

# CHAPTER 8

The first thing they did was hike. Every morning, trainees like Robert who had passed SOE's psychological and character assessments woke at 6 a.m. and headed out on two- to three-mile walks, which soon became fifteen to twenty, with full rucksacks strapped to their backs. This was in Inchmery, near Southampton, on the coast of the English Channel in southern England, the home of R/F agents' basic training. But La Rochefoucauld wouldn't have known that because SOE staff was adept at keeping certain details from its foreign trainees, for security purposes. (La Rochefoucauld thought the majority of his training took place in Manchester, some 225 miles north.) The secret organization kept many secrets. Agents after the war recalled being grouped during training by nationality or skill set—radio transmitters, industrial saboteurs—but never knowing a fellow trainee's name. Only aliases were used. Any letter written home was censored by SOE officers. Even the daily hikes served an ulterior motive: The staff wanted to see which trainees were drunks or addicts and therefore unsuitable.

Basic training lasted around three weeks, at which point the real commando lessons began. Robert moved on to Scotland, to the wild and stunning western coast of Inverness-shire, and the massive country estates there, which SOE head Colin Gubbins knew well and which was, as one agency historian put it, "secure from inquisitive eyes." Inverness-shire had few roads and, because of a nearby naval base, it had been declared a restricted area by the Admiralty. Not everyone found it as perfect as Gubbins did. In the fall, a Dutch agent described it as a "wretched, barren countryside, thinly populated; rain fell from a heavy sky that never cleared completely . . . a most depressing place."

La Rochefoucauld and the roughly thirty prospective agents in his class learned the skills that hinted at the war awaiting them: how to jump from a train moving at thirty miles per hour and roll away unharmed; how to crawl on their bellies and grow accustomed to live rounds being fired above them. The staff encouraged them to try escaping without getting caught, to live in the wild, to read maps and compasses. SOE personnel gave trainees a number to call in case they got in trouble, but, naturally, no name to ask for.

They learned to sabotage almost anything. The main training explosive was a plastic detonator consisting of cyclonite mixed with a plasticizing medium, one of the safest explosives to practice on, because it wouldn't ignite even if a rifle was fired at it. It needed a detonator in the mass of the explosive to set itself off. Plus, it could be molded into almost any shape, like dough. Perfect for a would-be saboteur.

The don of industrial sabotage was Lt. Col. George T. Rheam, and as the agents moved through their paramilitary courses, they split off into specialty schools like Rheam's on demolition, an advanced class at Special Training School 17, in Brickendonbury Estate. Tall, somber, even forbidden-looking, Rheam was an inspiring teacher. Students not only learned to blow up trains and railways and bridges—the targets of saboteurs since T. E. Lawrence's day—but gained a supple understanding of when to detonate what, with which means, and where. For instance, it was far better, after targeting a train or bridge, to also sabotage the cranes that cleared the derailed locomotives; that could truly slow the Nazi war machine. One could blow up a row of electric poles stretching to the horizon, or one could target the single squat transformer from which the lines derived their power. Sabotaging the whole of a Nazi munitions factory might be good for the spirit of an occupied people, but it was far more efficient and destructive to target only a vital, difficult-to-replace component of the factory, which meant versing oneself in the architecture and engineering of industrial plants. As the SOE historian M. R. D. Foot wrote: "Anyone trained by [Rheam] could look at a factory with quite new eyes, spot the few essential machines in it, and understand how to stop them with a few well-placed ounces of explosive." Rheam had personally instructed the Norwegians who went on to sabotage the heavy-water cells at Norsk.

Rheam taught that bombs could take on all shapes and could inflict damage that wasn't always measured in material losses. SOE agents in the field once stuffed rat carcasses with plastic explosives; though the mission largely failed, German administrators still inundated local secret police with dead vermin that they thought held clues to the nationality of the saboteurs. In another instance, SOE operatives camouflaged explosive materiel as coal; when a German fed it into a furnace the tiny bombs not only totaled a plant but left many workers afraid to return to the job. Rheam loved that sort of ingenuity.

The art of hand-to-hand combat was just as inspired—and just as savage. SOE adopted the teachings of W. E. Fairbairn and E. A. Sykes, two former policemen from Shanghai, who patrolled the port city when it was possibly the most dangerous in the world. Fairbairn knew multiple forms of martial arts and had also picked up French savate, Cornish wrestling, and English boxing. Sykes was, simply put, the best marksman anyone had seen. La Rochefoucauld was stunned by what he learned.

In the war's early years, by way of introduction, the pair would stand at the top of a staircase in one of the Inverness-shire estates, a class of agents sitting below, and would fall down the steps, tumbling to the bottom and landing in a battle crouch position, a gun in one hand and a knife in the other. They would then rise, so the prospective agents could take their measure.

Fairbairn was the older of the two, a lean and hard fifty-eight.

He had been in more than six hundred street fights in Shanghai and, twenty-five years later, during the course of SOE training, said little more to prospective agents than "Stick a knife in here," and "Now, put your thumb in his eye." Sykes was different. He looked like a retired bishop, observers wrote, a little shorter than Fairbairn and a lot more personable. Would-be agents came to the plumpy Sykes, fifty-six, with questions that Fairbairn and his tough demeanor didn't invite. Both wore glasses and battle dress with a webbing belt.

By the time Robert de La Rochefoucauld reached Inverness-shire, in the spring of 1943, Sykes and Fairbairn had revised the course syllabus based on the experiences of agents in the field, and Sykes oversaw the training alone, as Fairbairn had moved on to a special ops training ground in Canada. But the lesson plan still honored the collaboration between the men.

La Rochefoucauld and prospects like him learned to shoot a handgun, an automatic Colt .45, from a slight crouch, firing from the navel as Sykes preferred, two quick pops because a quick shot was better than an accurate one—and besides, accuracy came with practice. Sykes taught prospective agents how to keep the lower body tense but the upper loose and yet centered, and from there how to kill up to four people while falling down. He constructed a "house of horrors" for his would-be assassins. They busted open a door to see a dummy connected to wires leap at them from the bedroom; agents had to quickly gun him down. Then a trapdoor opened and more dummies emerged. Some sprang from beneath tables. Bottles and chairs came hurtling at the prospective agents' heads. They had to shoot everything. They had to adapt quickly, too, because on another day there was a second house, with new horrors, then a third, a fourth and fifth, the intruders coming from above them, below, lifelike and inventive in their attacks. Always, the prospects were graded for their efforts and accuracy.

Fairbairn and Sykes had developed a knife in Shanghai whose

blade was thin enough to puncture a man without leaving a mark and yet strong enough to reach his organs. SOE prospects learned to carry it in a sheath in their left hip pocket—the right reserved for their gun—and to flick it at an enemy fighter as if it were a paintbrush, in an upward motion that began at the testicles and ended at the chin. The blade did a nauseating amount of damage. La Rochefoucauld learned that in close combat a man who wielded a knife well was the most dangerous man of all.

In fact, the only good defense against a knife attack was a wooden chair, the four legs upturned and jutting at the opponent. This was part of Fairbairn and Sykes's defense training, which even Fairbairn called "gutter fighting." The main point was that one always had a weapon at the ready. The shovel or pick ax with which many nations outfitted soldiers could split a man's skull. A stick as small as four inches long could be turned into a nasty switch that was more painful than a punch to a face. The corner of a matchbox, held between the second and third fingers of a fist, could puncture a man's skin when he was punched—or, if delivered as an uppercut to the nose, could come close to killing him. A well-folded piece of newspaper could do the same.

Then there were the surprise moves. These were known as the Silent Killing techniques because the attacks opened with an unarmed maneuver that might end with a quick flick of the knife across the throat—or might not require the blade at all. Agents learned that slamming one's cupped palms against the enemy's ears would break his eardrums and perhaps concuss him. The thrust of an agent's open palm against a combatant's nose should conclude with the agent jamming his fingers into the enemy's eyes. Once an enemy fighter was on the ground, an agent should jump and drive both his heels into the man's diaphragm—at a minimum, the enemy is left without breath; at most, he has organ damage. If an agent was behind a man and had him in a sleeper hold, the agent should push forward on the back of the enemy's neck. The motion might paralyze, if not kill, him. Punching the enemy in the Adam's apple might kill him, too.

On and on the lessons went—testicle kicking, thumb bending, back breaking. "Your aim is to kill your opponent as soon as possible," the SOE syllabus said. "A prisoner is generally a handicap and a source of danger." As Fairbairn himself wrote: "The majority of these methods are drastic in the extreme. They are inspired by judo, but in contrast to judo, they recognize no accepted rules . . . The methods . . . enable a young man of only average strength to overpower a much stronger opponent."

The techniques became so well-known that in 1942 the Germans published a manual about how to counter these Silent Killing methods, which the Nazis called "savage." In fact, some scholars contend that Hitler's Commando Order—an October 1942 mandate stating that all captured Allied special operatives be executed—sprang from Hitler either obtaining the SOE syllabus or, at least, growing familiar with its passages on Silent Killing. "From captured orders," Hitler said, "it emerges that [Allied soldiers] are instructed . . . to kill out-of-hand unarmed captives who they think might prove an encumbrance to them, or hinder them in successfully carrying out their aims. Orders have indeed been found in which the killing of prisoners has positively been demanded of them." Hitler's mandate to immediately execute imprisoned operatives was a violation of the Geneva Convention, but, then again, so were Fairbairn and Sykes's training techniques. Hitler appeared to be speaking directly of SOE agents when he said, "In future, all terror and sabotage troops of the British and their accomplices who do not act like soldiers but rather like bandits will be treated as such by the German troops, and will be ruthlessly eliminated in battle, wherever they appear."

The threat was real. Beheadings, firing squads, and the slower death of the camps awaited many captured SOE agents. But they parachuted back into their native countries unafraid, in part because of the very training that incensed Hitler. "I think the great advantage of the advanced assault course," SOE agent Henry Hall said after the war, "was that . . . you knew so many more tricks of the trade and methods of attack, demolition and causing havoc and destruction that you became super confident . . . The answer to whatever attack you were up against would be an instinctive reaction. You just took it as something as natural as drinking a cup of tea or making a sandwich." As another agent, George Langelaan, put it, the self-confidence Fairbairn and Sykes gave trainees "gradually grew into a sense of physical power and superiority that few men ever acquire. By the time we finished our training, I would have willingly enough tackled any man, whatever his strength, size or ability. [The instructors] taught us to face the possibility of a fight without the slightest tremor of apprehension, a state of mind which very few professional boxers ever enjoy and which so often means more than half the battle. Strange as this may seem, it is understandable when a man knows for certain that he can hurt, maul, injure or even kill with the greatest of ease, and that during every split second of a fight he has not one but a dozen different openings, different possibilities, to choose from."

Summarizing all he learned and the edge it gave him, Robert de La Rochefoucauld said with his characteristic understatement, "The English were great coaches."

The preparation didn't end there. La Rochefoucauld and his class traveled to Manchester and its Ringway Airport for the most terrifying of lessons: parachute drops. It started simply enough. La Rochefoucauld learned to jump from a six-foot-high trampoline and roll properly onto the ground. Some agents from previous classes recalled the staff asking trainees to watch sandbags attached to parachutes drop from the sky. "A good half of the parachutes did not open," one agent said, "and the bags thudded onto the ground with a dull, flat noise that brought us no confidence at all." The surviving SOE records show that by 1943 the staff seemed to have done away with the airbags and just put the agents in the sky. A hot-air balloon tethered to the ground hoisted La Rochefoucauld and an instructor more than five hundred yards up. "I don't really know why," La Rochefoucauld later said, "the rope under our feet reinforced the feeling of empty space and gave me terrifying vertigo." That first time, Robert sat at the basket's edge, staring down, frightfully down, the distance between him and the earth shocking and disturbing. But the only way to learn was to do, and when the instructor commanded him to jump, he found it within himself to push off.

It wasn't awful—at least, that's what he thought when he landed on the ground. But he never grew comfortable with the particulars of parachute jumping—every time he "felt more and more afraid," he said—and one sentence in his military file might explain why. In early 1943, while training, La Rochefoucauld was knocked unconscious and broke his wrist. The report offered no further explanation, and perhaps one couldn't be expected given the clandestine nature of Robert's work. But it seemed possible that those injuries occurred on one of the four or five parachute jumps that each SOE agent was asked to perform before entering the field.

In some sense, Robert was lucky. SOE's French sections recorded six fatalities from parachute drops, though none during training. After La Rochefoucauld's injuries healed, he moved on to SOE's finishing schools, a euphemistic play on the peacetime connotation: Some of these institutions were literally run by convicts. SOE thought it important for prospective commandos to learn to crack safes and pick locks, and the agency employed burglars on special leave from prison. "They knew how to open the safes better than anyone," La Rochefoucauld said. The British seemed "concerned with working all of our skills to the maximum."

Another finishing school parachuted would-be agents into the middle of the countryside, and demanded they return to camp, some sixty miles away, without maps or compasses and while evading the police, who had been tipped off to their mission and worked to catch them. One time Robert and the other trainees saw an approaching patrol car and stripped down to their boxers, posing as joggers out for a run. When the cop reached them, "We'd start to shudder with big heaving breaths, like athletes in training," La Rochefoucauld wrote. "It wasn't a complete lie."

On another occasion La Rochefoucauld parachuted with a trainee on a similar mission—a race where teams competed to get back to camp on wits alone, avoiding arrest—but La Rochefoucauld's coconspirator landed awkwardly on his drop and sprained his ankle. He couldn't walk. Wanting to win, La Rochefoucauld stole a military police truck. Hours before anyone else returned, La Rochefoucauld and the man with the bad ankle stepped out of the government vehicle they'd stolen, and the SOE staff, astonished, decided the theft was as ingenious as it was illegal—the mark of a true agent—and did not punish La Rochefoucauld.

At another finishing school Robert learned how to withstand torture. The section heads themselves often participated in the mock interrogations. Maintaining silence during imprisonment was vital to the agency's success. "These rehearsals were grim affairs," F Section head Maurice Buckmaster later wrote, "and we spared the recruits nothing. They were stripped and made to stand for hours in the light of bright lamps and though, of course, we never used any physical violence on them, they certainly knew what it was to go through it by the time we had finished."

La Rochefoucauld's instructors told him to get angrier than his questioners. "When you become angry, you don't feel the blows anymore," he said. "This was one of the central trainings. And of course we were not supposed to say why we were there, where we came from, what we did." Piquet-Wicks outfitted his agents with clothes and cover stories, "all the intricate planning for a successful mission," he said, in the hope that the lies agents would convey to the Germans were believable. In fact, the SOE staff assessed agents on their contrived credibility. Stutters and cracks in cover were grave offenses. "On occasion, from perhaps as few as twenty available men, only four or five finally could be entrusted with missions," Piquet-Wicks wrote. He was a man who abided by the SOE adage, "He that has a secret should not only hide it but hide that he needs to hide it." These finishing schools taught La Rochefoucauld how to look and act ordinary while doing extraordinary things.

And when all else failed, Robert learned about the final redemption of the cyanide pill. It should be on an agent at all times, the staff directed; swallowing it would kill a man in minutes.

Though the passing rate of SOE trainees was low—in Robert's class of thirty, he was one of seven to become a saboteur—the last lesson of the agency for a graduating class was humility: Many great commandos had come before, and some had faced impossible circumstances, which had forced them to gulp down the pill. New agents should be prepared to do the same.

# CHAPTER 9

With the light of the moon guiding it, the four-engine plane crossed into occupied Europe one summer night in 1943, its lights flicked off, its pilot nosing the bird toward the faintly lit contours of central France and the region above the Morvan. La Rochefoucauld sat inside the plane, confident, even arrogant, and above all anxious to begin his first mission: helping to train Resistance fighters in the lethal tactics he'd just learned. He was not yet twenty years old.

He had been given French clothes, a French watch—everything that would obscure what he had spent months in Britain training for. He would hide his noble identity and deadly expertise in the dress and demeanor of a Burgundy laborer. On the tarmac just before takeoff, a colonel had stopped him to say La Rochefoucauld wasn't leaving to get himself killed; he had to be brave, be daring, but the colonel counted on seeing him again.

And yet as the plane crossed into France, the Germans on the ground spotted it, and their antiaircraft gunners opened fire. The plane dipped first one wing and then the other to avoid the rounds, but the bullets pockmarked its frame. The metal-shredding ping terrified La Rochefoucauld as much as the plane's swerving maneuvers. The craft at last rose, beyond the reach of the Germans but also above the outline of the landscape, and stayed there for minutes, flying blind. Everyone listened for the heavy drone of an approaching Nazi fighter. But none came. And so the Halifax descended to its steady cruising altitude, having endured surprisingly minimal damage. La Rochefoucauld tried to act with a similar resilience, but quietly shook with fear.

It would not be much better on the ground. Robert was joining a decided minority of the population, the 2 percent of Frenchmen who actively participated in the Resistance. The guerrillas the Germans captured, they killed, because a *résistant*'s mission—anarchy by any means—wasn't covered by the international treaties that protected prisoners of war in their official military fatigues. The *résistant*'s civilian clothing was itself sometimes all the goading the Nazis needed to send another suspected saboteur to the firing squad. While special operatives like La Rochefoucauld seldom fought at any front, their war was in some respects more dangerous than an Allied soldier's, because the standard rules of combat did not apply. Even British handlers said an underground man could make it only six months in France. After that, the law of averages worked against him.

Robert looked out his window at a country that was far different from the one he'd escaped. The North African landings in November 1942 had led a furious Hitler to declare the whole of France occupied. In February 1943, the Vichy government, by then openly Fascist, shipped French workers to Germany to aid the Nazi war effort. Eventually 650,000 Frenchmen would depart for the factories and mines; by the end of 1943, the French would build 42 percent of Germany's transport planes. Of course, this Service du travail obligatoire, or mandatory work order, worked against the collaborators in Vichy and Paris, too. The STO disrupted the lives of hundreds of thousands of people, and awakened in some the urge to rebel. They simply refused to honor the order and took to the mountains, where they trained as *résistants*, returning to the lowlands to sabotage everything German. The French began calling these fighters *maquis*, a Corsican term for mountainous scrubland. "The concept did not exist in January 1943," the historian Rod Kedward wrote. "It was everywhere by June." Maquis men, and really any Resistance group, organized by the British or forming organically in France, identified with de Gaulle, who said of the open collaboration between Vichy and Berlin: "Sabotage their plans and hate their leaders. National liberation cannot be separated from national insurrection." The German ambassador to Vichy counted 3,800 sabotages in France between January and September 1943. Even Défense de la France, a Catholic group that had once called for nothing more than "spiritual resistance," approved of Nazi assassinations in 1943, and ultimately stated in its underground newspaper, "Kill the German to purify our territory."

The Nazis were not unprepared for this uprising. They had handed over the policing of France in 1942 to the dreaded brutes of the Sicherheitsdienst, or SD, nominally an intelligence service, though in practice much more. By the time of La Rochefoucauld's drop, this secret police force had organized into a head office in Paris, and seventeen regional and forty-five branch sections in the provinces. The SD's reach covered the whole of France, aided by the collaborating and anonymous Frenchmen who sent up to five million denunciatory letters during the war, enough to turn the country into what the French scholar Michel Foucault would later call a state of "permanent, exhaustive, omnipresent surveillance."

And yet, angered by the persistent sabotages, the Nazis and the Vichy government created still another police force, the Milice, staffed by collaborating Frenchmen whose job was to hunt down resisters. In some sense, the Milice men were worse than those in the SD, who were ostensibly concerned with information; the thirty thousand members of the Milice, many of them former criminals, turned their job into barbaric fun, subjecting those they arrested to occasionally harsher torture than the Nazis themselves. As more French police refused to do their jobs to Germany's liking—a form of passive resistance—the Milice filled the void.

This was the country into which La Rochefoucauld was parachuting.

The plane circled around the Yonne department in central France, looking for the *résistants* on the ground who had helped organize the landing. A drop like this required twenty-three different steps, and the Brits and French were now near the end of the checklist. Each side operated with a wireless radio called an S-Phone, developed by SOE, which allowed both parties to speak on a secure airwave. The men on the ground had brought portable lamps and flashlights and organized themselves in formation, trying to catch the pilot's eye. After two passes, the plane swinging ever lower, the pilot saw them. The airplane's hatch opened and La Rochefoucauld moved to its edge. He sat down, his feet dangling into open air. Straight ahead of him were two lights: The red meant *don't jump*, the green meant *do*. The red one was lit and La Rochefoucauld stared at it, nervous.

Then it turned green.

He landed, uneventfully, and a dozen men helped him fold his parachute and gather the bags and weapons that had fallen after him. They worked quickly, afraid that Germans had heard the plane as it whined and circled or seen the parachutes bloom in the moonlight. They moved to trucks idling on a road near the woods and headed out.

These men were mostly from the local chapter of the Alliance, a nationwide resistance and intelligence group formed by Marie-Madeleine Fourcade, a beautiful milky-skinned mother of two. Before the war, she had served as the secretary for a magazine, *L'Ordre National*, which published the battle plans of Hitler's land, sea, and air forces. The magazine built up an intelligence network that after 1940 found a purpose outside journalism. With the majority of the magazine's staff fighting the Germans, Fourcade decided to head the intelligence network herself. It was the perfect cover: No one in wartime France would expect a woman to be capable of such covert work. Over the next few years, she slipped across the demarcation line stuffed in a postal bag, escaped Nazi arrest on multiple occasions, helped her own children do the same, grew the network from a handful of agents to a thousand. She gave her people the code-names of animals and watched as the network's actions became so notorious the Nazis took to calling it "Noah's Ark." By 1943, it was the only Resistance network covering all of France.

La Rochefoucauld rode in the pickup for an hour with these *résistants*, the landscape on the headlight's periphery rising gradually to the hills of the Massif Central, then narrowing as great forests crowded the road and blocked the light of the stars. The trucks slowed to negotiate turns and switchbacks carved out of the thick groves of trees, the road itself becoming a shabby path until at last the men arrived in a remote camp deep in the woods south of Avallon, near a village called Quarré-les-Tombes, named for the Gallo-Roman tombstones near its church. The sun rose above the forest line as twenty men clustered round. La Rochefoucauld distributed the cigarettes and chocolates he'd brought in his bag.

The Alliance's local boss was a vicar from a nearby cathedral, Father Bernard Ferrand, a forty-three-year-old with failing health and what some thought to be monarchist views, who hated the Germans and had joined the Resistance in 1941. Swarthy and bifocaled, Ferrand emerged as a leader because of his seniority—most Resistance fighters were, like La Rochefoucauld, young—and also because of his profession. Just as people thought Fourcade's gender prohibitive, many didn't think a man of the cloth capable of commanding saboteurs. He had a quiet intensity and a priest's righteousness. He didn't seem to mind that among his scores of fighters were socialists and even atheists. To Ferrand, only reclaiming France mattered, and so he recruited other holy men to his cause, convincing them to hide out *résistants* or downed British pilots in cathedrals or rectories.

La Rochefoucauld's job in Quarré-les-Tombes would consist of training Ferrand's men, and those from other Resistance groups, in the use of explosives. They would learn to place bombs against power plants or railroads; the Frenchmen who had the daring to become saboteurs often lacked the technical skills. La Roche-foucauld would fix that.

But as the sabotages had increased in central France, more Nazi agents had gone undercover and found their way into groups. "Arrests," Fourcade later wrote, "became a nightmare." Her people needed to speak with London by radio, but the Nazis knew the frequencies the combatants were likely to use and had developed tracking equipment that quickly isolated the neighborhood, then the block, and, finally, the apartment with the wireless transmitter. Radiomen were to keep communications to seconds, but most needed far more time to relay their information. "Our radio operators were the real frontliners, the first to sacrifice their lives," Fourcade wrote.

The SD unraveled many Resistance groups in the summer of 1943. The brilliant SD head in Bordeaux, Friedrich Dohse, flipped a fighter, which led to the dismantling of a massive network in southwest France called Scientist. In Paris, SD agents infiltrated and tortured members of the city's largest Resistance group, Prosper, which crumbled in July. Even the most important figure of the Resistance, Jean Moulin, who had persuaded France's eight largest Resistance networks to align themselves under one heading, was betrayed and arrested in June 1943. He died after weeks of torture, at the hands of the infamous SD agent Klaus Barbie.

The Alliance suffered that summer, too. In July, just as La Roche-foucauld was establishing himself in country, Fourcade agreed to leave it. The threat to her life was too great. "I was deeply afraid of what lay ahead," she later admitted. She fled to England, to command the network remotely. The dismantling of so many groups, the partial compromising of still more, and the arrests of hundreds of people led to a "total stagnation" in leadership in 1943, said Jacques Bingen, a formative *résistant* who survived that summer's arrests—only to be betrayed and arrested himself.

The fallow period meant the fighters who remained—courageous or naive or both—had to play outsized roles in the rebellion. Robert, all of nineteen, soon found himself training and leading forty men and getting pulled aside by a captain of a Resistance group, a man in his forties calling himself Pius VII. He "very insistently told me . . . he was painfully lacking in arms," La Rochefoucauld wrote. Could Robert help to supply him? The two first ran an inventory to see what was needed, and La Rochefoucauld found the chapter "truly weak, in weapons and in explosives." So, with the help of a wireless man, Robert contacted an R/F agent in London with the code-name Henri and requested an immediate drop.

Henri said multiple containers of explosives and small arms could be parachuted—but the date and time remained to be decided. For two weeks, Robert waited until he received word. The mission at last appeared a go for the following night.

Six arms drops occurred that summer in the region, and though three of them could have been La Rochefoucauld's, the one that most likely involved him was scheduled for July 22, in the small village of Chassy, an hour from Quarré-les-Tombes.

To communicate with the Resistance, SOE used not only encrypted radios but very public ones. The BBC, in fact, put out communiqués meant for the underground, in its daily "personal messages" segment. These were outright bizarre missives that aired on the broadcaster's English and French services—phrases that sometimes meant nothing but other times, if résistants had been warned in advance by their British handlers, meant that a mission was on. The evening of the proposed Chassy drop, during the personal messages segment, amid dozens of coded phrases—like "Romeo is kissing Juliette" or "Esculapius does not like sheep"—résistants in central France and SOE agents in London heard a message that was their cue: "The collaborators already have sad faces."

Well after nightfall, a handful of men drove their pickups from their camp to the drop zone, trees clustered here and there but the plains otherwise stretching to the moonlit horizon. The mission would be overseen by two local Resistance fighters who worked closely with SOE, Alain de la Roussilhe and Pierre Argoud. Soon their transmitter had contacted the pilot's. The men turned on their electric lamps and within moments heard the whine of the plane, and then saw its outline. It traveled, as ever, with its lights off. The bomber missed them and circled back, flying lower now, no more than a few hundred feet above the ground. Then its hatch opened and seconds later the men saw the familiar bloom of opened chutes. There were many of them—too many to count as they drifted downward. Strung beneath each was a three-foot metal cylinder that held up to four hundred pounds of cargo. When the bounty struck ground, the men folded the still-billowing parachutes and immediately took the arms with them. "It would do no good to wait where we were," La Rochefoucauld wrote. They drove to the safety of the Yonne's unending forest, and took stock.

It was stunning: fifteen containers of submachine guns and plastic explosives and ammunition and money—even chocolate and cigarettes. "Everything we needed to wage war!" La Rochefoucauld wrote. Some members of the Alliance looked at Robert in awe: How did a kid like this help to pull off a drop like that? It gave La Rochefoucauld a cachet with certain fighters, and the mystery of this young instructor lured local *résistants* to him; many knew he had parachuted from London but knew little else. So as his training continued in the days after the drop the men listened to him, even if they were nearly double his age. He confidently told them how to mold plastic explosives, where to place them—a smaller sabotage against key equipment was sometimes better than a massive, fiery one. "In a few weeks, they became excellent pyrotechnicians," La Rochefoucauld wrote, "and, at the end of August, they knew the ins and outs of using explosives. Now we had to get down to our main mission."

The hope was to sabotage the power plant that supplied electricity to portions of the nearby city of Prémery, and also a factory that repaired German equipment. A camaraderie grew among the men as they anticipated their mission, and those who trained under La Rochefoucauld began to think of themselves as part of Groupe Roche, according to Robert's military records, suggesting the brash young man relayed not only the secret techniques of sabotage but a bit of his personal history. It must have been hard for the nineteen-year-old to remain discreet that summer. At last, he was fighting the Germans, sending his men on reconnaissance missions of selected sites, discussing plant layouts and engineering and when the Nazis stood watch and when they did not. "Chance is the most extraordinary thing you can have in your life," La Rochefoucauld said, "and you should know how to take advantage of it." He positively thrummed with energy.

One night in September, with the power plant transmitter unguarded, La Rochefoucauld and his men placed their plastic explosives against it, and against the surrounding inflow power lines. They set their timers and ran. The explosion downed the lines and tore up the transmitter. "Everything went perfectly well," La Rochefoucauld later wrote, with a touch of English understatement. A few nights later, La Rochefoucauld said the men did the same to the German-occupied grounds that repaired equipment. They sabotaged the plant so that workers spent their days piecing it, and not the instruments of war, together again. Victory was now a nectar with a sweet aftertaste. The men next sabotaged two railway lines simply because they felt like it.

La Rochefoucauld's saboteurs were not alone. That August and September, the Yonne's Nazi-friendly politicians counted sixty acts of sabotage in the department, the work carried out by British-organized groups like Robert's, as well as Communist, Socialist, and French nationalist ones. Each sabotage seemed to embolden the next, and as they increased in frequency and intensity they tinged each day in the shades of hope—or, conversely, despair. The *sous-prefect* of Avallon, a Nazi collaborator, wrote in September 1943:

"Automobile theft, criminal attacks . . . fires, theft of food and sabotages are events which for two months have completely changed the public and created a small white terror amid our people." Another collaborating politician in the Yonne reported nineteen injuries and twenty-seven deaths as a result of these "terrorist acts." In response, a "special brigade" of German military police deployed to the northern half of the Yonne, armed with guns and even grenades. In the southern half, where La Rochefoucauld hid out, the Milice and military police made strong shows, appearing in what were formerly rural and unpatrolled municipalities. In Quarré-les-Tombes, for example, a village small enough for the "commercial district" to comprise a few shops, guards nevertheless stood watch at two stores day and night.

**B**ut the Nazis deemed even this increase in manpower insufficient, and the German high command in Berlin asked the head of the Abwehr in Dijon to intervene. The Abwehr oversaw German military intelligence and its man in Dijon, Oberleutnant Kurt Merck (aka "Captain Kaiser"), was one of the best in France. He was a thirty-six-year-old whose strong build belied his asthmatic wheezings, and who favored a silk scarf with his uniform.

Merck thought the best way to destroy Resistance groups was to infect them, and so he enlisted J. P. Lien, a dashing *résistant* from Combat, one of the first Resistance groups, whose underground newspaper Albert Camus edited. Lien had been turned during the war—perhaps under torture, though the historical record doesn't offer irrefutable evidence—and now worked as a double agent for the Abwehr. Merck asked Lien to infiltrate the Alliance. He said the Nazis would handle the arrests.

The German high command had threatened to ship Merck to the cold and bloody Eastern Front if he failed in this mission, which was soon called Operation Gibet, and so he'd chosen Lien carefully. Many *résistants* in the Yonne department and throughout the country knew of Combat and its bona fides, but none knew it had a double agent. As summer turned to fall, Lien developed more and more relationships inside Alliance, his credentials aiding his secret hideouts. The Alliance even gave him the code-name Lanky.

At 8 a.m. on September 16, 1943, as La Rochefoucauld basked in his success in the Yonne, SD men at a train station outside Paris arrested the Alliance's top deputy, Marie Fourcade's right-hand man, Commandant Léon Faye, on his way into the city. That morning, the agents also nabbed the Alliance's head of operations, its head of security services, five radio operators, and seven more people who helped with transmissions, finding "arms, ammunitions [and] a large sum of money," according to a German report. By the afternoon, a high-ranking Alliance man with the code-name Hedgehog sent a message to all local chapters: "Do not try to contact any member of our group stop examine ways of parachuting and rendezvous at sea stop . . ." Hedgehog thought the leak might be contained. He was wrong. Three days later, SD agents arrested two men in Paris who oversaw intelligence. Then Merck deployed his men to move through the provinces.

Young lieutenants from Lyon, radio operators, fighters who called themselves the Apaches—all of them were arrested. Parachuting experts who attempted to shoot their way out were killed. In the mountainous town of Volvic, in south-central France, SD agents surrounded the hidden headquarters of another Alliance cell, arresting a colonel who called himself Cricket, his lieutenants, radio operators and other agents, about twenty people in all. "Warning," Hedgehog said in a message, "do not contact Cricket's sector any more stop all captured stop . . ." In Autun, in the Burgundy region, the local boss's wife, aware of the arrests, anxiously awaited her husband's return from business in Paris. When she saw an unknown car slam its brakes in her drive, and then saw the felt hats and Macintosh jackets of the secret police stride toward the house, she threw her husband's radio transmitter through a back window, and followed it out. But it was too late. The SD men surrounded the home, and they then paraded out her handcuffed husband and his second in command, a banker, who had chained to his neck the two pistols he had tried to hide from the Nazis.

On September 22, the SD came to the Yonne. In Sens, in the north of the department, secret police found two brothers and Communist *résistants* in a safe house. The rebels opened fire on the advancing secret police. One of the brothers and three of the Germans were killed, but the Nazis continued their push south. They arrested, among others, a man and his family in Chapelle-sur-Oreuse, two more brothers in Brienon, and attacked and "annihilated," in the words of a subsequent report, a small group of Maquis fighters in Mount-Saint-Sulpice.

In Avallon, in the Yonne's southern third, Father Ferrand spent the day learning to work a transmitter, near a secluded cemetery. The SD men found him there. They arrested him along with François Robb (likely Ferrand's transmitter instructor), and a seventy-one-year-old priest named Froment. Panic spread through the remaining network.

Marie-Madeleine Fourcade followed the news of Ferrand's arrest, and so many others. "Treachery," she later wrote, "left us completely defenseless." Approximately 150 people were arrested in the span of a month. "There was no end to the list of names that I had to erase on my network chart . . . Each time I crossed out the name of a friend I experienced the feeling of having wielded the executioner's axe," she wrote. "I was dying of grief."

Merck, meanwhile, dined happily one night at a private banquet in Dijon where J. P. Lien was the guest of honor. Lien was given the German Iron Cross with Sword, and two million francs. "The Alliance," one Abwehr man pronounced, "the Noah's Ark that we have been fighting since 1940, has been destroyed."

La Rochefoucauld's subset Groupe Roche was dismantled, and Robert himself stayed to the woods, contacting the R/F agents when he felt it safe and pleading with them to get him on a return flight to London. He was not yet six months in country and already felt the odds, as his SOE handlers had told him, working against him. But no plane could be spared. The almost ceaseless arrests—the SD nabbing fourteen more Alliance members after Ferrand's imprisonment, and a Yonne *résistant* who under torture gave up twenty men across multiple Resistance groups—left a terrible impression on the Royal Air Force. Why help these irregular fighters? They seemed too poorly trained to avoid imprisonment, so why risk planes and pilots on them? The RAF had other excuses too. The weather in the last months of 1943 turned awful; the rain and snow blotted out the moon. Many arms drops were canceled. In fact, in all of northwest Europe, the RAF went on only twenty-three missions in November and December. By comparison, from July to September 1943, the British made 327 parachute drops in France alone.

The high plateau of the southern Yonne is a cold place to spend a winter. The protection the forests offered from German eyes also served as a threat to one's existence. It was difficult to walk amid that much snow, and the steep incline of the terrain was not only treacherous but made it difficult to hunt. Resistance groups shared what stores they had—often slaughtered cattle from sympathetic farmers—but food grew scarce. Men developed the rashes and skin diseases that came from too much time in the same clothes and too few baths. Sleep was fleeting, either because of the fear of nighttime capture or the impossibility of staying warm. A campfire was risky because its smoke could be seen by Germans or their French collaborators. La Rochefoucauld needed cover from the elements and found a deserted barn on an acreage outside Quarré-les-Tombes. He snuck there each night and moved his remaining stores of weapons to the site, too, so that none of his war materiel could be captured by the Germans who, with increasing efficiency, discovered the Alliance's forested hideouts. When he needed to go into Quarré-les-Tombes for everyday provisions, he wore the outfit of a laborer and tried to act like one. He could not shake the suspicion that each of the village's thousand people stared at him as he passed, especially as the arrests climbed. Torturous interrogations led to the betrayal of seven more *résistants* in the Yonne in November. Fourcade literally lost count of the Alliance members captured nationwide—was it four hundred? five hundred?—and took to calling 1943 "the terrible year."

One day, La Rochefoucauld walked into Quarré-les-Tombes and broke SOE protocol by phoning his mother. The agency strictly forbade its fighters from contacting their families. Doing so increased the likelihood of the Germans discovering these ties, and if that happened the Nazis grew monstrous, threatening the lives of loved ones who sometimes stood before the captured agents, unless those agents talked. People died and missions were exposed when *résistants* contacted their families, but Robert did it anyway—only to tell his family nothing remarkable. Just that he was doing well. He didn't tell them where he was and kept the call to a few minutes. But it was the first conversation he'd had with his family in nearly a year.

He surely missed them, but he never said why he phoned; the omissions from that period are their own revelations. He was scared, as *résistant* after *résistant* disappeared, never to be seen again, and maybe he wanted to hear his mother's voice before he too was captured. In that winter without end, still hoping for spring and a London-bound plane, he felt many conflicting emotions. Fourcade, even from the remove of England, complained of going a week without sleep as the arrest tally climbed and thought she was going mad. The anxiety, the tipping mental imbalance for agents in country, was far worse. The cold forced La Rochefoucauld more than he liked from the woods into a rural society where every glance, every smile, carried possible malevolence. Who would help him? Who would betray him? The questions were infinite and without answer, and so he spent what time he could in the barn, trusting only himself. But seclusion invited contemplation, and that was no better than strolling through Quarré-les-Tombes in a worker's costume. Alone, fighters dealt not only with the paranoia of *Am I next?* but with the guilt of *Why have I been spared?* The Resistance leader Henri Frenay put it best: "I felt overcome with fatigue. Crushed, oh, I was utterly crushed! . . . One by one the faces of all those dear comrades rose up to haunt me . . . I felt ashamed to be free . . . Should not I too be among them? It would have been so simple for me to surrender to the police, and I would have found such peace."

It seemed it would be December forever.

One night in the barn, fast asleep on a bed of hay, something jostled La Rochefoucauld awake. He blinked and saw a half circle of uniformed Milice men and the overcoats and felt hats of SD officers. For a moment, no one moved. Robert tried to hide the fear already warming his cheeks. The Nazis looked at him, curious. Then the blows fell. After a stretch, "They tied me up like a sausage," Robert said, and then began searching the barn. They seemed to know what they were looking for, and in a moment they found the arms.

"I had nothing to do with that," La Rochefoucauld said. "I was sleeping here because I was tired."

The Nazis didn't buy it. They put him in the back of a vehicle idling outside and headed out.

His mind raced: How did they know where to find the arms? Who had given him up? Someone in the village who'd tracked him? Another *résistant?* But soon those thoughts gave way to darker ones: Where were they taking him? And what would they do to him when they got there?

# CHAPTER 10

Already they were beyond the forest, and in the moonlit view that blurred past him he saw a flattening of the terrain, with trees huddled together at the horizon, as if sheltering from the cold. The car appeared to be heading northward, through the Yonne's farm country, whose barren fields in this season were as uninviting as the men driving him. They moved past more groves of trees, the road undulating slightly, the plots of land shrinking, more houses appearing, and then more houses than land, and then more factories than houses, the commercial and residential districts blending, in a town of some sort now, down streets where rooftops peeked out over ancient walls that had once protected the city from invaders, but not anymore. And then they were on a major thoroughfare, and then they were slowing before some sort of compound—it took up half a block. A mighty stone and brick barricade rose at the perimeter to guard what was inside. Two red doors opened to let the German vehicles through. La Rochefoucauld saw rings of barbed wire and a two-story building, with three lower-slung ones connected to it, and beyond that the lookout tower of the prison in Auxerre.

They hauled him out of the vehicle and down a wide hallway, into the stale administrative office. They took his shoelaces and his belt, but otherwise kept him in his clothes. The night clerk made a note that it was December 7, 1943, and La Rochefoucauld did something curious: He told the truth. Not the whole truth. But the prison registry showed that this new inmate said his name was de La Rochefoucauld; no first name entered the rolls. La Rochefoucauld would never say why he did this—he could have used one of his aliases—but perhaps it was because it allowed him to lie about other things, most notably that he was a simple woodcutter from Quarré-les-Tombes. The clerk bought the story and noted his occupation as a lumberjack.

Still, the guns in the barn suggested he was more than he appeared, and so the lumberjack La Rochefoucauld was not led to the wing that housed common criminals, but escorted to his right, toward the B wing, the building reserved for political prisoners and terrorists, where the Germans paid very close attention to each inmate in their care. La Rochefoucauld most likely spent that first night in Auxerre as many political prisoners did: in solitary confinement, without pen or book, little food or water, with no contact from the outside save the howling, sometimes unending screams from a nearby "interrogation" room.

Auxerre was some fifty miles from Quarré-les-Tombes, a town of 21,000 that predated Julius Caesar and was now the Nazi's local headquarters. The prison was constructed in 1853—with turreted roofs and a promise to reform criminals. The Nazis called it by their own name, Stalag 150, and made no attempt at progressivism.

One day soon after Robert's imprisonment, a guard opened the door to what was likely the holding cell, and La Rochefoucauld squinted at the flood of light filling the room. Such confinement tended to soften inmates, suddenly desperate for human interaction, a return to how things had been on the outside. The wails coming from nearby heightened a prisoner's despair. The Auxerre rolls were full of inmates who had short prison stays, presumably because they said what the Germans wanted to hear. But La Rochefoucauld said nothing. So a guard ordered him to his feet and led him out, where Robert saw the prison's interior: an open floor plan, two stories high, with narrow metal walkways at each level, snug against cell doors. The doors themselves were wooden, with a peephole at eye level and three metal locks running down the left-hand side: the middle one requiring a massive key and the outer two fastened by impressive cylindrical bolts. There was a low buzz of noise, as the people behind those doors talked to each other, or to themselves, or shifted about in their rooms. Even the airy interior stank of unwashed humanity. Roughly two thousand people cycled through the B wing during the war—the prisoners leaving for the concentration camps or firing squads or, if their information helped the Nazis, to a shameful kind of freedom. At any one time the Germans held between two and three hundred people in the B wing, the men and women doubling and sometimes tripling up in its seventy-two cells. The guards stopped La Rochefoucauld before one of the doors and did the extensive work of opening it, swinging it wide to reveal a thirteen-by-six-foot room. It was wanly lit by a skylight, with metal beds on either side and a slop bucket in between. The room was unheated, and La Rochefoucauld must have been glad he'd been arrested in his winter jacket.

A man on the bed propped himself up to study Robert. People were detained for making bombs or running guns or cutting power lines, but La Rochefoucauld only wrote one thing of his own cellmate: He was an epileptic. One day, perhaps not long after Robert's arrival, he had a violent seizure. "So I yelled to alert the watchman," La Rochefoucauld wrote. "He came to help me put my poor cellmate on his pallet, then went to find a doctor." It's unclear if the cellmate continued to share the room with Robert.

Other people occupied his mind anyway. Soon, La Rochefoucauld endured a session of German "questioning," no doubt led by Dr. Karl Haas, the local SD head. He was a forty-six-year-old with the blunt, too-large features of a man not aging well. With skin bloated and mottled, Haas had taken to sweeping his hair straight back and parting it down the middle, as if to center his disproportionate, rotund appearance. He smiled maniacally and had a mouth full of gold teeth. He liked his colleagues to refer to him as "Doctor" even though nothing in his personal file suggested he'd earned the title. The German high command didn't trust him. Major developments in the Yonne weren't adjudicated by Haas but by the aforementioned Abwehr head in Dijon, Kurt Merck, who in launching Operation Gibet and the double agent Lien had done far more to fill Haas's Auxerre prison than had Haas himself. That was fine with Dr. Haas. He was a man who took extreme delight in driving the couple of miles from the SD's local headquarters to the prison, so he might torture inmates like La Rochefoucauld, even though he had five or six capable noncommissioned officers beneath him.

But Haas was not simply a brute. He did study the monthly terrorist reports he received and he did build his network of informants inside and outside the prison. He and the German staff joked that their French informers were "Gestapistes," and he even tried to launch a Resistance group composed of double agents. Depending on Haas's whim, an inmate's first interrogation might be just that, Haas feeling out his combatant, and the fighter returning afterward to his cell, unbloodied and still silent, awaiting the fetid soup from the prisoner who pushed the hospitality cart door to door. But ultimately the most that could be said of Haas's network of French sources was that he tried but could not eliminate the bad intel. When he was reminded of that, when the evidence rebuked him and affronted him, he turned violent.

La Rochefoucauld witnessed this firsthand. In his interrogation, in a small room on the first floor near the entrance, Robert watched a proud and haughty Haas in one session reveal that he knew La Rochefoucauld to be a Communist. This baffled Robert. *A Communist?* He countered that the Germans had the wrong guy. And soon the assault began.

Haas wanted information. He kept shouting, "You Communist thug!" So Robert turned to his countervailing training in England. "Not all Communists are thugs but all thugs are Communist! And

I am neither!" he yelled back amid the blows. It was at once an accurate and brilliant play: Denying his role in thuggery or Communism would only push Haas to prove La Rochefoucauld's involvement in both, and leading Haas down those avenues would keep him a great distance from the truth.

Pain, of course, was the currency paid for Robert's tactic. These interrogations could last up to ten hours, and Haas didn't carry them out alone. As the blows fell on La Rochefoucauld, from Haas or a second, third, or fourth man, as they jarred Robert's teeth loose and he spit out the shards or whole molars in streams of blood, and then even later, as he faded in and out of consciousness, La Rochefoucauld took what pride he could in saying nothing of value. His body, however, resembled a carcass.

This was not his last trip to the torture room. The Germans held weekly interrogations of their prisoners. It is likely a reflection of La Rochefoucauld's upbringing, and his parents' dictum to never cry, complain, or even discuss one's suffering, that Robert said little of what happened in those sessions with Haas and his staff. To do so would have awakened "the brutal return of past despair," as a survivor of Haas put it. La Rochefoucauld, like other inmates, was called repeatedly to the interrogation rooms, one in the prison, the other across the street, in the basement of a psychiatric hospital the Germans had commandeered for their purposes. The French prisoners liked to joke, *Would you rather be in this prison, or that hospital?* In other words: Would you rather be beaten here or go mad over there? For any *résistant* who stayed in Auxerre long, the question was hard to answer.

The Nazis in their interrogations routinely forced a prisoner to kneel on a bench while a German climbed his shoulders, sending extreme pain shooting through his joints. Or they suspended the man from the ceiling, his arms tied behind his back, until "you feel like you are being dismembered and torn apart for good," as one inmate in Auxerre put it. In those or other susceptible positions, Haas accentuated the suffering: He brought out the wooden bludgeon he favored. The people who received its blows describe a dry, flashing, almost electric pain that was distinct from that of the rubber bludgeon Haas also used. The rubber bludgeon's blows were muted, but one felt them much longer, especially if Haas had ballasted the bat with lead.

The prisoner who stumbled to his cell after a session in the interrogation room often needed guards to support him. The other inmates peered out from their peepholes, the halls suddenly silent, as if members of a requiem Mass were parading by.

The weeks passed, and Robert's questioning continued. The techniques to extract information likely grew more grotesque. Haas enjoyed waterboarding inmates, a singularly terrifying experience where the Nazis pushed a man's head backward into a tub of water. "I was helpless," wrote one prisoner who endured it. "I panicked and tried to kick but the vise-like grip was such that I could hardly move. My eyes were open. I could see shapes distorted by the water, wavering above me, my lungs were bursting; my mouth opened and I swallowed water. Now I was drowning. I put every ounce of my energy into a vain effort to kick myself out of the bath, but I was completely helpless and swallowing water. I felt that I must burst. I was dying, this was the end."

It was not. The inmate was then pulled above water, allowed to gasp for air, and plunged back under. Haas added a note of shame by filling his tub with trash and feces. "I told myself that this was surely the kind of torture it would be the hardest for me to endure," wrote Jorge Semprun, a novelist and *résistant* who was held in Auxerre at the same time as La Rochefoucauld. "And indeed it was. There is nothing more to say."

Throughout his lengthy stay in the prison, La Rochefoucauld maintained a stubborn silence, but Haas was a patient man. He liked to brandish a pliers-like tool and hold down a prisoner's hand, pulling out one nail, and then another, and then a third. Haas's

outside intel did improve during La Rochefoucauld's imprisonment, and soon he was asking about the Resistance captain Pius
VII, and if Robert received his arms from the British. But La Rochefoucauld just yelled back—he had been taught, after all, that anger
lessened pain. He said that the man they called Pius was actually
named Pope, which he knew the Germans wouldn't believe. The
penalty for such defiance was still-harsher treatment. Haas often
attached an electric wire to the ankle of a stubbornly silent inmate,
and then a live wire to the man's testicles and turned up the voltage. One survivor of Auxerre said Haas and his men even sat some
inmates bare-assed on toilets, beneath which starving rats swam.
The screams were worse than those that had come from the most
deranged invalids at the hospital. "Those who are overwhelmed by
the pain of torture," wrote the Resistance fighter Jean Améry, "feel
their bodies as they have never felt them before." Or, as Semprun
put it: "My body . . . asked—demanded—that I give in to torture.
To win this contest with my body I had to subdue it, master it . . .
But it was a pain that had to be won over and over again, minute
by minute, and a victory that mutilated me by making me hate
an essential part of myself that I had experienced until then in a
carefree, physical happiness." When a session concluded, no one
else could enter the interrogation room until it had been scrubbed
clean of blood.

Meanwhile, for the prisoner, the depravity continued. In the
basement of the psychiatric hospital, the Nazis often permitted an
inmate to rinse himself off, at a basin near a stairwell. At the top of
the stairs, the collaborating nurses took the opportunity to ridicule
the wounded man.

It was little better when a prisoner returned to his cell. Many inmates had no change of clothes and lice scurried over their bodies.
The filth of the prison, in contrast to the cleanliness of the torture
chambers, did not allow open wounds to heal properly. Medical attention was as thin as the nightly soup. The smell of pus and drying

blood and sickness never left the wing, in fact it became as much a part of it as the bolts on the door.

The one kind gesture the Germans extended to those in their care were the packages. The prisoners, even political prisoners, could receive small parcels at the administrative office, provided they were censored and from a source the Nazis knew. A battered La Rochefoucauld would periodically be escorted to the front desk and there see, standing alongside a German guard, a small, black-haired Frenchman, whom the Nazis said was the proprietor of Auxerre's Hôtel de la Fontaine, a restaurant they liked. The owner would bunch his round cheeks into a warm smile and give Robert a wrapped present. Sometimes it would be toiletries, sometimes chocolates. Always, the Nazis opened the package, studied it, and then slid it across the table to La Rochefoucauld, satisfied that it contained nothing of consequence. A guard would then walk the hotelier back out the front door and Robert would return to his cell, wondering why this man sent him anything at all. The owner gave packages to many inmates in the prison and the Nazis thought he was simply a soft-hearted collaborator with too much time on his hands. But La Rochefoucauld wondered if that were a cover. Could this man be a member of the Resistance? It was such a bold act, to hand a rebel a care package in the presence of Nazis. Even the Germans didn't take it at face value. But wasn't that the brilliance of it too? La Rochefoucauld tried to dwell on the hotelier in the long black hours in his cell as he awaited the next round of questioning.

December turned to January, and January to February, and still the sessions continued. *Where did you get those arms? Who are you working for?* Some Nazis favored slashing the soles of a prisoner's feet and forcing the man to walk on salt. Others liked to dab wool in gasoline and place portions of the soaking fabric between a prisoner's fingers and toes, and then light each piece. Punches to the face and body never seemed to end, and when a prisoner fell to his knees, the Nazis kicked him in the stomach and testicles. Hemorrhages and hernias and cracked ribs went untreated. Many times the Germans threatened a prisoner's family with similar methods; in this way Robert was lucky. He had been naive enough to give his real name to the Auxerre staff, but it had been dumb enough to not find any La Rochefoucaulds. Some Nazis filed down prisoners' teeth. One SD agent grew so mad with a *résistant* from the Alliance that he gouged out his eyes. One Milice leader carried a star of David in his wallet made from the skin of a Jewish man.

"No one can foresee or protect oneself from the possible revolt of one's body under torture," Semprun wrote, "blandly and bestially demanding of one's soul . . . to surrender unconditionally: a shameful, yet human, so very human surrender."

And that's all the Germans wanted of La Rochefoucauld: *Tell us. Tell us what you know and this—all of this—stops.*

"[One] needed a fantastic morale and a superhuman will not to yield during the interrogations and to reveal the names of friends who were still at large," wrote Jacques Delarue, a Resistance fighter and author of a history on the Gestapo. "Some, broken morally and physically, collapsed. Who would dare to judge them?"

La Rochefoucauld, in session after session, told Haas nothing.

Many *résistants* who did not want to expose their comrades saw one other way to end the suffering. There was a reason the Auxerre staff confiscated belts and shoelaces as soon as prisoners were registered. Many Resistance fighters, wary of their weakened bodies, committed suicide to fend off betrayal. Jean Moulin, before he became the most effective Resistance organizer in France, was beaten so severely by the Germans that he took a shard of glass on the ground and cut his throat. His life was likely saved by the return of a German soldier who wanted to keep him talking. Pierre Brossolette, a journalist and Paris Resistance leader, regained consciousness after one interrogation and found himself still in the room, alone. He jumped out the window, five stories up, rather than endure more.

In Robert's cell, minutes felt like hours and hours like days. His strength, his very sense of self, collapsed and that alarmed him. He looked and felt like some sort of disfigured beast. His Catholic faith would not allow him to go the way of Brossolette, but Robert knew that with a few words he could earn a smile from the Germans and maybe walk out of here. He could then regain his strength and perhaps in time return to the frivolity of his old life, before a warm fireplace at Villeneuve, staring at the embers and above it the family crest, which the generations of La Rochefoucaulds had interpreted as an allowance to live indulgently, to explore all of life's delights, a sentiment echoed in the family creed: "It's my pleasure." In this almost libertine environment, no one would need to know, or perhaps even care, about his secret.

At the same time, the trappings of Villeneuve and in particular the "It's my pleasure" motto carried a second meaning. The La Rochefoucaulds had split generations ago into four branches, and Robert was of the oldest line, the one descended from dukes. The dukes served in France's royal court and *C'est mon plaisir* also meant, "It is my pleasure . . . to serve the king." To give of oneself and to do what was best for France.

This commitment to honor the family by serving *La France* explained why Robert had joined the Resistance. But he realized he could honor it again by remaining a silent man, here in Auxerre.

February turned to March and the smell of roses from the adjacent garden wafted through the prison windows. He had been imprisoned for four months; most inmates didn't make it half that long. His bushy beard indicated the passing time, and he resolved to defy the Germans until the end. They acted more feverishly with La Rochefoucauld now, looked more confused around him. He began to see that, even as the Germans tried to break him, *he* was in fact breaking *them*. "Every hour of silence I won from Dr. Haas's henchmen," Semprun wrote, "made me realize with ever greater certainty that I was at home in the world." La Rochefoucauld showed

Haas that oldest of truths: Freedom is an idea that torturers cannot mangle, and a faith in it can help one stare through death. It took a certain type of person to believe in this freedom in early 1944, and La Rochefoucauld was not about to betray others who felt as he did. "The experience of being tortured does not imply just the abominable solitude of suffering," Semprun wrote. "It is also an experience of brotherhood. The silence that we hang on to, against which we brace ourselves with clenched teeth, trying to escape by imagining or remembering our own body, our wretched body, this silence is filled with all the voices, all the lives it protects, and allows one to continue to exist . . . It is a co-existence, whose individual, possible, probable death nourishes life."

The Nazis had to make a choice about La Rochefoucauld. One day he and some of the prison's guards took a three-minute drive to Auxerre's Palais de Justice. It was a former abbey transformed in the nineteenth century into a proper house of law, with rising Greek columns and rows of windows on either side carved in half circles. The Germans pushed Robert inside, where, in a stately room with high ceilings, crown molding, and gold walls a Nazi military tribunal sat beneath a chandelier that glimmered in the daylight. Here La Rochefoucauld would learn his fate. One judge was a German officer, the second a noncommissioned officer, and the president of the tribunal in 1944, Dr. Karl Haas himself, showing his gold teeth through a smile. A man named Ribain, the president of the Auxerre bar, was to defend La Rochefoucauld before the tribunal, but the Germans didn't give Ribain a chance. In a matter of a few minutes—the amount of time in which the judges resolved most cases—La Rochefoucauld was tried for sabotage and hiding arms and sentenced to death. He was to be executed by firing squad.

Word spread quickly in the B wing when a man departed for the tribunal. The prisoner Jean Léger wrote about how the wing was seldom quiet; throughout the day there were conversations between cellmates and at night speeches to continue the fight. The exception was when a man returned from his trial. Léger said two brothers, in the time before La Rochefoucauld's sentencing, came back from their own case and everyone in the wing waited for them to say something. At last, another prisoner shouted, "Well?"

One of the brothers said, "Death for us both."

No one spoke until the evening.

The prisoners no doubt honored La Rochefoucauld upon his return with the same silence.

He moved to another cell, one reserved for death penalty cases. His execution was set for March 20 at 8 a.m. A German priest early on the assigned morning gave La Rochefoucauld his last rites.

All that time in Salzburg learning German, Robert thought wryly, and still he didn't understand a word the priest said.

# CHAPTER 11

Just before 8 a.m., two guards escorted La Rochefoucauld out of the B wing and to the bed of a waiting truck. They told him to sit on a coffin lying there. Robert saw another coffin next to him, and here came a second prisoner pushed along by guards, onto the box that he, too, would soon fill. Robert did not know this man, and as the guards hopped in the back, high-powered rifles in their arms, he didn't see the point in introductions. The truck belched into low gear, and the red doors that had closed behind La Rochefoucauld four months earlier parted to let him out.

The truck stopped before Route Nationale, the city's major thoroughfare just beyond the prison, whose northbound lane directed one to Paris. The truck, however, turned right, south, toward the Yonne's rural countryside. They were headed for a series of dirt paths off Route Nationale, each narrower and bumpier than the last, the terrain moving from uninterrupted wheat fields to groves of trees to a fork in the road, where the rightward path drove one ever deeper into woods, until a clearing came into view, where the road ended. There, against three trees pockmarked with bullet holes, La Rochefoucauld would be told to stand, and he would look out on the distant brush and listen to the birdsong, while the Nazi guards took their aim. Forty-three people would be executed here during the war.

As the truck started out on this path, passing the brown-stone chapel on the grounds of the psychiatric hospital, La Rochefoucauld had a thought. *Why give in to the Nazis now?* He had spent the last four months ignoring the basest screams of his body because he could not fathom giving the Germans anything they wanted. Now they wanted him dead. But he did not wish to die.

He looked at the road beneath him, rushing past—and noticed the Nazis' one mistake. The Germans had never learned much about him, which meant they never understood the extent to which he'd been trained to maim and kill. Robert kept his eyes on his wrists. There were no handcuffs on them.

He glanced at the guards and saw their guns resting on their laps. If he couldn't succeed, he thought, he wanted to die as he'd lived: fighting. He looked at the other inmate, who sensed Robert calculating something. "Even if it means being shot," Robert said to the other Frenchman, "I'd rather be shot right away. I'm getting out!"

The prisoner stared at him, astounded. Traffic was light and the truck moved at a brisk pace. The guards didn't speak French, or at least didn't hear La Rochefoucauld over the wind in the open-air bed. Neither Nazi stirred himself to attention.

The other inmate said: "You're crazy. It won't work!"

In a moment, La Rochefoucauld sprang himself on the nearer guard, plowing into him and then jumping from the truck, rolling and somersaulting just as he had been trained in England. When his momentum stopped he shot to his feet and broke into a sprint. He heard angry shouts behind him, and then the even louder reports of rifles. The first bullets missed and he looked behind his shoulder to see the truck's driver, startled by the firing, slam on the brakes. The sudden stop threw the guards headfirst over the truck's hood.

Robert sprinted down one street, then turned onto a second, then onto a third. He did not know Auxerre; he had spent the last four months in his B-wing cell. So he just ran, mindlessly, and as fast as he could. He ran until his weakened legs burned and he gulped at the air, and then kept running. He ran onto one street, Avenue Victor Hugo, and came upon a guarded villa of sorts, bedecked in swastika flags and banners: the SD's headquarters.

La Rochefoucauld stopped cold. Should he turn and run the other way? If he did, would *that* be more suspicious than just trying to walk past the enemy HQ? Had someone inside the building already seen him? And where was the truck?

La Rochefoucauld decided to continue down the street, despite his heart's drumming in his rib cage. He walked as casually as a man trying to escape his execution could walk. As he approached the building, he saw a Citroën sedan, with swastika pennants on the fender, parked nearby. He stole a glance inside the car—keys in the ignition. He looked around and saw a driver, maybe thirty feet away, pacing back and forth, waiting for someone to emerge from the building. Just then La Rochefoucauld heard distant shouting. *The truck!*

*Now*—he had to decide now. He moved closer to the car and swung the door wide and threw himself in. He started the engine and peeled out before the chauffeur realized what was happening. La Rochefoucauld looked quickly in the rearview mirror and saw the man draw a pistol from his coat pocket and fire twice, but it was too late: Robert had escaped, the Nazi pennants whipping in the wind.

Back through the streets of Auxerre now, down one street, then another, looking for something to direct him out of here . . . and then—there!—a sign: Paris, this way. The road was none other than Route Nationale, and in a moment he saw the Auxerre prison itself—and sped right past it.

The open highway, with the pedal to the floor, and seconds becoming minutes and still no one trailing him. He might actually make it! He had never felt so alive! More time passed and Robert even began to relax behind the wheel.

But soon he noticed traffic ahead of him slow and saw in the distance a roadblock, a wooden beam stretching across the highway. The Germans must have put all neighboring jurisdictions on high alert, and now they planned to stop each vehicle that passed until they had their man.

Robert edged closer and saw two heavily armed soldiers manning the blockade, asking every driver for identification. Robert was in the garb he'd worn for the last four months. He stank. He had a full beard and cuts and bruises across his face and body. There was little hope of him fooling the soldiers, even in his Nazi sedan, maybe especially in his Nazi sedan, if word of the vehicle being commandeered had spread.

He couldn't turn around; turning around would draw too much attention. So he inched closer, shifting the car down into second, the soldiers' faces visible now, seemingly inquisitive, asking him to stop.

That's when he gunned the engine, smashing into the blockade and one of the soldiers, who flipped over the hood. The second opened fire and La Rochefoucauld ducked, the bullets ripping into the car's frame; Robert kept his head low and his foot on the pedal. The rat-a-tat-tat of more angry shots followed the initial volley, but the car sped ahead. When Robert at last sat up, the car was not smoking, was still on the road—and, just as important, was beyond the reach of the Germans' guns.

He checked himself. Somehow, he was unharmed. For the third time that morning he had avoided German fire at something close to point-blank range.

He saw a gravel road ahead and took the turn as fast as he could, plumes of dirt kicking up behind him. He had to put distance between himself and the Nazis. The road soon rose and fell beneath him and La Rochefoucauld hummed over it. He noticed smoke billowing from the hood, but he kept on until the smoke grew coarser and blacker and he had no choice but to slow the car. He saw a quarry up ahead, a mineral excavation site, just off the road. He stopped before it and got out. He listened. Nothing. Yet. The best thing to do was to crash the Citroën in such a way that the Germans might overlook it as they drove past. So he put the car in neutral, got behind it, and pushed it into the quarry.

The car fell, falling into one of the deepest voids and crashing in blooms of dust and smoke. When it cleared, he saw the outline of a crumpled, charred mess. *They'll never get this one*, he thought. He ran off into a nearby line of woods, his new plan to hide and await a nightfall that could not come fast enough.

He spent the next hours in anxious solitude, and when stars at last filled the sky he made his way again, a strong moon guiding him but once more aimless. He did not know where he was. He walked under branches and through thickets and among groves of trees; he walked for what seemed like hours, with the idea that he might find a *résistant* in a small town or a sympathetic family in the countryside or even another abandoned barn. Something that would serve as a temporary base where he could get a few hours' sleep and perhaps a meal before sneaking his way—by who knew what means—out of the Yonne.

At last, in the distance, he saw lights. They multiplied as he walked toward them and became the nighttime view of a city. *Maybe he knew someone here*, he thought. La Rochefoucauld approached with caution and saw a sign at the town's edge:

Auxerre.

He was back where he started.

# CHAPTER 12

The longer he stood there, in the glow of the city, the more he realized the situation wasn't as bad as it seemed. If the Nazis hadn't seen the crashed remnants of the car in the quarry, they were likely to think La Rochefoucauld was hundreds of miles away by now. The Germans would have broadened their search, perhaps even leaving Auxerre understaffed. What's more, the one person who might feed and hide La Rochefoucauld was here, in town: the owner of the Hôtel de la Fontaine, who had given him those care packages. Robert had no proof that the man was a *résistant*, but he knew no one else close by who could be. He could either walk through the night and gamble that an unknown farmer might be brave enough to shelter him, or he could walk into Auxerre, as crazy as that sounded, and test his luck by finding the owner of the hotel.

He walked into Auxerre.

For the second time that day, he tried to move about its streets with insouciance, as if he were something other than an escaped "terrorist." Few people were out, and so he didn't feel as frightened as he had that morning—of course, he didn't see any German soldiers this time either.

He needed a phone book, so he could find the hotel, but didn't see any telephone booths around; the Yonne remained an agrarian and somewhat antiquated department in the 1940s. Up ahead, however, he saw a grocery store with its lights still on.

The clerk at the front paid him little mind when he walked in. La Rochefoucauld asked for a phone book and the grocer pointed to the back of the store. Robert flipped through the pages until he found the address—then realized that, while he could walk to the hotel, it might be more discreet to place a call and get a sense for the owner. If he suspected that the man was in fact a *résistant*, he could ask to meet him. If the call went poorly, however, La Rochefoucauld could hang up without disclosing his location. He dialed the number.

The employee who answered said the owner had gone home for the night. Should a message be left for him? "It was hard to explain to the person on the other side why I needed to talk to him," Robert later remarked. He said there was no message and hung up.

One option was to return to the woods—but he was hungry and thirsty and exhausted. Besides, even if he spent the night there, he would still have to walk back into Auxerre tomorrow and get to the hotelier during the day, during business hours. That wouldn't work.

He stared hard at the grocer at the front of the store. *What if . . . ?*

Robert's relative, François de La Rochefoucauld, wrote in his acclaimed book of *Maxims* that "one cannot answer for his courage if he has never been in danger," and perhaps nothing—not fleeing to Spain or training in England or bombing a power grid or escaping the firing squad—was more dangerous than what he considered doing now. In those other instances Robert had placed his life in his own hands. Now he thought about placing it entirely in someone else's. *What if I asked this stranger for help?*

The grocery store was closing and La Rochefoucauld watched the other customers pay and leave. He debated his move. He was twenty years old and had already been denounced twice by his countrymen. Then again, those same countrymen had helped him flee to England and sabotage German war materiel.

The store's last patron walked out the door.

La Rochefoucauld moved with purpose to the front.

He put his hands on the man's shoulders. "Are you a good Frenchman?" he asked.

The grocer stared at him, baffled, and a little angry. "Of course I'm a good Frenchman," he barked.

La Rochefoucauld took in a sharp breath.

"I escaped," he said. "And I'm being chased by the Germans."

The man looked at him, his eyes widening. "Well, I'll be," he said, and then with curiosity: "So it was because of you that there's all that nonsense in the city since this morning?"

La Rochefoucauld gave the man a slight nod.

"You can trust me," the grocer said, his face suddenly sincere. "You're at home here."

Robert exhaled.

His name was Monsieur Séguinot. He closed up shop and took La Rochefoucauld to his nearby house, where Robert met Madame Séguinot, who hugged and welcomed him as one of her own and began preparing the *résistant* a plate of food. She "served me a meal big enough to choke on," La Rochefoucauld wrote. She told him that if the Germans came, he could escape through a door at the back of the house. When he finished eating, Madame Séguinot said she had no room for him other than a bed that her paralytic father occupied. Robert, grateful for anything, soon climbed in, the old man neither moving nor uttering a word. "I fell asleep, exhausted, as if I had been sleep-deprived for several months," La Rochefoucauld said.

The next morning, he faced a troubling reality. He knew he was endangering the Séguinots by staying, but he also knew he risked his own life by being out in public. He had to find a Resistance member who could get him out of the Yonne. The Alliance had been decimated months ago, and even if he found an old comrade, he wouldn't know if he could trust the man, given the double agents in France. La Rochefoucauld explained to the couple about the care packages, and about his suspicion of the hotel owner's secret life. He didn't want to risk placing a phone call in the grocery store during the day, so Robert asked Séguinot a difficult question: Would he talk to the hotelier? Séguinot agreed to do it.

That evening, Monsieur Séguinot asked La Rochefoucauld to come to the back room of the store. So Robert walked into the night, onto a street where he had the familiar sensation of thousands of eyes following him, and then quickly into Séguinot's grocery. There, in the back, he saw the hotel owner, his round cheeks bunching themselves again into a smile. The man moved toward La Rochefoucauld and gave him a hearty embrace. He said his name was André Bouy and Robert had been right about him: He came with clothes and a plan for escape.

It would not be easy. La Rochefoucauld's face was plastered on posters throughout Auxerre. So Bouy said the first thing to do was nothing at all, to wait a day or two until the fury to find La Rochefoucauld dissipated. But Bouy would check in with him, and he would shepherd Robert to safety.

Bouy was thirty-eight that spring, a short but powerfully built man who encountered the world with an arched eyebrow and that warm smile, which served him well in his chosen field. His parents had owned the Hôtel de la Fontaine since 1925, a three-story, fifty-room neoclassical beauty on Place Charles Lepère in Auxerre. Bouy had been a curious boy and voracious reader but found the life around him the most fascinating of all. After high school, he earned a business degree from the École supérieure de commerce, in Paris. He spent the last of the Roaring Twenties working in big hotels around the city, before moving back to Auxerre. By the outbreak of World War II, the family business was effectively his.

But he didn't want it alone to define him. He enlisted in the army, something no Bouy had done before, his patriotism fueled by the military histories he'd read and the love of a country that had allowed him to thrive.

France's quick defeat ashamed him, angered him, and he vowed to fight on, even as he returned to his hotel and found German officers billeted there. The businessman in him catered to them; throughout the war, various Nazi officials frequented his establishment, dining there, sleeping there, reserving the banquet room and celebrating there, drinking and shouting and stomping their big heavy boots well into the morning. The patriot in him abhorred this, but he never let it show. Instead, he and a few friends—an attorney, a bailiff, and a farmer—joined an underground group and spent their evenings and off-hours shuttling parachutists to Resistance camps and hiding weapons in nearby gardens. The hotel, even with the Germans there, became a meeting point for Bouy and his close friends to discuss which *résistant* needed transport, which one a shipment of arms, and which a care package, like the ones Robert received while in prison. The Germans knew Bouy and soon all his respectable friends, and the Nazis suspected little while mingling in the lobby or walking to the restaurant for a meal. Why should they? Only a fool would plan such operations from a German-occupied hotel, and Bouy was no fool. His food was quite good and he and his staff were always hospitable to the Nazis. He even spoke a little German.

Bouy cultivated this image, the obeisant businessman, because it kept his wife and three children safe. He never stocked his hotel with anything but German-censored newspapers, never flipped on anything but Vichy-approved radio, never even told his wife all he was doing. He tried to be absolutely discreet. But discretion was not the same as inaction, and talking about rebel missions in hushed and coded phrases did not protect him from the fear of repercussions, even if he was clever enough to carry out those conversations in the one place Germans would not suspect. As the "terrorist acts" spiked in the Yonne—sixty in one month in 1943— Bouy watched the prison fill, the Germans ever more suspicious, and their anonymous French conspirators affirming that paranoia with each new denouncement. Bouy had long thought there was safety in transparency: That if he delivered a care package to the

B wing with a German officer at his side, his true intent would remain hidden. But by 1944, with the war worsening and the prison rolls adding more and more names, he questioned his cleverness. One day he told his wife everything. He feared reprisals, he said, and wanted her and the kids to move to Valençay, in the Loire Valley, where Bouy thought they would be safer. Françoise Bouy, ten at the time and the oldest of the children, only remembered her parents telling her that she and her younger brothers, Jean Pierre and Claude, were moving with their mother, until the war was over. No one explained why they needed to go to Valençay, nor why their father would remain behind.

After their departure, André Bouy did not cease his involvement with the underground. If anything, he acted more boldly.

After meeting La Rochefoucauld, he took Robert's existing identification papers and in a day had a new false set for the young man, made out once more under his pseudonym of choice, René Lallier, since the Auxerre prison staff knew him by his given name, La Rochefoucauld. Bouy then finalized his plan to get him out of the Yonne.

Three days later, the hotelier pulled his vehicle up to the Séguinots' house. Bouy had been given an *Ausweis*, a travel permit the Germans approved for certain Frenchmen in good standing, which allowed collaborators or small businessmen to travel beyond their towns, a practice that the Germans otherwise forbade the populace in 1944. Bouy had gained the *Ausweis* for legitimate reasons: He really did need to pick up food and supplies for the hotel. But he had never attempted anything like what he was about to do. In fact, for all Bouy's secret meetings, for all the weapons he buried in gardens, this would be the most valiant act of his war: transporting a man the Nazis had condemned to death in a vehicle they approved for travel. Bouy likely told no one about the mission, and he entrusted only himself with La Rochefoucauld's passage because he alone wanted to be punished if he were found out.

The plan was simple enough. Bouy would hide Robert in the truck and take him to the nearby town of Monéteau, where he'd purchase a train ticket that would get La Rochefoucauld to Paris. The difficulty lay in the military checkpoints. The truck was almost certain to be stopped outside Auxerre by the gendarmerie, the French military police who since the Occupation worked alongside the Germans. Sometimes officers checked vehicles thoroughly, and Bouy's truck ran that risk because of both its size and the news of an inmate's recent escape. He and Robert could do nothing to evade a search.

They could only hide him well. Bouy explained that he grazed sheep outside Auxerre and often loaded his truck with bales of hay for them. La Rochefoucauld would hide behind these bales in the truck's covered bed. If they were stopped and any officer asked, Bouy would have a ready-made and quite legitimate answer: *The hay is for the sheep I graze, monsieur.* The only problem, the biggest problem, lay in police pulling down the bales.

If they made it to Monéteau, Bouy would park at the train station, walk inside to buy a ticket, and make sure he saw no German soldiers or French policemen on the platform. When the train came, he'd race back to the truck, and send La Rochefoucauld on his way, with his new clothes, false ID papers, and rail ticket.

Robert listened to the plan and nodded, grateful. He had washed himself, trimmed his beard, and treated his wounds, so, if he got that far, he would look like any other passenger on the train. He turned to the Séguinots and began the elaborate process of expressing a gratitude that could not be stated. Then he left with Bouy.

He slid into the back of the truck, situating himself between bales of hay that Bouy stacked around him and over him. The hotelier closed the truck's rear door and La Rochefoucauld's world turned dark. He heard the engine fire and now the hum of tires on the road beneath them. Monéteau was roughly five miles away.

La Rochefoucauld could not quell his nerves, and he and Bouy were barely on the road a minute when he felt the truck slow, and then stop, and then heard a voice: "Papers!"

Everything slowed down.

"Here you are, sir—my *Ausweis*," he heard Bouy answer, in an attempt at nonchalance.

More time passed and then: "Where are you going?"

"To feed my sheep for my hotel. I own the Hôtel de la Fontaine in Auxerre."

"The Hôtel de la Fontaine is very good," the officer said. Another silence, this one somehow longer. Was the exchange over?

No. La Rochefoucauld now heard the officer move to the back of the truck, linger there for a moment, and then open the rear door.

Fear shot through him.

The officer took his bayonet and thrust it through a bale, missing La Rochefoucauld by inches. He dared not move or breathe. The officer pulled his blade out.

A moment later he closed the door. "Go on," the officer called out, lazily.

Bouy tried not to speed away too quickly.

Minutes later, he parked at the train station and told La Rochefoucauld they'd arrived. He left to buy a ticket. When he returned, he said the train was coming and he saw no Germans or cops on the platform. Bouy had purchased a third-class ticket for La Rochefoucauld, not to be cheap, he said, but because a third-class car was often the most crowded.

La Rochefoucauld eyed the hotelier with his round smiling cheeks and thanked him. Bouy told him to go; the train was here.

Robert ran off and, at the platform, mixed in with other travelers, lines of them shuffling closer to the open train door, until an attendant stamped La Rochefoucauld's ticket. He got on.

Masses crowded onto the third-class car, and La Rochefoucauld squeezed his slight frame into one of the few remaining seats, next to a traveling businessman. Robert kept glancing out the window. He waited, but the train would not move. He tried to will it forward, *this close* to freedom.

When it at last lurched ahead, he exhaled. He watched the trees blur by his window.

But then the train reached the next stop, Laroche-Migennes, some ten miles on, and Robert saw clusters of German soldiers and policemen on the platform. He asked the man next to him: Why such a show of force?

The man didn't know, but said it had been like this for three days.

Three days?

Fear seized him again. He had his fake ID, his beard, and a pair of eyeglasses that helped mask his appearance, but what if any of the officers had seen the posters plastered throughout Auxerre and saw the resemblance when they looked at La Rochefoucauld?

He quietly excused himself from his seat and strode down the walkway. Already soldiers had filed on, one of them on either end of his car checking passengers' papers. In the middle of the carriage, however, stood a bathroom. The older, cheaper cars still had a restroom positioned in their center, and La Rochefoucauld moved toward it as quickly and inconspicuously as possible.

The restroom's dimensions were small, a toilet ahead of him and the sink behind the bathroom's opened door. La Rochefoucauld decided to crouch down and settle himself beneath the sink. He then quickly pushed the door closed. Any officer who opened it would see only an unoccupied toilet. But if the German then walked into the restroom and peeked behind the door to the sink, well, then La Rochefoucauld would face another death sentence.

Cold droplets of sweat poured down his face. Anticipating what might happen next— not even on the day of his execution had he been this scared.

Suddenly a Nazi shoved the door open. La Rochefoucauld braced himself for what might—what must?—come. He heard the man step into the bathroom, the door separating the two men by inches. And then . . . La Rochefoucauld saw the door close again.

He tried not to shudder.

Minutes passed and the train still did not move. Why was it taking so long? Would the Germans still be there when La Rochefoucauld stepped out of the bathroom? *Should* he step out of the bathroom?

At last the train started, and he decided to face whatever appeared on the other side of the door. He washed his cheeks and forehead to compose himself and walked out.

He saw . . . nothing. No Germans in his railcar. No Germans on the train. He had somehow eluded them again.

Three hours later the train arrived at Gare de Lyon. When he reached the Paris streets, Robert started giggling, "drunk with freedom," he wrote. "I started to shout, to roar with laughter." People stared at him but he didn't care. "I was as happy as a king and singing like one too."

# CHAPTER 13

I t had been eighteen months since he'd last been in Paris, and the city was stranger now. He noticed the change even in his giddy state. People looked . . . thin, as thin as the prisoners he'd lived among. Four years of rationing, of subsisting on a 1,300-calorie diet, of children told by the government to forage for acorns, had all affected the populace. La Rochefoucauld's emaciated features didn't look out of place in Paris, a city that didn't have the tillable soil of the agrarian departments and didn't have the more abundant—if unsanctioned—meals of the countryside either. And yet, in other ways, the capital remained rather remarkably its prewar self. The heavy bombing campaigns suffered by London and Warsaw had never reached the City of Light. "Paris was arguably the safest place in Europe," one historian later noted, in part because the major manufacturing bases the Allies might target—specifically Dunlop, Renault, and Citroën, which were in fact bombed in 1943—lay in either the outer reaches of the city or the suburbs. Furthermore, the German military officers who'd clustered in Paris at the start of the war and remained there now, administering the state, had forced Resistance groups to the provinces. Sabotages and other "terrorist acts" occurred with far greater frequency in central and southern France. Saboteurs still found ways to damage the German war machine in Paris, but it looked more like 1938 here—if one ignored the swastikas.

Robert headed to the other side of the city, a young man out of the Yonne but not out of danger, with little money and a chilly night settling in. He walked to the eighth arrondissement, on the right bank of the Seine, where on rue Paul-Baudry, a few blocks from the Arc de Triomphe, lived an aunt and uncle of his. Monsieur and Madame Gotz did not have children and had once already taken Robert as their surrogate: During his student days in Paris, at the start of the war, he often stayed with the Gotzes. He endangered their lives by knocking now, but he knew nowhere else to go.

He approached the Gotzes' stately apartment, and when he rang the bell, he left the eyeglasses Bouy had given him perched on his nose. Geoffroy answered, and despite Robert's eyewear, the gaunt cheeks, the beard, and the feral look, Gotz recognized him immediately. *Robert?*

Gotz asked what Robert was doing, a trill of shock in his voice, as he invited him inside and hugged him. Before Robert could say much, Geoffroy pushed him into the living room, where Madame Gotz, the cousin of La Rochefoucauld's mother, sat in an armchair, working her needlepoint. She raised her eyes and stared.

"Robert!" she said, and raced to hug him.

"For me, it was a marvelous moment," La Rochefoucauld wrote, reunited after a year and a half with family in a quiet and warm house that the Gotzes, as the evening progressed, refused to let him leave, in spite of the risk he posed to their safety.

They had so many questions, so he started at the beginning: the denunciatory letter, the flight to Spain, his first imprisonment, training in England, parachuting into the Yonne, his Groupe Roche missions, and then a second and far worse detention, leading to his escape from his own execution and, ultimately, his arrival here. The Gotzes listened "in the utmost silence," La Rochefoucauld wrote, and when he finished, Geoffroy Gotz said, quietly and humbly, "Well, we're very lucky that you're here tonight."

They had a full meal and lively conversation, including talk of how Robert's father had returned home from his POW camp due to a German-approved rule that allowed the release of aging French officers with more than four children. Then La Rochefoucauld returned to the room where he'd slept as a student. It felt odd to be there. Nothing about the room had changed, and yet everything had. Four years had passed and though he was not yet twenty-one, he was in no way the young man he had been at seventeen. The room seemed a remnant—it *was* a remnant—of another age, another life. He mourned what he'd lost even as he felt safe enough to fall asleep.

It was very late the next morning when his aunt woke him. She brought in a large breakfast, larger than he expected and likely more than the Gotzes could part with, given the rationing. But Madame Gotz insisted on La Rochefoucauld eating what was before him. She told him that Geoffroy had gone to call Robert's parents; as a precaution he hadn't phoned from the apartment but walked to a public booth at a post office.

Geoffroy returned with good news. La Rochefoucauld's parents would come to see him the next day. Robert was so happy he paced and grew restless and found he needed something to occupy his afternoon. He decided to call a friend: Princess Salomé Murat, then a stunning eighteen-year-old whose great-grandfather, Joachim Murat, had fought alongside Napoléon and married the emperor's sister, Caroline, before Bonaparte named Joachim the king of Naples in 1808. Salomé Murat lived now with her family on rue de Constantine, in the seventh arrondissement, a few blocks from Invalides, where Napoléon was buried. She invited La Rochefoucauld for a drink.

"The entire Murat family welcomed me beautifully," La Rochefoucauld wrote, bringing him sweets and spirits, "vying with each other to be the kindest to me." They insisted he dine with them, so that he might tell his story and share what little food they had.

In his afternoon and evening with the Murats, the conversation kept returning to the mood in the country. People no longer resigned themselves to the Occupation; they fought against it. That month, in fact, Pierre Pucheu, Vichy's former minister of the Interior, who had fled France after the North African landings, was arrested in Casablanca. The Free French state of Morocco tried him for treason, found him guilty, and sentenced him to death. General de Gaulle refused to pardon Pucheu, saying, "I owe it to France." Pucheu became the first Vichy politician to be executed under de Gaulle's provisional rule. Also that month, de Gaulle's National Council of the Resistance, composed of various bands of sabotage-minded men and women, drafted a charter that called on trade unions and political parties to "declare their wish to set the motherland free by collaborating closely with the military operations that the French army and the Allied forces will undertake on the continent." The hoped-for Allied landings in France were a constant topic that night. "We could feel victory coming," La Rochefoucauld later said.

But that's not to say Frenchmen idly waited for it. In the first fifteen days of March, the German military command in France reported nearly seventy trains disabled on the tracks by explosives and nearly fifty derailments. With most of France's nationalized rail shops out of commission, these trains could not be repaired. And with the country's transportation network largely out of service, several industrial plants had closed, causing total production for the Nazi war effort to decline by 30 percent. Heinrich von Stülpnagel, the Germans' high military commander in France, announced that the Reich faced "a very grave crisis." Even the prefect of police in Paris said that the Gaullist and Communist *résistants* would soon contribute to a "national insurrection and the German defeat." That night at dinner, La Rochefoucauld and the Murats discussed how the mandatory work order, or Service du travail obligatoire (STO), which now sent some men as old as sixty to Germany, worked completely against the Vichy politicians who had established it. Many people escaped, "returned to France and either joined the Resistance or went into hiding," as La Rochefoucauld wrote of the conversation.

One of the people to escape Germany was his older brother,

Henri. At the outset of the STO he'd fled to Lorraine in northeastern France and worked under an alias in the mines that his mother's family, the Wendels, owned. On his off days he biked some 185 miles back to the family chateau in Villeneuve. His younger siblings would see him approaching, his face blackened by soot, which showed either his anxiousness to return (he hadn't even bathed first) or, conversely, how thoroughly he'd planned the trip home (the soot was a good cover from any inquiring police officer). But Henri, like his younger brother, could only flee for so long. He would join the Free French's Second Armored Division in 1944, and fight in Lorraine, not far from the mines in which he'd once worked.

Robert, even in this elegant home, and despite all he'd endured, felt the urge to fight again too.

The family rendezvous occurred the next day at L'hôtel Wendel, the neoclassical hotel that his mother's family built in the 1860s behind the Paris Opéra, in the quite fashionable ninth arrondissement, not far from rue de La Rochefoucauld, the street named after the paternal side of his family. Olivier and Consuelo invited many members of the clan and planned to hold, in a private banquet room, an impromptu party. To be safe, the couple had not told their guests what the bash was for. Robert's younger sister Yolaine, then fifteen, just heard that they were all going to Paris. The La Rochefoucaulds found their seats at the banquet's large dining table, gathered there for reasons no one explained, and began talking as if all this were normal.

Around that point, Robert walked in. Yolaine immediately noticed his beard and mustache. It had been nearly two years since she'd seen him, the brother who used to protect her in the siblings' backyard brawls. He went around the table, greeting and kissing everyone, and Yolaine eagerly awaited her turn. The beard gave him a maturity, but something, some grave quality in his gaunt face, also announced he was no longer a boy.

Robert smiled and laughed as he moved through the room, accepting the comments about his changed appearance and thinking how surreal it was to see his entire family, not even a week after his would-be execution. The surprise party overwhelmed him. And to hug his father again, thin but indomitable—he could later only write that he felt "such emotion" that day.

But as he swapped stories with his family, he thought about the war. At one point he told his parents that he couldn't stay long in Paris. He planned to contact his handlers in London. As long as the Germans remained, the fight against them had to continue. His mother seemed to have expected as much from him and, ever practical, had even drawn up an itinerary. Robert would see a doctor first, she said, so he might be cured of whatever diseases or infections he'd contracted. She then recommended he phone a cousin, Gabriel de Mortemart, who lived in Saint-Vrain, a somewhat rural suburb outside the city, where the Nazi presence was minimal. The message for Robert was clear: Rest up, and then battle on.

When someone said a German had entered the hotel, Robert looked at the suddenly somber faces around him and left the room.

It was the last time Yolaine saw him during the war.

The doctor told Robert he had scabies. He wrote down a prescription and recommended Robert do nothing strenuous for some time. Robert then followed his mother's other command and called his cousin. Gabriel de Mortemart agreed to take him in the following week, and La Rochefoucauld spent the next few days shuttling between the elegant salons of the Murats, the Gotzes, and Robert's grandmother's on avenue de la Motte-Picquet, where his parents came to see him.

It wasn't safe to move about like this. The French-run Milice, the nationwide militia headed by Joseph Darnand, a World War I hero who had pledged loyalty to Hitler, and who staffed his group with thirty thousand borderline reprobates, had begun collaborating with the SD in January 1944. Week by week arrest totals climbed, and in March alone, the Milice or their German counterparts detained ten thousand Frenchmen; the year before, it had taken the Nazis three months to reach the same figure. Everyone knew someone who had disappeared—Robert wasn't even the only La Rochefoucauld to be detained. His distant uncle Bernard and aunt Yvonne were members of the Parisian Resistance group Prosper; in 1943 the Germans flipped some of its fighters under torture and brought down the whole organization. Bernard de La Rochefoucauld was sent to the Flossenbürg concentration camp, where he died. Yvonne—who also worked for SOE—survived the war only after enduring the experiments of the Nazi doctors at Ravensburg—eight injections of poison in her right eye, which blinded it; more injections in an ear, which deafened it; typhus shot into her blood to make serum. She was then thrown into a block of cells in which inmates were not fed. One of Yvonne's last memories of the camp was feebly fighting off an equally weakened inmate, who was so hungry she tried to eat Yvonne.

And yet, for all the danger, pacing the streets of Paris that spring was an oddly civilizing and even sensuous affair. The Paris Opéra, next door to the Wendel hotel, staged six ballets and works by Gluck, Wagner, Verdi, Guonod, Berlioz, and Richard Strauss. Meanwhile, the Opéra Comique presented two operas by Puccini (*Tosca* and *La Bohème*), two by Bizet (*Carmen* and *Les pêcheurs de perles*), two by Massenet (*Manon* and *Werther*), and Debussy's *Pelléas et Mélisande*. Then there were the forty-four theaters that put on plays and musicals, the comedy clubs, nightclubs, cinemas, and restaurants. In March, a Parisian boxing exhibition celebrated the fiftieth birthday of the former French champ Georges Carpentier, a onetime opponent of Jack Dempsey's. The German heavyweight Max Schmeling sat ringside.

It must have baffled La Rochefoucauld, moving about in the

disguise of his glasses and beard. Despite the despair of the Occupation, or perhaps because of it, nightlife in the capital thrived—
even with the 10 p.m. curfew. How strange to be in a place where
the threat of absolute menace lay just beneath the promise of airy
entertainment. It was best not to dwell on it, so La Rochefoucauld
went from party to party.

The scene was different at Saint-Vrain when Robert arrived the
following week. His cousin Gabriel de Mortemart's country estate
was "charming" but remote, about forty-five minutes outside Paris.
Gabriel himself welcomed La Rochefoucauld but remained publicly distant around him. He'd explained to his young children that
he was taking in a temporary laborer, whom they all called, simply,
"monsieur." Privately, Mortemart insisted Robert spend most of his
time eating and sleeping, but La Rochefoucauld kept up the cover
by trimming a few hedges. In those celebratory days in Paris, he
had contacted a member of the Resistance who had in turn reached
the R/F administrators in London. After roughly a week in Saint-
Vrain, La Rochefoucauld received word to return to the capital, for
reasons unstated. He thanked the Mortemarts for their hospitality
and headed out.

I t wouldn't be easy to get back to London. "The first three months
of 1944 were disastrous from the point of view of supplying SOE
agents and circuits in Europe in general, and France in particular,"
one historian later noted. The weather was bad, and few planes
could fly to France. The fighters waiting for them there felt abandoned.

Some people began moving by sea, which SOE years earlier
conceived as the main means of getting clandestine agents into
occupied France. But the surprising, if relative, success of moonlit
airplane drops had eclipsed the seafaring option and its logistical
nightmare of getting fast boats to safe beaches. Not that such travel
via the English Channel was ignored. The Allies attempted around

120 missions on the north and west coasts of France alone during the war.

La Rochefoucauld later wrote that the plan was to sneak him back to London via submarine, but top-secret British records, disclosed decades later, did not show any submarine embarkations from the French coastline in April 1944. There were, however, three missions to pick up French clandestine agents that month by motor gunboat, a vessel of equal daring whose small size and high speeds made it difficult for the Germans to gun down. The fog of war was at its densest here, but the facts of one embarkation align themselves generally with La Rochefoucauld's view of events, published decades later.

"The procedure I was to follow was similar to that of my passage into Spain," La Rochefoucauld wrote. Contact a member of a Resistance group in Paris, who would in turn put him in touch with another *résistant* along the coast, this time at a place called Beg-an-Fry, near Guimaëc, northeast of Morlaix, in the Brittany region of northwestern France, according to British records. The problem was that this part of the country abutted the "prohibited" area, which comprised the coastal towns and cities hard against the so-called Atlantic Wall—a structure the Germans constructed to defend occupied France from an Allied onslaught. The wall itself was a three-thousand-mile collection of minefields, fortified artillery emplacements, concrete barriers, bunkers, and barbed-wire fences. Travel through the area was strictly prohibited. But that didn't mean it didn't happen.

La Rochefoucauld took a train from Paris to a small town just inland from the western coast. He then biked roughly eleven miles to a village redoubt where he says he met a Resistance fighter named Jean-Jacques. After a brief introduction, the two set out again, still on bikes, down country roads and dirt paths, making stops at inns where everyday Frenchmen much like André Bouy whispered what they knew of the Germans' positions.

With that information, the duo reached a hideout in the woods about a half mile from the ocean, where they found a collection of men. With them was a small rubber boat, which, when the coast was clear of Germans, they planned to set down in the sea and paddle to a motor gunboat, which would then take them to England. The plan was to communicate with the bigger boat by light signals: If their electric-lamp greeting was returned by a quick burst from the sea, the operation was on. If the men on land saw no such light, the mission would have to wait until the following evening.

The first night, a moonless night, the men moved to the coast at a designated time—at some point in the small hours—and sent out a quick signal. But they received no response. They resigned themselves to another day in the woods, sleeping when they could and otherwise scanning the horizon.

The next night, April 15, the men once more put out their light and this time—yes!—saw a return signal. Already the skiff was in the water, the fighters "paddling like madmen toward the open sea," La Rochefoucauld wrote. The ocean was calm that night and now they saw a follow-up signal, which oriented the men toward the boat that would take them to England. They had timed it just right: They heard no German shouts, saw no German boats. A few minutes later, they were aboard His Majesty's vessel.

There were, in fact, two boats out that night to collect men, according to British records: Motor Gun Boat 502 and Motor Gun Boat 718. The evening's mission called for placing six SOE agents on French soil, which the boats had done in the moments before they sent out signals to take in La Rochefoucauld and the other men. Now with Robert and the other fighters aboard—British records indicated roughly twenty people, SOE agents and Royal Air Force airmen between them—the vessels turned north toward England and freedom.

"There was a brusque change in ambiance," La Rochefoucauld wrote. The captain and crew greeted the men warmly and in a moment a sailor had procured large tumblers into which he mixed tea and whiskey. "We joyfully raised our glasses to the health of England and her sovereigns, convinced that, a few hours later, we could tread upon British soil," La Rochefoucauld wrote.

Then the boats came under heavy German fire. The cramped contours of the boat, the claustrophobia it induced, led to something like asphyxiation as the hail of enemy gunfire focused its aim. "I'd never been so scared in my life," Robert said, "to the point that I eventually convinced myself that I wouldn't come back from the expedition alive." Ultimately, the English outran the German boats—so fast that the Brits never actually opened fire—and the exchange ceased. But not, alas, without damage. On one of the boats, the crew suffered a casualty, a young sailor.

The vessels motored on, mourning their loss but otherwise judging the mission a success. And when they reached land again, three weeks after La Rochefoucauld had dared to escape, he had at last arrived in England.

# CHAPTER 14

The first thing they did was quarantine them. The British interrogated La Rochefoucauld and the other French agents—to see if they'd become German spies—but it was a pro forma exercise and soon they "gave us a royal welcome," Robert said, where "whiskey flowed like water . . . and I saw a few of the instructors I knew." They reveled in his story: the sabotages, imprisonment, escape. One officer in particular would have loved to hear it, but Eric Piquet-Wicks, the man with the goofy smile who'd recruited La Rochefoucauld to SOE a year and a half earlier, no longer worked in London. The stress of building the R/F network, the horrifying reports of agents who were tortured and killed, men and women whom he'd recruited and viewed as kin, seemed to affect him even more than his diagnosis of TB. His health worsened with the booze he drank, and he was removed from active service, in such a poor state that he relinquished his commission in September 1943. Piquet-Wicks wanted badly to return to SOE, and by the spring of '44, he had, but as a junior assistant working out of the British embassy in Madrid, where staff thought the climate might help him convalesce. In London he had developed a reputation as a more or less functioning alcoholic, drinking for reasons that were not discussed, and in Madrid doctors ordered him to work fewer hours, sleep well, and resist the soft nights' seductions. Piquet-Wicks promised he would. And yet reports soon surfaced of him staying out until 6 a.m. or taking his car a few streets from the embassy and driving it in reverse, "the worse for drink," noted one memo. At work, he couldn't encipher telegrams and he complained that traveling to Barcelona and back was too much for him. People in the office, who still found him charming, and liked him as much as the French agents he'd once recruited, kept excusing his behavior. But "it seemed quite evident," one visiting supervisor wrote, "that [Piquet-Wicks's] presence . . . far from assisting the general work, resulted on all sides in a considerable loss of time." He lasted in Spain six months before returning to England without a posting. Not every casualty, it seems, is listed.

La Rochefoucauld, meanwhile, went to some of his old training sites and met with other commanding officers. They knew of his imprisonment and admitted they thought he'd ended up like so many before him, one of the 75,000 French Resistance fighters to die at the hands of the Germans during the war. "To them, I looked like a ghost," La Rochefoucauld wrote. His resurrection called for celebration, then, and as Robert's story spread through the ranks, the Brits made it a point to feed him and show him a good time— every night. "We were endlessly invited to the best houses," he wrote, "and women fell into our arms!"

Rationing had not ended, the bombs still dropped, but life and London in this moment in May came furnished with a certain joie de vivre. "Hope was prevailing," Robert said. The Germans had overreached in Russia, and the Allies had fought their way north from Africa, and soon the European landing would come, had to come. "The hope of a victory people wanted to believe was near," La Rochefoucauld wrote.

He wondered how he would contribute to it. His hatred for the Germans and shame of his collaborating countrymen had not abated, and now—more than ever—he longed to prove to himself and the enemy that deprivation and torture could not break him. There was honor in that, especially for a man whose country had so often acted dishonorably. There was—and he liked this, too—a great deal of fun and adventure in another posting. He wanted to return to work in France, to be there when the Allies landed.

One day he was called to meet with an SOE major, who told

him his assignment: La Rochefoucauld and a small team would sabotage a munitions factory the Germans operated outside Bordeaux, in a town called Saint-Médard-en-Jalles. Saint-Médard's factory was less a plant than a compound: three massive buildings, barracks for officers and 5,500 laborers, the whole of the works covering 684 acres, or more than one square mile of suburban Bordelais real estate. Already, this plant had been attacked. On April 29 and 30, seventy-three British planes dropped 268 tons of bombs on the grounds, severely damaging its northeast wing, boiler house, and some ancillary buildings and leaving throughout fires that burned well after the bombing ceased. The damage was in no way complete, however, and eight days after the raid, the Germans had large parts of the works operational again. It would be La Rochefoucauld's job to cripple what the errant British bombs had not. The mission would take time, of course, and the Saint-Médard job wouldn't be Robert's only responsibility. He was to bring mayhem of all varieties to southwest France, working within Resistance outfits as he tried to find a way into the munitions compound. From there, he could figure out where charges might be laid.

The major recommended La Rochefoucauld reacquaint himself with the nuances of plastic explosives.

# CHAPTER 15

On May 7, two Halifax bombers idled on a runway outside London, crews loading three tons of arms, explosives, wireless devices, and radios into their bellies. With midnight approaching, La Rochefoucauld and his radioman squeezed into one of the planes. Moments later, they took off.

Once at cruising altitude, the pilot turned around to tell Robert he could take a nap; they wouldn't be to Bordeaux until nearly dawn, and their landing site was ninety miles south of there. But "I didn't sleep a wink during those tense hours," he later wrote.

Bordeaux was a different beast than the Yonne, more volatile and yet more cosmopolitan, and La Rochefoucauld was a different man now, still eager to fight but aware too of the consequences. This mission would be more dangerous than his last. The Nazis already had large parts of the "old" factory in Saint-Médard operating—its output had armed the French during World War I—and with each day, Robert assumed, the plant gained more functionality.

Bordeaux itself accentuated the peril of the assignment. The city had a reputation among Resistance fighters as a place where Nazi repression was at its worst. Bordeaux's port was a significant U-boat base. Its SD agents had been there since August 1940, longer than in any other provincial city, and these men now knew the region well. The Resistance leader Albert Ouzoulias said Bordeaux was "a cemetery of the finest fighters."

In part this was due to Friedrich Wilhelm Dohse, who oversaw the regional German police structure, coordinating all espionage, counterespionage, and security activities for the Nazis across southwest France. His portfolio included the military intelligence of the Abwehr and Feldpolizei, and the secret policemen within the regional SD offices. He was precocious, thirty-one in the spring of 1944, and in surviving photos bald and grimacing, as if the responsibilities of his post had aged him. Dohse spoke fluent French, dressed extremely well, and had single-handedly dismembered Bordeaux's largest Resistance group, Scientist. "This is a man who got results," a Bordeaux police officer later said. "He was an evil man."

The plane drew ever closer to Bordeaux. Soon it flew over the reclaimed marshes on which the city lay, where even the topography worked against *résistants*: The surrounding hills scrambled many of the wireless transmissions sent to London, and so drops like this one moved to the forests south of Bordeaux, to clearings in the terrain that only locals knew. La Rochefoucauld's landing would occur in the neighboring southern department of Landes, in a town called Mugron, amid its vineyards and groves of pine and fifteen hundred sleeping residents.

The plane swooped low, nearly skimming the tree line, five hundred feet off the ground. The pilot saw a formation of lights in an opening in the forest—the local *résistants*—and established radio contact with them. The bird swirled round and headed back for the formation, and La Rochefoucauld moved to the plane's hatch and stared at the red light opposite him. He waited, just as he had done in the Yonne, for the light to turn green.

It did.

Despite how little he liked parachuting, he once again landed without difficulty. His radioman, however, sprained his ankle. About a dozen *résistants* emerged from the trees to greet the men and helped them fold their parachutes. All around them fluttered down the ammunition, explosives, and wireless sets, floating to the ground in black containers that were each the size of a man and carried up to four hundred pounds of supplies. It was a massive haul, and took the men hours to ensure no trace of it remained behind.

When they were finished, La Rochefoucauld and the fighters of this Resistance group, Léon des Landes, departed on bicycles, the radio guy in a truck. They headed toward one of the group's hideouts.

Léon des Landes was led by one Léonce Dussarrat. Though he was an excellent shot, and even once taught a shooting course at the elite Saint-Cyr military academy, the forty-year-old was not a military man. He was a hardware store owner and a widower, who'd remarried and had four children. He'd joined the Resistance late, unaware that his business partner, Léon Baraille, was the local chief of the Organisation civile et militaire (OCM), a nationwide Resistance network. Baraille was sick and near death in 1943 when he revealed his involvement to Dussarrat, and asked him to carry on the fight when he couldn't.

What turned Dussarrat from a jovial shopkeeper to a Resistance mastermind occurred moments after Baraille's funeral in September of that year. André Grandclément, the regional head of the OCM in Bordeaux, had been flipped by the Germans and quite openly discussed his betrayal; he worked with the Nazis, he said, because he believed the Communists to be the real danger to France. Grandclément visited Dussarrat at his office and asked him to turn over the OCM's weaponry in the Landes. If Dussarrat failed to do so, well, Friedrich Dohse himself waited on the street.

Dussarrat stared at Grandclément—and refused. He would honor Baraille, his deceased friend. What followed is a bit unclear: Either Dussarrat narrowly avoided his arrest or Grandclément, in a moment of conflicting loyalties, allowed him to leave through a back door. But in the days ahead, Dussarrat's escape from Grandclément and Dohse became a one-way track to the underground, because now the SD knew who he was and where he worked. His refusal to turn over arms meant that he had no choice but to use them. So he put his family into hiding and began to learn the black arts of anarchy.

His former life helped him. Dussarrat knew the Landes, and its people, and as he met with them in secret, he began to construct the Resistance hierarchy, placing his group at the top of it, thanks in part to a store owner's sense for building inventory. To wage war one must collect weapons, and Léonce Dussarrat relied on a conviviality he'd perfected to cajole people to give him what he wanted. Then he expanded his new business, bridging his group beyond the department—working with major Resistance outfits just to the north, in Bordeaux—until Dussarrat's OCM chapter was larger than Baraille's had been: seven hundred men in spring 1944, and growing to an estimated five thousand by summer's end. As it grew, it transformed—Dussarrat collecting and distributing ever more weapons and planning ever more sabotages, finding a raison d'être in his new career—until it was no longer fitting to call Dussarrat's group an OCM chapter. Its members rechristened themselves Léon des Landes, an homage to their captain.

The Mugron parachute drop was Léon des Landes's fourth in three weeks, and the sabotages started soon after: the destruction of 328 yards of rails and 150,000-volt power lines in Saint-Paul-lès-Dax on May 20; a sabotage the following day in Mont-de-Marsan on two more power lines; and then, on June 3, cutting an underground cable between Dax and Bayonne. The successful missions helped to draw other groups to Léon des Landes, and before La Rochefoucauld could venture north to Saint-Médard and the munitions factory, he was asked to contact a second band of *résistants* about a sabotage. The details were unclear, and La Rochefoucauld was supposed to learn more when he met with the other rebels, and explained his expertise and available arms.

He was not the only agent that spring to parachute in with a skill set and supplies. Almost too many SOE *clandestins* dropped into France that season. By the middle of May, F Section had 75,000 men in country, R/F Section 50,000. The drops from RAF planes had increased from six tons in the last quarter of 1943, to 172 in the

first quarter of '44, to 794 in the second. In 1941, SOE's first trans-
mission station had only twelve channels; by June 1944, there were
fifteen circuits and 108 channels.

This had profound effects on France. The stream of weaponry
increased Resistance recruitment. Resistance groups became networks and networks an underground army. In May 1944, the Allies
gave General Marie-Pierre Koenig command of the newly formed
French Forces of the Interior, or FFI, which attempted to coordinate rebellious acts against the Germans, in anticipation of the Allied landing in France.

The Nazi reprisals in Bordeaux and the Landes turned even
more vicious. The Germans could sense victory slipping from
them and wanted revenge. Rebels heard savage stories: SOE agents
disemboweled or the Nazis draping a French fighter's corpse across
the front of a German truck on patrol. As Robert and two other
Léon des Landes men walked toward their rendezvous point, to
meet the saboteurs from the second group, they moved quietly, all
too aware of the repercussions for failing to do so.

But something, some snapping twig in the forest's underbrush
perhaps, betrayed them. "We fell upon some Germans," La Rochefoucauld said. The fight was brief and favored the overwhelming
number of Nazis. One *résistant* fled when the skirmish could not
be won, but Robert and the group leader were captured and sent to
a command post the Germans called Bouriotte-Bragence, a sort of
mini-Kommandatur staffed by a handful of soldiers.

La Rochefoucauld couldn't believe it: jailed in a second fortress.
Because of the tales of atrocities, "I was convinced my friend and
I would lose our lives here," Robert wrote. After a few hours, the
Nazis led him and the other *résistant* to a room on the ground floor,
where a confused interrogation began, the Germans not speaking
French well, and the French not wanting to answer.

But then, just beyond the shouted questions, the fighters heard
a car screech to a halt. In a moment three men peered through the

window of Robert's interrogation room. They wore plain clothes and, suddenly, raised submachine guns from their side. La Rochefoucauld hit the ground, crawling behind an upturned table. He grabbed his fellow *résistant* by the collar and dragged him close, more and more bullets tearing up the floor, ripping through walls, and narrowing their makeshift protection. The Nazis fell around them.

The men doing the shooting seemed to be from Léon des Landes. The problem was, in the confusion of the moment, they shot indiscriminately; the angry hiss of bullets zipped by La Rochefoucauld's ears. He tried shouting *I'm on your side*, but couldn't be heard over the guns' motorized roar. In such a confined space, it became "blindingly obvious," he thought, that he would die here, at the hands of his own comrades. Robert switched tactics, hoping it would stop the barrage. "We give up! We give up!" he shouted. At last the firing ceased.

His ears rang. The room smelled of gun smoke. He rose slowly from behind the table and saw the shooters, the thin skeptical lines of their mouths widening now into smiles, recognizing that La Rochefoucauld was one of theirs. They looked around the room, triumphant. Robert stepped over the corpses on the floor.

At 8:15 in the evening on June 5, the BBC sent a coded message meant for all fighters of the French Resistance. *"Blessent mon cœur/D'une Langueur/Monotone,"* whose literal translation was "Wound my heart/With a languor/Monotonous." These passages, from Paul Verlaine's poem "Autumn Song," were lines *résistants* had been waiting years to hear and had spent months planning for. D-Day had at last arrived.

The next morning more than 5,000 ships, 13,000 aircraft, and 160,000 Allied soldiers attacked the coast of Normandy. Hundreds of miles south, the men of Léon des Landes, like *résistants* throughout France, carried out missions their commanders had been organizing.

In the hours following the landings, Léon *résistants* ambushed German formations, slaughtering five here and dozens there and forty-two more at a command post outside Nanoose. But what really aided the Allies crawling on the beaches in northern France were the sabotages. From June 7 through June 10, Léon des Landes carried out more than two hundred. Rebels like Robert cut down power lines, blew up bridges and railroads, hid in trees that hung over major thoroughfares and fired at the Nazis as they drove by. They abided by the golden rule of irregular warfare: Kill the enemy, and when the enemy cannot be killed, delay his passage.

Every hour the Germans' forces were held up gave the Allied fighters bellying along the Cotentin peninsula that much more hope of taking the beach. There were, nationwide, up to a thousand sabotages on June 6 and the day after. A heavy emphasis was placed on blowing up rail lines, because 90 percent of the German army in 1944 moved by rail or horse. Throughout France train traffic collapsed by 50 percent. In Toulouse, one SS Panzer division equipped with the latest in armored tanks hoped to reach Normandy in three days. It took two weeks. Resistance fighters and Allied pilots first bombed all bridges heading to the beaches and all oil dumps where tanks might refuel. When Nazis tried to move north by railway, *résistants* sabotaged the networks of lines. Without fuel or rail transport, the Germans took to marching. Here, they walked into collections of snipers who, like those in the Landes, took aim behind strategic trees, or buildings, or hills. This played out in city, after town, after village. As Allied Supreme Commander Dwight Eisenhower later said, "I consider that the disruption of enemy rail communications, the harassing of German road moves and the continual and increasing strain placed on the German war economy . . . played a very considerable part in our complete and final victory." Eisenhower later estimated that the Resistance in France after D-Day was the equivalent of fifteen extra divisions, or up to 375,000 soldiers.

For La Rochefoucauld in those furious days of exploding power lines and quick-strike ambushes, a member of a secret army that was no longer so secret, he longed to complete the mission that had sent him back to France. One he hoped would cripple the Nazis and bring about their final defeat.

# CHAPTER 16

R obert and his radioman headed north, to Bordeaux, joining a group called Charly, led by the theater director René Cominetti, who had been involved in the Resistance since 1941. Cominetti had formed Charly with the help of a lawyer and banker, and by the summer of 1944, it had nearly 950 fighters. They roamed the terrain, taking up the battles of their neighboring underground tribes as well. Charly shared some of its *résistants* with a parent group, Groupe Georges, also operating near Bordeaux. It was led by Alban Bordes, a twenty-five-year-old as vicious with the Nazis—he admitted to carrying out hits that "God himself cannot pardon"—as he was fearful of them. He respected SD agents' intelligence and lived in secret, knowing the reprisals that awaited his capture.

In July, La Rochefoucauld met with someone who was likely, according to the historical record, a top Georges lieutenant and some of his staffers. This was in a group safe house, a cave outside Bordeaux, where the top man brought a bottle of wine and glasses and laid out his plan. He said three men from Georges had recently begun working at the Saint-Médard plant, scoping out its parameters and committing the layout to hand-drawn maps. La Rochefoucauld would meet these men when their shift at the factory ended. Because Robert knew how to lay plastic explosives, he would work at the plant alongside them. With the Allies moving inland from Normandy and the Germans fighting desperately to retain ground, there wasn't time to train men to do the work that La Rochefoucauld could do himself—if he just got inside the plant.

Robert loved the idea. He had not parachuted into France so that he might supervise someone else's job. Pleased with the response, the lieutenant left the men to their bottle of wine and open-ended afternoon. Soon thereafter, they themselves departed on bikes for a hideout closer to the factory, about ten miles west of Bordeaux.

The beauty of the vineyards in sun-dipped and fragrant July masked the danger of the Occupation. Robert and the rebels took a careful if not circuitous route, off the main roads where people looked friendly but might secretly work for the SD chief Dohse. A short while after they made it to the house, the three plant workers joined them, and they all decided to celebrate their mission. From the vague phrases La Rochefoucauld later wrote, it appears the *résistants* took him to Bordeaux's finest brothels that night. "We were perfectly received," said Robert.

The next day, Sunday, was not a day of rest. The Georges men and La Rochefoucauld gathered round a table at the safe house, maps spread before them, everyone hunching over. The munition works was massive: on the northern and eastern half of the compound sat the "old" factory, next to a railroad track that had shipped the works' supplies for generations; the "new" one was on the grounds' western and southern half, built in advance of World War 1; and the so-called "pearl" factory, constructed at the start of this war by two thousand imprisoned Spanish Communists, bordered the two other factories. The compound was surrounded by twelve workers and officers' camps where some Germans and many of the 5,500 laborers lived. In total, the grounds encompassed more than a square mile. From the aerial maps, the Saint-Médard factories and their surrounding barracks resembled less a place of labor than a city unto itself.

La Rochefoucauld's job was not to blow it all up. The massive bombing campaign in April hadn't even done that. Robert's task instead would be to place pinpoint bombs at key positions throughout the compound, crippling it from within. As the British sabotage instructors had said: *It's better to target small but vital components of a factory. This is the mark of a true saboteur.*

To get inside the grounds, La Rochefoucauld first had to replace one of the three factory workers. A man named Pierre, who
unloaded trucks at the plant, looked the most like Robert: roughly
his height, dark hair swept back off his forehead. Pierre's best feature was his glasses: black-rimmed and big enough to obscure the
shape of the face behind them. Did Robert look like Pierre when
he put on the glasses? Not really. But he looked nothing like anyone else there. So Pierre handed over his plant ID card—reissued
every two months for factory security—and La Rochefoucauld
and the other *résistants* did the hard but also routine work of making a fake ID, of transferring La Rochefoucauld's photo from his
identification to Pierre's factory card. At long last they had it. The
ID looked authentic.

The men then began thinking how to traffic explosives past the
German guards. No single idea had everyone's support until, at last,
someone said they should put the bombs in their food—specifically,
in the round loaves of French bread that each man took with him
for his midday meal.

The *résistants* set about kneading dough to see if it could work.
When the loaves came out of the oven, the men slowly, delicately,
carved open the top of each one, cutting out the moist middle and
dropping in a couple pounds of plastic explosives. They then set
the severed top back on the loaf and studied it. From the outside—
*voila!*—it looked like lunch.

La Rochefoucauld arose early Monday morning and got dressed.
Many factory workers favored denims and newsboy caps, and
Pierre's big-rimmed glasses further hid Robert's features. As he
put on his clothes, he couldn't help but worry that the disguise
was not enough. In fact, that's what everyone worried about. The
Georges men, as a precaution, had decided to arrive separately
at the plant, lest all three *résistants* be implicated in a La Rochefoucauld arrest.

He steeled himself and set out on a bicycle for the munitions compound, carrying a bag with a loaf of bread in it. Robert arrived at the factory alone, around 7:45, fifteen minutes before the plant opened. He saw the two other Georges men standing together, but tried not to stare at them. Everyone formed into a line, which began moving at 8 a.m.

La Rochefoucauld shuffled along, in a "delicate" state, he wrote. He slung the bag that held his lunch—and so much more—over his shoulder, just as the rest of the men did. He tried to look bored. *Shuffle left, shuffle right, stare absently. Shuffle left, shuffle right, ignore the rising panic.*

Soon there was one man ahead of him, and then the German asked for La Rochefoucauld's plant ID. He willed his hand steady and gave the guard the papers.

The Nazi glanced at them, then at La Rochefoucauld. The German looked sleepy, or maybe just disinterested. He handed the plant ID back to Robert, then motioned for the next man in line.

It was that easy. He crossed the factory's threshold, trying very hard to hide his excitement.

His job was to unload the trucks that had arrived at the grounds the night before and carry the boxes and crates throughout the compound. It was an ideal task for a saboteur. Robert walked through the wings, noting every aisle and crevice, mentally matching it against the maps he had spent Sunday studying: a fuel warehouse over here, metal presses and sieves there, a survey of the plant's "most vulnerable spots," La Rochefoucauld said. He also studied the Germans. They seemed an old and largely uncaring class of soldiers. The Nazis had hired a French firm called OPA at the start of the Occupation to oversee the Saint-Médard compound and two other nearby plants. The Germans demanded OPA acquire experienced workers, but the firm, perhaps as an act of passive resistance, instead hired ex-cons and prostitutes. They allowed, knowingly or not, *résistants* like the Georges men to comprise about one-fifth of the labor force. Plant production suffered, the workers delivering anywhere from one-quarter to one-third of the war-machinery tonnage the Germans annually expected. And yet few repercussions fell on the laborers. The Germans were primarily concerned with security at the plant, and in this they were successful: There were no labor uprisings, no fiery sabotages, and even the more subtle resistance of lethargic work habits could be explained by the aging and outdated equipment. By 1944, the German attitude seemed to be, *As long as they are here, working, they are not elsewhere, plotting. And as long as they are here, they are working for us.* So the Germans tolerated the lowly sixteen tons of supplies delivered—they may have even been impressed by it, if the effort to get the plant operational after the British bombing was any indication.

Because of the Germans' lax oversight, La Rochefoucauld left the grounds Monday night feeling he could case the plant as he wished, unimpeded, and decided to use more than just bread to do it. That week, he and the other *résistants* also slit holes in the heels of their shoes that allowed for another pound of bombing materiel.

The following days, then, fell into a routine: Arrive at the plant early, shuffle in nonchalantly, pass the hours ostensibly in the Germans' employ—but then, with no one looking, twist the top off a loaf of bread or open the heel of a shoe and deposit explosives into hiding spots. Anxiety trailed Robert everywhere at the plant, sure, but it was also fun and somewhat easy work in this laissez-faire factory, even if it meant eating little more than bread crusts for lunch. At night at the safe house, to celebrate their deception, "There was always a bottle of very good wine," La Rochefoucauld said. "After the schnapps, we would go out." He was not yet twenty-one, doing the work of a lifetime and feeling so very alive. He would show the Germans, he would punish them, he would leave his impression on this war. After seven days, La Rochefoucauld and the two other Georges men had smuggled in roughly forty pounds of explosives.

The sabotage was set for a Thursday. The plan was for Robert to work a full shift and, at 6:30, a half hour before the plant closed, activate the first fuse near a fuel warehouse, with a one-hour delay. He'd hide out on the grounds until the compound locked its doors at 7 p.m., then set surrounding detonators, all of them with a half-hour delay. To get out of the factory he had already stacked crates and boxes next to a high window that looked down upon the plant's courtyard. He would climb the crates, open the window, and jump into the courtyard. The courtyard itself had high walls, about twenty feet tall. The Georges men would be on the other side and toss a rope over the wall's edge. La Rochefoucauld would grab it, hurry over, and run away before the fireworks began.

At last, the appointed day arrived. The tension of what lay ahead drained La Rochefoucauld even as it energized him. He seemed to have the flighty unfocused quality of someone given too many cups of coffee. The hard work lay in concealing his frayed state.

When 6:30 p.m. approached, he walked to the fuel depot. With no one looking, he positioned himself behind it. In a moment he had assembled the first explosive and embedded the charge in such a way that it would not explode outward, but inward and toward the depot. He set the time-delayed fuse for one hour and quietly reemerged from the shadows.

Near 7 p.m., he crawled into a crook of the factory, a hiding space where no one could see him, but where he could watch as two Germans made the day's final patrol. Then a siren sounded and the workers meandered out of the grounds. In a few minutes the guards exited and locked the front gates behind them. La Rochefoucauld crawled out.

Every saboteur is an artist, casing his target as he sees fit with the materials at hand, the marks he leaves as idiosyncratic as his own fingerprint. There were about eight positions Robert needed to case inside the factory—water mains and conduits and so forth—

and he wanted to time the detonators inside the plant to explode as the charge at the fuel depot did, about one hundred yards away. The most effective sabotages were simultaneous ones. So, inside the plant, he placed each detonator against its target, syncing the charges, one to the next, with a detonator cord that burned at 22,000 feet per second when ignited. He then set a time fuse within each explosive that would burn until 7:30, when the fuse at the fuel depot ignited the bomb.

When he had cased everything, he still had about ten minutes until the fiery explosion. He hurried to the crates he'd piled next to the high window, his escape window, and climbed up the boxes. He looked out to the courtyard a short distance below and quickly broke each pane of glass and then the window frame. He climbed up onto the windowsill and jumped.

He thumped to the ground, unharmed. His skin crawled with the strange but quite reasonable sensation that he was in mortal danger. He ran to the courtyard's wall and just as he reached it he saw a rope, hurtling up and over and tumbling down to him. "Never in my life," La Rochefoucauld wrote, "neither before nor after, have I scaled an eighteen-foot wall at such a speed." On the other side, he fell into a Georges worker's arms.

The *résistants* had brought a bicycle for Robert, and now the men pedaled away furiously. When they'd put enough distance between themselves and the plant they slowed, and then stopped, the anticipation overwhelming.

Then—a great concussive boom. It shook the ground on which they stood. And then a second explosion, just as angry. The men exchanged brief, *holy shit* looks and kept biking, giddy boys suddenly, racing to their hideout.

They reached it, laughing and celebrating and recalling it all. Bordes had already arranged a feast: enough food, wine, and merriment to last into the next day. La Rochefoucauld ate and drank, but soon realized he didn't have an all-nighter in him. "I felt immense fatigue more than anything," he wrote. "I thought only of sleeping."

Just as he was settling in Robert remembered he still had to send word to London. He removed the radioman momentarily from the festivities and together they crafted a succinct note, the better to avoid any Germans monitoring the airwaves:

"Operation . . . successful."

The reply was even terser: "Congratulations."

With that, "I collapsed onto a straw mattress," La Rochefoucauld wrote, "and instantly fell asleep."

# CHAPTER 17

The morning after the mission he awoke to the dusty throbbing particular to the overserved, but the sound of success—those concussive booms—lingered in his head, coursing through the body like caffeine, freeing him of his hangover. The Georges plant workers surveyed the factory and reported back the level of destruction: water mains and conduits leveled, buildings charred. According to two subsequent British reports, the factory would be out of commission for fifteen days, a week longer than what the British bombing campaign had mustered. When one considered that this sabotage had not terrorized the people like the bomber fleet—where Frenchmen had run for cover with saucepans on their heads and farmers had found the limbs of their livestock in nearby trees—the July sabotage could only be judged as something close to flawless.

The Georges men began to plan their exits. Everyone assumed the streets would fill, were perhaps already filled, with vigilant Germans twitching to catch the *résistants* who'd pulled off the job. After a few days, the group decided La Rochefoucauld would be the first of his team to sneak to Bordeaux, to a second safe house, where a man with the code-name Jean would help smuggle him back to London.

La Rochefoucauld spent the downtime sleeping well and learning the backroads between Saint-Médard and Bordeaux. On the designated night, when it seemed safe to head out, he said his farewells and left on a bicycle, without headlights but with the bends and turns of his darkened route memorized.

It was not only Friedrich Dohse who made La Rochefoucauld's

trek to Bordeaux dangerous. The whole of the German army fought dirty now. The 2nd Panzer Division Das Reich had rumbled into a small village, Oradour-sur-Glane, in June on the rumor that a Resistance group held a German officer captive. But the Germans found no jailed Nazi and no sign of a Resistance group. Instead of leaving, the Nazis ordered all men into the village's central marketplace. The Das Reich regiment raised their machine guns and mowed down the male population. Then the Nazis turned to the town's women and children, herding them all into a church. The Germans encircled its grounds and set it on fire. In all, 642 people were murdered in Oradour. It was the worst civilian massacre of the German Occupation of France.

Resistance fighters whispered about other barbarities, too, as they waged war that summer: the Nazis coldly assassinating thirty-six ailing *résistants* who had turned a cave into their makeshift hospital; the Nazis gang-raping women, dismembering men. Everywhere were stories of "terrorist" roundups and mass executions by collaborators who were now as desperate as the Nazis. They had picked the wrong side, and knew it, and their resignation gave them the permission to fight with a feral cruelty, a cornered panting prey.

Pierre Poinsot was one of them, the commissioner of Bordeaux's police department. Even now, he retained in his full cheeks the cherubic look of the seminarian he'd once been. But Poinsot was the man who, in 1941, made sure the Nazis received each of the forty-seven hostages the Germans wanted dead, in reprisal for a French Communist's assassination of a Nazi officer. These forty-seven included people whom Poinsot in theory protected as commissioner, twelve of whom even he later admitted held no Communist views. Poinsot had the cruelty to send them to their deaths regardless.

At the prefecture of police, Poinsot and his associates hung the men they interrogated from their thumbs, waterboarded them, burned them with cigarettes, forced their wives to listen to their animalistic screams—women who were in turn stripped of their clothes and made to kneel on the floor. The torture did not cease until the interrogated betrayed their fellow *résistants* or, at length, died. Poinsot "massacred" people, a Bordeaux police officer later said.

Soon he had an impressive and quite nuanced understanding of rebel groups in southwest France, which endeared him to someone like Friedrich Dohse. They became a formidable duo as the war ground on, systematically infiltrating and killing most of the region's Resistance cells. For Poinsot's assistance, the Nazi secret police brought him into their ranks, even giving him a number, member 192. He earned it. By that desperate summer of 1944, as La Rochefoucauld pedaled toward Bordeaux, Poinsot had helped to deport 1,560 Jews, 900 Resistance fighters, and had executed 285 people. All this despite having fewer than twenty men under him in his so-called Brigade of Killers.

As La Rochefoucauld biked, he saw no one, which he knew wasn't the same as no one seeing him. So he moved at a measured pace, straining to see and straining harder to hear. Behind him, suddenly, was the sound of an approaching vehicle. He threw his bike into a ditch and followed it in, a reaction so swift and instinctual it surprised even him. He heard the low rhythmic hum of tires and burrowed down deeper to avoid the sweep of passing headlights. When the car passed him, he peeked up and watched it fade in the distance, waiting until he heard nothing but the rush of silence in his ears. He then slowly and carefully set out again. Minutes later came the whine of a second far-off engine—back in the ditch, hiding out until he thought it was safe.

For a long time thereafter, he saw and heard nothing on the road. Soon he was a few miles from the city. Robert followed a bend, moving now between two farmsteads and something else—

He broke hard and nearly slammed into a roadblock. Two

German soldiers flashed their lights and raised their submachine guns, yelling at him to stay where he was. La Rochefoucauld stretched his arms to the sky and assumed the practiced, panicked hysteria of a civilian: *Don't shoot! Don't shoot!* In bad French, the Germans asked him what he was doing tonight. Did he have permission, an *Ausweis*, to be out this late?

No, he said. He told them the response he'd been mulling in his mind: He was returning from the woods. He had been with his girlfriend, you see, making love. And he was just on his way home now.

The Germans were suspicious. *Why not fuck your girlfriend at home? Or in a hotel? And even if you did take her to the woods, where was she now?* The questions rattled him more than they should have, and La Rochefoucauld stammered out responses. He sensed they weren't satisfying. Suddenly, he was no longer assuming the role of the panicked Frenchman: He was one. With each meandering statement the Germans' skepticism grew. "I knew I was damned," Robert later said.

The Nazis handcuffed La Rochefoucauld and loaded him into the vehicle just beyond the roadblock. Moments later Bordelais storefronts rushed past, the truck turning down one street and then another and stopping at last before an imposing multistoried brick and concrete enormity, with a high stone wall surrounding it. The engine clicked off and the guards led La Rochefoucauld inside Fort du Hâ.

# CHAPTER 18

France's King Charles VII had ordered its construction in 1453 along the ramparts of Bordeaux, at the end of the Hundred Years' War, to protect the city from future British invasions. An imperious and stately compound rose from the earth—and in the centuries to come dukes and mayors and barons would call it home, despite its primary function as a barricade. In the eighteenth century, and largely in response to the French Revolution, Fort du Hâ became a prison, its hulking three-story towers the last stop for dissidents—journalists, lawyers, even the mayor of Bordeaux—before the guillotine. After the Reign of Terror, the government partially demolished the structure, to allow for a courthouse and new prison, built around two of its original towers. By the middle of the nineteenth century, Fort du Hâ had become a symbol of progressive reform, modeled after the penal infrastructures in Pennsylvania, where prisoners were not shackled or bunched together in common areas but separated into small cells, in which reflection and (one hoped) rehabilitation could take root.

Fort du Hâ's standing changed again after 1940. It housed the political opponents that Poinsot and the Nazis interrogated and thus became a savage symbol of torture, of firing squads and, for some prisoners, of deportation to concentration camps. La Rochefoucauld did not need to be told into which prison the Germans escorted him. Fort du Hâ's reputation reached beyond its stone walls.

The heavy door to the outside world thudded closed behind him. The Germans pushed him up a flight of stairs and down a humid corridor to a processing room. Signs on the wall said in French, German, and Spanish that prisoners could not talk. A sergeant and

166 | PAUL KIX

two clerks awaited him behind three vast tables and, despite the order on the wall, La Rochefoucauld spoke up, trying to explain that he was there by mistake, attempting to tamp down the notes of hysteria climbing out of his voice. He was traveling at night by bicycle—he did not deny that—but it was completely for personal reasons. The administrators, however, were no more romantic than the soldiers had been. They sniggered and ignored him. They had a protocol to follow, after all. They told him to empty his pockets. They then counted the money he had on him, and asked him for any valuables or jewels, keeping it all.

After that, the administrators gave him a paper to sign, which asked if he were part of France's secret army or the French Forces of the Interior. La Rochefoucauld's military records made clear his involvement in the Resistance, but he was not about to mention this to the Germans.

And they seemed to suspect as much, because the sergeant on duty told him to save his pleas of innocence for the interrogating officer. The man would return in two days' time, the following Monday morning.

That interrogating officer would be none other than Friedrich Wilhelm Dohse.

What made Dohse dangerous, what made him so good at his job, was his detachment from it. He was born in 1913 in the suburbs of Hamburg to a professorial father, and this last bit of biography explained a lot of why Friedrich Dohse later excelled: In a field ruled by visceral reactions, Dohse questioned *résistants* academically, distancing himself from the emotion and even brutality of the interrogation to observe his suspects, to see what motivated them, which was a more useful insight than what frightened them. Given that his father had taught French, Dohse went into every interrogation with a cultural understanding of the man or woman opposite him. His ease with the language made him all the more lethal.

He was not an imposing man. He had a slight frame and easy smile. Though he dressed well, officiously, always in a suit with a tie and collar cinched tight to his skinny neck, he was not handsome. He looked sickly even, with deep lines under his eyes and a bald pate that seemed almost alien in its dimensions, a bulbous forehead barely corralling his big brain. At the age of twenty he had enrolled in Hitler's Fascist party, and by 1936, at twenty-three, was a member of the vaunted Schutzstaffel, or SS, the führer's elite Praetorian guard, which soon assumed intelligence operations and ran the Reich's concentration camps. Membership in the SS required an ancestry free of Jewish forebears, but the anti-Semitism rampant among its ranks was not shared by Dohse, who joined the service almost exclusively for career advancement. Even at that young age, then, Dohse was not motivated by the baser urges of the Nazis and their attendant ideologies. Because the SS was less an agency than a club, Dohse apprenticed within the Abwehr, Germany's military intelligence apparatus. He took a post in Denmark and, in 1941, Paris. In the capital he worked alongside Karl Bömelburg, the head of the city's SD Section IV, which snuffed out the saboteurs and helped deport France's Jews. Bömelburg was a complex man. In an earlier life, he had been a great law enforcement agent, thriving within the Internationale kriminalpolizeiliche Kommission (IKPK), the forerunner to Interpol, where from his office in Vienna he'd developed relationships with French policemen, conferring with them in their native tongue on the subtleties of international law. Years later, in his mid-fifties, he worked to stifle the very ideals he had once defended. There was no indication that that pained him. In fact, Bömelburg turned to Dohse because he saw a kindred soul, another man whose capacious intellect could hold and not be troubled by opposing moralities. Bömelburg became Dohse's mentor.

In January 1942, Dohse received orders to do in Bordeaux what Bömelburg did in Paris, and oversee southwest France's SD

Section IV. The existing chief there, Herbert Hagen, who lived on a yacht that belonged to the king of Belgium, did not take kindly to Dohse's encroachment. Hagen was so standoffish in their initial meeting that Dohse left Bordeaux the same day he'd arrived. Back in Paris, he reported his interaction to Bömelburg, who, displeased, said he would take care of it. By the time Dohse returned to Bordeaux, Hagen warmly welcomed him—and soon thereafter left his job. "Commandant Bömelburg," Dohse later said, "loved me like his son."

Dohse occupied a strange position. The nominal chief of Bordeaux counterespionage—the Kommandant overseeing all SD sections—was Hans Luther, a crew-cut, big-eared man with a background as a civil magistrate. But Dohse, just twenty-nine upon his arrival in Bordeaux, soon became the real head of power. What made the arrangement even more remarkable was that Luther far outranked him. Dohse entered the war as a Hauptscharführer, which meant he wasn't even an officer—though he was later promoted to SS Untersturmführer, the rough equivalent of a second lieutenant. Luther was a captain, two rungs higher than Dohse, and yet Luther deferred to him. Dohse was widely read and applied his towering intellect to the psychology of the *résistant*, so good at questioning suspects that soon Luther ordered all incoming "terrorists" to be grilled by Dohse, a stunning honor in a region of roughly 290 competitive agents. Dohse almost expected the commendation: He believed he was the intellectual better of every German in Bordeaux. This annoyed Luther, but, then again, Dohse *was* too smart to be overlooked and too valuable to be punished for his arrogance.

Interviewing all suspects gave Dohse the power to shape all investigations, and armed with such authority he effectively minimized Luther. Bordeaux became Dohse's town, and *résistants* soon feared the sickly man in the well-tailored suit, for he seemed to know everything and to destroy what he wished. Perhaps nothing better illustrates his prowess and intellectual finesse than his inter-rogation of André Grandclément.

By day Grandclément worked as an insurance-salesman-cum-broker, and in his off-hours he led the Resistance group Organisa-tion Civile et Militaire (OCM), which over the course of the war helped civil servants and military officers take the fight to the Ger-mans. He oversaw five combat groups, one team of parachutists, and recruited promising young men to a secret school in Bordeaux, where they learned how to operate the saboteur's weaponry. He claimed to have forty thousand fighters at the ready. This was likely an exaggeration, but London respected OCM and by April 1943 Grandclément's group and other Resistance outfits in the region had been the beneficiaries of 134 British air drops. By one account, Grandclément soon had enough weapons to supply a division, or as many as twenty-five thousand soldiers.

In the summer of 1943, SD agents infiltrated and destroyed Paris' massive Resistance group, Prosper. One of the arrested Prosper *résistants* flipped under torture and revealed André Grand-clément's name and his address in Bordeaux. The Paris SD, and perhaps Bömelburg himself, notified Dohse, who descended on Grandclément's house with a search warrant. Though the Ger-mans did not find Grandclément and his wife—they were visiting friends in Paris at the time—they found something much bet-ter: the ledger in which Grandclément had written many OCM members' names and their addresses. The SD arrested more than eighty people, including, ultimately, Lucette Grandclément, An-dré's wife, when she returned from Paris ahead of her husband. She was thrown with the others in Fort du Hâ.

Questioning the arrested *résistants* methodically, Dohse learned a great deal about Grandclément. Dohse learned that he was the son of a French admiral who'd spent his formative years moving between universities and military schools, seldom finishing what he started and entering the army as a soldier in 1928. Grandclément ultimately became an officer but left the military after a nasty fall from a horse. What buoyed him through a rather pedestrian life—he joined numerous insurance outfits—was a conservative ideology common to those of his station. It was little coincidence, in fact, that Grandclément joined and then thrived within OCM, which began the war as a notorious right-wing group.

Here, Dohse saw his opening. When at last SD agents arrested André Grandclément and put him before Dohse for questioning, the SD chief knew that Grandclément wanted to clean out not just the Nazis but the Communists, too. Dohse planned to appeal to Grandclément's conservatism, and in so doing play a bigger game. What Dohse had in mind could only be revealed through conversational niceties, so he was not severe with the OCM chief. Dohse would later describe their first session as "a conversation on the general situation, the military situation, the chances of success for the adversaries [the Germans], the Resistance in France and the divergence in views within it." And it was around this last point that Dohse began to make his pitch. He knew that the Communists bothered Grandclément as much as the Fascists. Dohse could see why: In fact, to his mind, the greater threat to France was not losing a war to Germany but winning it only to be overwhelmed by agents from Russia. In an offer that would be debated and deconstructed for decades to come, Dohse told Grandclément he was willing to free OCM members, and his wife, if Grandclément agreed to drop the fight against the Germans and battle the Communists alone. Dohse would also want, in exchange for the freed prisoners, the locations of some of the arms the English had sent to the OCM.

Grandclément did not immediately say no, and so Dohse pressed. He already knew, he said, the real names of British agents, OCM agents, their rendezvous points. He already knew—because it was his job to know and because he was good at that job—the location of almost all the Allied arms anyway. He'd learned that a month earlier, after the first wave of OCM *résistants* were arrested. (Dohse was not bluffing here. A French report filed after the war said the Germans discovered "several" stockpiles of arms in August 1943, weeks before Grandclément's arrest.) All Dohse asked now was for Grandclément to give him a bit more information, and then Dohse would free his wife, his imprisoned fighters, and together, Grandclément and the new OCM could battle the Communist scourge.

Dohse knew he had him when Grandclément asked for twenty-four hours to consult his top two lieutenants, men named Chazeau and Malleyrand. The SD chief agreed to let him leave detention.

The Resistance boss and his men met at a safe house, where a fourth fighter joined them, Roger Landes, head of Scientist, an SOE-run outfit in Bordeaux. Grandclément made his pitch, but it did not go over well. Landes thought it an unequivocal betrayal and drew his automatic pistol. The only reason he didn't pull the trigger, he later said, was because two women were in the house, and he didn't want them implicated and questioned by the SD and Dohse. Landes said he wanted nothing to do with such a deal and was appalled Grandclément was considering it.

The next day, however, Grandclément dutifully returned to Dohse, his mind made up. He loved his wife and hated the entrenched Communists, and his rationale seemed to be that as long as he and his freed fighters battled someone, the battle for France was just. He did the deal with Dohse. Grandclément gave up the locations of arm stores, and Dohse freed dozens of prisoners, including Grandclément's wife.

Grandclément then began meeting with *résistants*, pitching his fight-the-Communist-only campaign. The rebels were bewildered—some outright opposed his angle. And no wonder: Grandclément's collaboration with Dohse became quite transparent, Grandclément even going so far as to show two German officers *résistant* compounds. The threat of Grandclément's betrayal became even more effective than anyone he actually betrayed. Rebels fretted over whether he would mention their supplies or their names to Dohse, and fled or hid accordingly. That threat crippled the Resistance in southwest France.

And here we get to the game Dohse seemed to be playing all along. A traitor everyone knows can be as dangerous as a traitor no one does. Dohse didn't just want Grandclément to fight Communists; he wanted Grandclément to *tell* everyone he was fighting Communists. Viewed in this light, the brave and noble Roger Landes, who went from cell to Resistance cell warning men about Grandclément's deal with Dohse, actually helped the SD's efforts. Fearful of a Nazi arrest, *résistants* began to flee the region.

Dohse then pressed his advantage. First, he kept some OCM *résistants* behind bars, breaking his promise to Grandclément to free them. And then Dohse began to arrest more French agents, be they from OCM or Scientist or from other Resistance groups, the arrests and interrogations piling up by the dozens and then scores. All told, roughly 250 fighters were nabbed in the months *following* Grandclément's interrogation. Suddenly, Dohse didn't need Grandclément's intel. He had dozens more scared men just as willing to talk about the fighters still on the outside. Even circumspect SOE chiefs weren't safe: Roger Landes had to leave the country. For a period of a few months, Dohse single-handedly wiped out the Resistance in southwest France, the whole of his jurisdiction. No one, not even Bömelberg, could claim that.

Of course, no one, not even Bömelberg, had Dohse's autonomy. Dohse had allowed his best suspect to leave detention, and no other German agent had questioned his wisdom. He would have scoffed at the dissent anyway. Dohse hated military protocol, military dress. He almost never wore a uniform. He spent his weekends in the coastal spa town of Arcachon with his mistress, an hour's drive from the demands of the SD office. He secretly thought Hitler and the Nazis were done for in 1943, and even as he became known as

the most cunning Nazi of them all, he began dreaming of a civilian postwar life in which France were free and he imported champagne and cognac. He may have betrayed Grandclément as much
as Grandclément betrayed his *résistants*, but Dohse also treated
those he imprisoned with respect: He saw them as combatants to
be detained and not as terrorists to be tortured. Dohse even went
to the German high command with what would today be seen as a
successful counterinsurgency strategy. He claimed that he could be
more effective in Bordeaux if he could grant suspects the humanity
that was their right. If he could build a rapport with insurgents, he
could wipe out their need to rebel. The idea went nowhere in Hitler's Europe, but the respect he held for certain Resistance fighters
was real. "I found in you a dangerous adversary," a *résistant* named
Jean Duboué once told Dohse, "but an honest enemy with a strong
sense of honor."

At the same time, of course, he was not above using torture.
Dohse would go about his careful interrogation, but if the information wasn't to his liking, he brought in the brutes, a coterie of
henchmen who allegedly included a former trainer to the boxing
champ Max Schmeling. Dohse never harmed a suspect himself and
always left the room before the day turned nasty. Even here, by
leaving before the assault began, he was playing the angles, imagining how he might save himself in a postwar world in which Germany was not the victor. Literally keeping his hands free of blood
might keep him from any future war crimes indictment. Like a
mafia don, Dohse made it hard to trace the more horrific acts back
to him.

By the summer of 1944, *résistants* had returned en masse to Bordeaux, some emboldened by D-Day and others by SOE chief
Roger Landes, who'd reappeared and built a new Resistance group,
Actor, which by June comprised two thousand men: British-trained
and Gaullist fighters or people who were otherwise smart and

brave and discreet. Dohse wanted to nab Landes, a man as cunning and powerful as he, more than he'd wanted to destroy OCM and Grandclément. He said he would pay any sum for Landes's capture. But from secret hideouts, Landes avoided Dohse's detection and approved the mayhem that so infuriated the SD chief. Landes's people didn't act alone. Other groups had nearly the size or strength of Actor, still more were Communist outfits, and other cells were so small and secretive that neither London nor de Gaulle's forces knew of them. Dohse battled in that decisive summer a determined and invisible army.

Which is another way to say: The arrests and interrogations did not let up. The cells in Fort du Hâ, in fact, had one of three colored cards affixed to each door, to categorize for Dohse and the prison staff the sort of inmates found there: common-law prisoners got the green one, Communists or Gaullists the red, and *résistants* the yellow. This last group was seen as the most dangerous, and no crime was more serious in Bordeaux in 1944 than sabotage, which didn't bode well for Robert de La Rochefoucauld.

After his processing Saturday night, a German guard marched him down a narrow high-ceilinged corridor, which gave way to a small wing and its twelve holding chambers. These were separate from the general prison, with its three floors of cells and up to twelve hundred inmates. The long-incarcerated of Fort du Hâ called the holding rooms the "reception centers," but there was little to welcome a new inmate. Each was roughly six feet by three, equipped with not so much a bed as "cage-like things," in the words of one prisoner, made with unfinished wood, "topped with moldy straw sewn into decaying canvas, letting off a vile odor." In the corner was a rusted, dented, very much used bucket, to relieve oneself. Overhead was an electric lamp and high on the wall a barred window, with a limited view of Fort du Hâ's courtyard and Bordeaux beyond. The guard shoved La Rochefoucauld into his cell; he would stay here until Dohse interrogated him Monday, after which he would be given an identification number and enter Fort du Hâ's rolls.

The guard closed the heavy door and in five minutes the overhead light automatically shut off. On many nights prisoners would sing after lights out, the walls outside the courtyard heightening the acoustics, a full-throated concert rising into the night in French, Czech, Polish, Spanish, Portuguese. But no chorus reached La Rochefoucauld this night, and he sat in the dark with only his anxious monologue as company.

Could he endure more? That seemed to be the big question. Torture changes everyone, and it had changed La Rochefoucauld. He remained committed to a free France but also knew the fallout of that commitment. "Anyone who has been tortured is incapable of feeling at home in the world afterwards," wrote the Resistance fighter Jean Améry, who survived Buchenwald. It seemed surreal, or abstract, or at the very least something that no one else could understand, those sessions with Dr. Haas and his men in Auxerre. But La Rochefoucauld understood it even if he couldn't verbalize it, and that knowledge had led him to plea—to plea with the Germans in Bordeaux that he was an innocent man, a half-maniacal alibi whose stumbling inconsistencies showed he was not innocent, and which might yet tie him to the attempted sabotage at Saint-Médard. *What a fool*, Robert thought. And then, again: Could he endure more?

Everything had happened so fast after Auxerre: the escape to Paris, the toasts with family, the return to London, the fight here in the southwest. But now in the hours before dawn it seemed that Auxerre had at last rushed in, its ghosts filling his cell. His thoughts circled around themselves and blackened with each turn. For the first time in his life Robert thought of suicide, and the cyanide pill that SOE staffers had given him, which he had slipped into the false bottom of his shoe. The pill would keep him from seeing Monday, from experiencing a pain sharpened by a new fear: the very real likelihood that Dohse and his men would get to Robert's family.

Bordeaux's Nazis routinely flipped *résistants* by finding and then threatening to kill a fighter's next of kin. If Dohse discovered La Rochefoucauld's real name, he would not make the mistake Karl Haas had. He would recognize the aristocratic forebears, and he would track Robert's family down. In chateaux throughout France, they would not be hard to find.

Could Robert withstand that? And if not, did La Rochefoucauld have the separate sort of courage necessary to swallow the pill? "I felt lost, totally lost," he wrote. The ghosts of Auxerre pranced around the room now, taunting him.

At dawn on Sunday a haggard La Rochefoucauld peeked out his window into the courtyard below and saw a few guards mingling. Whatever Robert decided, he needed to do it before tomorrow morning, when the weekday shift began and Dohse sat before him, opening the interrogation.

He did not want to die. He now knew that much. "I was strongly resolved to leave that pill in its hiding place," he wrote. But he also didn't want to see another room with a rack or leaded bat.

As the sun rose, he thought about something else in Auxerre. He had escaped death there, after all. Would it be too much to expect to do it again? He began to devise a plan as the day warmed his cell, one that seemed simple to execute but carried very little chance of success. He would walk right out of Fort du Hâ.

He remembered his cellmate in Auxerre, the epileptic who once had such a bad seizure that guards rushed in and escorted him out. Whether out of a sense of compassion or an obligation to keep prisoners alive and talking, the Auxerre staffers had momentarily seemed unguarded. For a few fleeting seconds the Germans had been as vulnerable as the man writhing in the cell. Robert could take advantage of that.

What if he waited until tonight and faked his own seizure? With any luck, a guard would run into his room alone, and Robert could surprise the Nazi, maiming or killing him, and taking his guns and prison keys. La Rochefoucauld could then break for it, sneaking his way through the grounds on the one night a week that Fort du Hâ wasn't properly staffed, rushing to the front gate, and turning the key into the lock that gave him passage to freedom.

It really was so simple. And yet—and yet if two guards came to his cell, well, could he expect to surprise and overpower them in a six-by-three room? Even if he did, wouldn't the noise attract whatever other guards worked the Sunday night shift? Or, what if he made it past one staffer in his cell, but then was chased down corridors by a few other men, their guns drawn? Or, to consider still another scenario, what if he faked a seizure and no one answered his door? That would be as bad as any outcome. He would be interrogated tomorrow, likely carded as a terrorist, and if he kept his silence through the torture sessions, either sent to the camps or the firing squad. Everything, then, had to happen tonight and everything had to break his way.

But as the day progressed, he settled on this plan. Just as he had done in Auxerre, he would make one more attempt at life. If he failed, if the guards threw him back into his cell, then he still had his little pill and he could swallow it satisfied that he had tried to live.

He broke off a large piece of wood from the cage-like bedding and hid it for the evening, the rest of his day passing in a stoic loop of what he planned to do that night. In a few hours he might be free, or he might be dead.

Around 2 a.m. he stretched out on the ground. He put the piece of wood behind his back, looked to the heavens one last time, and started to twist and shake and let loose a tirade of beastly screams. He contorted his body and kicked and moaned. He shouted, he writhed, he thrashed. Amid all that flailing, he saw the peephole on the door flip open. La Rochefoucauld increased his spasms. He heard a key in the lock, and then the creak of the opened cell. And then he saw the guard—just one guard.

He sprang to his feet and rushed him, not even registering if the man looked as confused as La Rochefoucauld had hoped. Robert pulled his piece of wood from his back pocket and clubbed the guard over the head with it. The blow startled the man and knocked him from his feet, and in that instant, La Rochefoucauld grabbed him, placed one of his palms over the Nazi's chin, the other around the back side of his head, and twisted violently, just as the Brits had taught him. He broke the German's neck.

La Rochefoucauld stood over the collapsed, suddenly formless body. Had he just killed a man? Paralyzed him? He didn't have time to think about it. He had to move. He searched for prison keys on the body, but couldn't find them. *Shit.* He ran his eyes over the guard but knew immediately what he had to do.

He had to find the prison keys. He had to find them whether they were on the door of the staff's quarters or in the pocket of another guard.

He looked again at the man on the floor. He stripped off the guard's jacket and shrugged it over his shoulders. If he were to escape, he would have to surprise the remaining staffers as much as he'd surprised this one. He looped the man's belt around his waist, and took the man's gun, cocking it.

Then La Rochefoucauld started walking.

He guessed he needed to move toward the center of the grounds, where the staff likely had its offices. The labyrinth was divided into five sectors that led to the infirmary, but La Rochefoucauld was able to navigate down empty corridors to what he thought was the middle of the complex, passing cell doors with peepholes that gave out a partial view of what passed. What any inmate saw looked only like a German on patrol, a gun in his hand.

La Rochefoucauld moved down one corridor and noticed, up

ahead, a wan light seeping out from beneath a closed door. The guards' quarters?

He walked slowly toward it, and when he got there prepared himself for whatever was on the other side. Freedom, or death, mere moments away.

He pushed the door open and saw two Germans slumped down in chairs, half asleep, neither paying much mind in the dimmed light of the room to the man in the jacket of a Fort du Hâ staffer. La Rochefoucauld walked quickly into the space and at point-blank range fired at one guard. He turned to the other, who struggled to stand up and take hold of his gun. La Rochefoucauld shot him dead, too.

The room fell silent.

He looked around him, for the second time that night surprised at all he was capable of. Two more men, just like that. He scanned his surroundings, looking for a key chain. He found it and walked out of the staff quarters, down hallways he'd just passed and into the empty prison courtyard.

He ran to the main gate and began jamming in keys. At last, one turned over, and with that, just as he'd hoped, Robert de La Rochefoucauld walked right out of Fort du Hâ.

# CHAPTER 19

No sirens sounded and no guard shouted for him to halt, but he took off at a dead sprint, in the jacket of the German he had likely killed, carrying the man's gun. He ran because his instincts told him to and because it felt good, given the dread of the last twenty-four hours. He needed to find the fighter with the code-name Jean, the one he was to have met two nights ago. La Rochefoucauld had memorized some of Bordeaux's maps, and the city remained still and silent, and soon he stopped running, catching his breath among the darkened shadows of the deserted streets. Walking would be less conspicuous, he realized, and so he set out on a long jaunt through the shuttered Bordeaux, which exhausted and began to relax him. The few people he encountered thought nothing of this patrolling guard. On a modest side street in Bordeaux's outer reaches, he found the address he had been given by his Saint-Médard coconspirators: a small house with a little garden, surrounded by a metal gate. He hopped over it and knocked on the front door.

A second-story window opened and a man in pajamas leaned out. He asked La Rochefoucauld what he wanted. Robert told him he was the *résistant* the man had anticipated Saturday night. "I got a little held up," La Rochefoucauld said.

"Oh my God!" he exclaimed. "I'll be right there."

This was Jean, and when he opened the door and introduced himself he took in La Rochefoucauld's outfit. Jean quickly pulled him inside. He was bewildered, staring at La Rochefoucauld, so Robert thought it best to start at the beginning.

When he finished, Jean shook his head, stunned, and then

asked for Robert's jacket and bunched it into a ball and threw it in the fire.

A short while later he returned with snacks and a bottle of wine. "To refresh us," he said. Jean wanted to celebrate what might be the greatest escape story of the war, he said. La Rochefoucauld appreciated the gesture but was bone tired. So Jean placed his drink down and led Robert to a guest bedroom, where his longest day ended.

When he awoke he found himself in the same position as Auxerre: He had escaped prison but not danger. Dohse would surely be looking for his convict. La Rochefoucauld and Jean thought the best thing to do was to get in touch with a man by the code-name Aristide, who was SOE heavy Roger Landes himself. Landes had worked with Groupe Georges and likely knew of the Saint-Médard job.

"First, I'll go see him," Jean said to La Rochefoucauld. "Rest while you wait. You'll find all sorts of police novels in the library. They tell stories much less incredible than yours, but they'll entertain you."

In Jean's day job he sold kitchen supplies door to door, which gave him an entrée into any home, and an alibi afterward. That would come in handy today, if Dohse had his men on high alert. Jean jammed catalogues into his briefcase, told La Rochefoucauld not to expect him until evening, and walked out.

He returned that night with news that he'd shown his papers twice. "Hard day," he said. Still, he'd met with Landes at his safe house. Landes had instructed Jean to wait a bit, just to be cautious. After a few days, if the German paranoia died down, La Rochefoucauld could meet with Landes, and Aristide would find a passage for him out of the city.

"Fate was thus offering me three days of relaxation," La Rochefoucauld wrote, "three days to sleep, read, eat my fill." Jean was gone from morning to night, and each evening the two discussed the streets, the city's milieu, and how to avoid German suspicion. It still seemed dangerous out there, menacing. Too many unhappy guards patrolling a town that remained firmly occupied. If he were to make it to Landes's, the men decided, La Rochefoucauld would need a disguise. They talked about what might work, but nothing seemed sufficient. Nothing hid the man fully enough to also mask his fear of being detected.

And then Jean had a "genius idea," as La Rochefoucauld later said. Jean's sister wanted to be a nun and was going through the rites of ordination. She had left a habit—in her rather large size—in Jean's house. What if La Rochefoucauld wore that?

Jean tracked down the habit and Robert tried it on. It fell a touch short, but the black wimple and white coif fit perfectly, and even accentuated and softened La Rochefoucauld's eyes. Jean found black stockings; Robert rolled them on. The two men sniggered at his transformation. With a rosary in his hand and powder on his cheeks, La Rochefoucauld would look every bit the sister Mary.

He disrobed and they hashed out the remaining details. They decided Jean should lead them to Landes's, walking ahead of Robert, maybe fifty yards, so no one would think the two together. They had faith in their bride of Christ, Jean said, but wanted to minimize the need for divine intervention. When Jean reached Landes's safe house, he would turn and subtly acknowledge it, then continue walking. That was the cue for La Rochefoucauld, who would enter the home alone.

At the end of the appointed day, the two set out, Jean in front, the nun trailing him, in her coif and wimple, and falling farther behind now. It was harder to walk in a woman's dress, even a flowing robe like this one, than La Rochefoucauld imagined. "I was getting somewhat tangled up in my habit," he wrote. The distance between them kept growing until Jean was roughly a hundred yards ahead. No one thought they were a pair now, which was perhaps

for the best: The city was teeming with guards and soldiers and police. La Rochefoucauld decided to continue in the role of the slow-
moving sister. The walk took much longer than either he or Jean
anticipated. But the glances La Rochefoucauld got from passersby
seemed blank, and he felt as if, despite its restrictions, he was pulling the ensemble off.

After an hour on the streets, Jean stopped to admire a house,
and then walked on. Moments later La Rochefoucauld arrived at
the front door.

A woman answered the bell. Robert, improvising, and in his
best approximation of a female voice, said he wanted to speak to
Aristide—figuring that the code-name would reveal the intent of
the visit.

The woman sized up the nun.

"Come in," she said.

This was likely Ginette Corbin, a courier in the Resistance and
the daughter of the police inspector Charles Corbin, who had fled
to Spain with Roger Landes after André Grandclément's betrayal
the previous year. Charles was a secret member of Landes's Resistance group, and his daughter Ginette was Landes's not-so-secret
love interest, whom many assumed to be his fiancée. The two married at war's end.

To La Rochefoucauld, the woman coyly said she was the lady
of the house. She handled Aristide's charitable groups. Robert realized he had fooled her; she thought he really was a nun.

"But I would like to speak personally with Monsieur Aristide,"
La Rochefoucauld insisted.

She gave him a puzzled glance. "I'll go look for him," she said.
"Please wait."

She walked out and closed the door behind her. La Rochefoucauld, impish, played up the sister act. He sat down gently,
crossed his legs and joined his hands in his sleeves, and assumed a
"meditative air," he said.

A few minutes later the door opened and Landes appeared, a thin man, five foot four, only twenty-seven that summer, who passed most days in his Basque beret. His eyes were alive to the world, taking everything in, and he often wore a sardonic half smile. He otherwise looked so unassuming—his diminutive stature, his olive complexion—that even the Germans who'd hunted him had repeatedly failed to recognize him. He once accidentally dropped a suitcase that contained a wireless set, and the man to pick it up was, to Landes's shock, a German agent. The Nazi simply handed the case back, unaware. Landes had made it to 1944 alive—escaping the dissolution of his Scientist network and the creation, that spring, of Actor—because his air of anonymity matched his discretion. He chose to lead *résistants* in Bordeaux on the rationale that he had too many loose-lipped friends in Paris, where he'd grown up. He never contacted fighters whom the Germans had freed, even if they'd been of great value to the Resistance. His parents, for the whole of the war, thought he was stationed in the Middle East.

Now, to La Rochefoucauld, and a bit fastidiously, he asked: "Can I help you, Sister?"

Robert got up, walked over to him, and patted him forcefully on the back. He dropped his voice to its natural register. "You don't recognize me?" he asked. "You were waiting for me."

Landes's face changed. "Well, I'll be," he said, amazed. "Your disguise—they didn't warn me you would be in a disguise." He said that when he heard a nun had demanded to see him, he was convinced that the sister brought news of La Rochefoucauld's catastrophic end.

The two laughed and embraced. The noise caused Lady Landes to reenter the room, even more puzzled now by the nun Aristide had his arm around. Landes introduced his guest, "explaining that I was indeed the boy he was waiting for," La Rochefoucauld later wrote. She let out a half shriek and ran to him, hugging him.

When the impromptu celebration ended and she left, the two set themselves to business. La Rochefoucauld said he hoped to return to London, but Landes scoffed. That was impossible, he said. Because of the European landing, the English did not have the time or spare planes to get a French agent to SOE headquarters. Aristide instead offered refuge with a certain Monsieur Demont, a forester in the wilderness to the south of Bordeaux, not far from where Robert had parachuted that spring, in the department that shared Landes's name. Thick stands of maritime pines covered roughly four thousand square miles of the Landes department, and La Rochefoucauld would work for Demont as a lumberjack. There, he would be safe from Dohse. And from there, when the time was right, he could contact London. "My orders," La Rochefoucauld wrote, "were to hide and wait."

Aristide kept the meeting brisk because he worked twenty-hour days that summer, losing nearly thirty pounds in the process, the stress of the war culminating that month when he gave the order to execute André Grandclément. Landes reached out to Grandclément and told him and his wife that a plane was coming to take them to England. On the fateful night, an associate of Landes's, Dédé la Basque, walked Grandclément on a tarmac, Aristide walking Grandclément's wife, Lucette, in the opposite direction. Basque killed Grandclément execution-style, and Landes did the same with Lucette, shooting her in the back of the neck with his .45 automatic, the bullet exiting through her throat and spurting a trail of blood over four-feet long. For the rest of his life, Landes would maintain that killing Madame Grandclément was necessary: She had known and conspired with the Germans in the same manner as her husband. Few in the military would disagree. After the war, Landes was highly decorated by the French and English.

La Rochefoucauld knew none of this, of course. Landes remained circumspect around him, revealing only what was necessary so the young fighter might make his escape. Robert said good-bye, thanking Landes again. Landes flashed him his classic sardonic smile.

A few days later, as instructed, La Rochefoucauld biked on seldom-traveled roads to the edge of Bordeaux, where one of Landes's vehicles waited for him. The driver was impressed with Robert's story but, when they reached Demont's camp deep in the forest, introduced him not as a *résistant* but a defector from the Nazis' mandatory work order. Even here, among friends, Aristide and his men favored discretion.

Demont welcomed Robert warmly and said he specialized in selling lumber that became pit props: the shafts of wood that prop up mines. La Rochefoucauld soon found himself in a demanding if monotonous routine: cut wood, stack wood, repeat. There was a restorative, comforting quality to the work; Dohse could not find him here, in the pine's long shadows. But as his shifts ended he began to almost miss the streets that had threatened him. Yes, he had escaped prison and his own death sentence three times, and, yes, because of that, he had been ordered to this exile, but he was twenty and impetuous and carried the belief—and not an unfounded one—that this was the defining season of his life. He wanted it to shape his future. He wanted to shape his country's future. It would be hard, but he could try to forget the terror of imprisonment; that could haunt him later. If he could just rejoin the fight now, he could perhaps even expunge his suffering, sanctify himself, really, in the glory of a lasting victory.

He tried and failed to contact his London handlers, growing impatient and then angry by the silence. He began to see Demont's camp as another imprisonment. If London did not want to let him out, then, as in Fort du Hâ, La Rochefoucauld would go in search of the keys to liberation.

One day, La Rochefoucauld decided to simply walk out of Demont's camp. He was on his own now, a freelance commando, a trained specialist, in search of a great and final battle.

# CHAPTER 20

The Landes department was a strange and dichotomous place that summer. The sabotages increased—one hundred to the railways alone in July, to aid the approaching Allied troops—and yet even with the British and American advance, the Germans remained unquestionably the occupiers, ordering the populace to equip the Nazis with supplies in case of a military retreat. People obeyed, but at the same time they could feel the power shifting, France beginning to redeem itself, a palpable but not quite visible reclamation. *Résistants* multiplied and those new to the cause and the ones who had been there, as the French said, "from the first hour," began to identify each other, openly and in broad daylight, as if they were fellow soldiers and not underground agents.

And yet that esprit de corps didn't unite the groups fighting the Germans. The Communist *résistants*, isolated in the north of the department, refused to speak with their SOE counterparts in the south, who denied them arms. The SOE groups weren't even talking among themselves; petty squabbles and competing aims kept them apart. The Gaullist cell refused to recognize anyone who was not a follower of Le Grand Charles. The best way to cleanse southwest France of Nazis was for each man to give himself to a cause greater than his self-interest. But one's self-interest, after four years of deprivations, seemed the primary reason to join the cause. The Landes was like so much of France that summer: Yearning for liberation yet begrudging the path to it.

Robert de La Rochefoucauld walked into this wild and coarse landscape. Eager to fight and to avenge his own pain, he saw the region only as he wanted to see it, which is to say in a blinkered, almost monochromatic light: The Nazis were bad and any group that fought them was good. So he rejoined his old group, Charly.

The size of the troop, nearly one thousand men, protected La Rochefoucauld and many others from René Cominetti's ultimate betrayal. After the war Cominetti—aka Charly, the leader of the eponymous group—would be convicted by the English for turning eight British aviators over to the Nazis, and sentenced to fifteen years of hard labor. He was dubbed a collaborator, but during that summer of 1944, one would never have known it. Charly ordered his men to fight fiercely: seventy résistants raided a munitions factory in Saint Hélène on July 23, killing one hundred Germans; seven Charly men ambushed a German post on August 16 in Le Moutchic, taking guns and three Nazis prisoner.

La Rochefoucauld found himself in many skirmishes that would never be named, ephemeral battles of rifle reports and fiery sabotages through a forested and surreal southwest France, the Germans on the run and the Allied objectives back at headquarters too slow to form to be effective. The fighting took on a tribal quality. He was part of Charly, and oversaw a small group of men as its sergeant, but he gathered with fighters from other groups, too, most notably a Jewish one whose men had joined the cause after an administrator in Bordeaux secretly warned them of a roundup. La Rochefoucauld's summer of war was "simultaneously intense and limited," he wrote, bursts of fire followed by hours or days of boredom. His weeks "essentially consisted of increasing skirmishes with [Nazi] troops at the borders of the zone they occupied." One day, for instance, carrying out a patrol near a German line, La Rochefoucauld approached an abandoned building. As he opened the door, someone else swung wide the back entrance. Across the poorly lit expanse neither man could immediately make out the other, but when Robert's eyes adjusted he saw he stood opposite a German—just as the Nazi realized he faced a Frenchman. La Rochefoucauld shot five rounds from his revolver as he ducked the German's fire. Not one bullet, however, hit its intended target. When the last reports echoed off the wall, each man found he had no other gun on him, and no more ammunition.

An awkward moment passed between them: What was called for here? A run at the other man? A run away from him, looking for more ammo? Finally, "as if in a properly settled duel," La Rochefoucauld wrote, each soldier decided with no fanfare to leave through the door he'd opened. The two never saw each other again.

The liberations came in August. Gen. George Patton and his U.S. Third Army had swept through the German forces in Normandy, moving southeast to the Loire Valley and Orleans, and then due east toward the Seine, south of the capital. They reached the boundaries of Paris on August 23, so close that Parisians heard the blistering squeals and thunderous reports of modern war, a sweet sound now, the city thrumming with anticipation. The police who worked for the Germans had fled, and those who'd passively resisted refused their patrols. There was almost no law enforcement presence. No Vichy broadcasts either: The collaborationist Radio Paris had been off the air since the seventeenth. The French Forces of the Interior called for a mobilization of all Resistance groups in the city. Soon, in the Latin quarter, 35,000 FFI fighters battled roughly 20,000 German troops. The Nazis had tanks and the FFI soldiers inadequate arms; the guerrillas' advantage in men fell away, the fighting fierce. Meanwhile, skirmishes flared in other neighborhoods, barricades of chairs and mattresses and tables rising on the streets, like an insurrection out of Les Misérables. By 6 p.m. on August 23, after pleas from de Gaulle that the French liberate Paris, the Allied high command ordered Gen. Jacques Leclerc's Second Armored Division to march on the capital. Leclerc's forces arrived on August 25 and met a weary and even disenfranchised German army—Hitler's order to blow up the Eiffel Tower had been ignored—and Leclerc's men moved quickly down the thoroughfares. Everywhere now the French reclaimed state buildings and hotels. Ernest Hemingway "liberated" the Ritz, either returning enemy fire from the roof or spending that increasingly celebratory day drinking in the bar, depending on the account one chooses to believe.

By the afternoon, the Germans surrendered at Gare Montparnasse, where Leclerc had set up his headquarters. De Gaulle himself arrived there at 4:30 and then moved to the Hôtel de Ville to meet representatives of his Free French forces and to make the first of what would be many speeches as the country's leader. "Paris!" he said. "Paris humiliated! Paris broken! Paris martyrized! But now Paris liberated! Liberated by herself, by her own people with the help of the armies of France, with the support and aid of France as a whole, of fighting France, of the only France, of the true France, of eternal France."

The following day de Gaulle organized a procession to move down the Champs-Élysées. "Behind him," one observer noted, "a human herd dances, sings, enjoys itself utterly; from it there stick out tank turrets sprinkled with soldiers and with girls whose destiny does not seem likely to be a nunnery." De Gaulle later estimated the crowd at two million, the throngs shouting *"Vive la France!"* and *"Vive de Gaulle!"* He was a long way now from the country's most junior general.

By the month's end the Germans' Western armies had lost 500,000 men, half of them as prisoners, and the Allied liberation of other French cities followed. Bordeaux was freed August 28, Dohse fleeing just before the Bordelais made a bonfire on the streets of whatever the occupiers left behind.

La Rochefoucauld was in Bordeaux that day. He tried but couldn't really share in the joyous mood. He sensed disingenuousness. Just weeks ago, after all, "I'd taken the same streets and crossed the same squares," he wrote. "Then, they were abundantly filled by the enemy army; you could barely make out any civilians. This time, you might have believed the entire French army, crushed by the heat, had besieged Bordeaux. Soldiers were everywhere, in full uniform on café terraces, heroically drinking their aperitifs, while others in battle dress, pistols in plain sight, patrolled through the city with a menacing eye. The heroes were surely tired, but why were there so many of them here, when the danger had disappeared?" This scene replicated itself so often across newly freed cities—French soldiers emerging when the Nazis vanished—that the natives found a word for it: *Napthalenes*, after the smell of mothballs that clung to a man's uniform. Even in liberation, then, there was shame for the French.

But not all of France was freed that summer. On the same day Parisians celebrated the Nazi surrender, the people of Maillé, twenty-five miles south of Tours, witnessed horror. A group of German soldiers, angry over *résistants* who'd bombed a car of Nazis, descended on the small town and lined up and shot dead disabled grandmothers and six-year-old girls and women who held children in their arms. The Germans bayoneted babies in their cribs and put guns to retirees' foreheads. The Nazis killed everyone they found, 124 people in all. They then razed the town and scrawled on pieces of paper near the murdered: "A punishment for terrorists and their assistants."

All over the country in that season of liberation many French towns felt only savagery and oppression: nineteen *résistants* assassinated in Carcassonne; thirty hostages executed in Rodez; more than one hundred prisoners shot in Montluc, their bodies burned. The road to freedom descended through a grotesque anarchy.

The liberators themselves struggled to impress onto the bloody land a rule of law. Resistance leaders refused to recognize de Gaulle's officer corps—*where had* they *been for four years?*—and many guerrillas became de facto mayors in the towns where Germans had fled. The Vichy officials who remained were often dragged into public squares to face the threat of firing squads. These purges, as they were soon called, drew crowds who had little patience for jurisprudence. Many suspected collaborators were denounced in the manner in which *résistants* had been: without supporting evidence and with grave consequences. Some cities attempted to stage makeshift trials, but people wanted revenge—they mailed collaborators miniature coffins—and Frenchmen killed their own quickly, and rashly, and with the full support of rebel leaders who reigned "like feudal lords," as one historian wrote. The number of French killed in the purges of August and September reached nine thousand. Some people who weren't executed were publicly shamed. Women thought to have slept with Germans had their heads shaved or their bodies tarred and feathered and painted with swastikas. All the while the waging of war continued, the battalions sometimes far more orderly than the cities they freed. On September 1, FFI fighters outside Lyons staged a "textbook battle" alongside U.S. troops, one historian wrote, pinning back the 11th Panzer Division and opening the road for U.S. forces. The FFI men looked "proud when you compare them to the green-uniformed [Nazi] cowards who fled," reported a local newspaper.

In theory Charles de Gaulle should have been grateful to the fighters who won his battles and accelerated his political ascent. But the haughty de Gaulle saw in each liberated city a threat to his power; many *résistants*, Communists in particular, wanted a revolution, freedom from the Germans and then the Third Republic, whose systemic rot had corroded France. De Gaulle hated such dissent. He planned to shape the state to his liking. He treated the *résistants* who angled for postwar authority with "lofty coldness," in the words of one of them, taking every opportunity to diminish their significance. In his "Paris liberated" speech, for example, he didn't acknowledge the role the Resistance played in the city's liberation. In Bordeaux, after its return to sovereignty, de Gaulle told the SOE boss Roger Landes he had two hours to leave the city.

Town by town, de Gaulle forced the Resistance to kneel before

him. A short time after the first French cities' independence, the
general ordered the dissolution of the French Forces of the Interior and other national groups that had organized sabotages before, during, and now after D-Day. If these *résistants* still wanted
to fight, de Gaulle reasoned, they could join his Free French army.
By November, more than 200,000 *résistants* had, La Rochefoucauld
among them.

He enlisted that fall in a reserve officers' school in Bordeaux,
École des Cadres de Quellec. La Rochefoucauld scribbled down the
lessons of army officers while in neighboring cities Frenchmen still
bore the Occupation's weight. One of La Rochefouculd's superiors
noted his "natural sense of command," an *aspirant* who had "already
acquired the experience" and the "incontestable qualities" of a leader.
For Robert, the officers' school epitomized the surreal illogic of that
fall. He was there to learn the skills he'd already gained in two years
of fighting, from staffers who out of humiliation preferred to act as
if La Rochefoucauld was not their better. *He* had fought these last
dark years while *they* had lost in 1940. "Will be an excellent reserve
officer," his superior wrote, the line a patronizing sneer.

His military records from this period, page after page, seemed
to praise La Rochefoucauld in a way that also belittled him. But
one remark suggested how even a jeering command corps recognized his true gift: "very 'cavalier,'" the note read. So adventurous,
in fact, that the twenty-one-year-old wasn't long for the École des
Cadres de Quellec. By November 1944, not two months after enlisting, he left the officers' school, having received orders to join
a commando troop. "I was tasked with instructing my men and
instilling in them the basics of commando combat that I'd acquired
myself in England," he later wrote. He would not sit in classrooms
or walk on manicured firing ranges while people very much like
himself settled the last of the war in nearby woods or marshes. He
would join one of the most selective strike forces in France.

He would also carry out his most daring mission yet.

# CHAPTER 21

T hough Hitler had ordered his troops to begin evacuating France, he also wanted the submarine bases on the Atlantic coast protected, which meant that in the southwest, and primarily along the Gironde estuary outside Bordeaux, as many as nine thousand soldiers remained through the fall. They built and then buried in the beaches explosive devices, and plunked sixteen-foot logs into the sand, connecting at their tips strings of barbed wire that would entangle the limbs of landing Allied parachutists. Up and down the estuary's coasts the Germans constructed no fewer than 218 casemates, the squat, scary-looking, cement-fortified antiaircraft artillery compounds that featured 280-millimeter guns. The Allies called the Nazi defensive positions "pockets," but really they were belts: long lines of nasty fortifications that stretched from towns like Royan, on the mouth of the Gironde estuary, north to La Rochelle and the Bay of Biscay, 35 miles away. The Germans had 210,000 mines in Royan alone, 800,000 overall; 137 bunkers; 80 pieces of artillery—an impressive defense for its submarine bases.

Maybe even too impressive, because the war moved east that fall, away from the Atlantic coast and toward a softening Germany. Yet the Nazi soldiers in that corner of the Gironde remained, peering out from behind their fortifications, wondering if they had safeguarded themselves out of the war.

They hadn't. These nine thousand Germans bothered Charles de Gaulle. He wanted a France cleansed of Nazis, and, more than that, a French-led victory on French soil. There were other considerations, too. The Nazis in Royan, the soldiers manning the smallest base in the Gironde estuary, had declared a state of siege, forbidding citizens the use of public transportation, or the right to heat or light their homes after dark, or draw any water at night. The Nazis forced eight thousand people to live as if they were in the Middle Ages: their days beginning and ending with the sun, drawing water from wells, and traveling by foot. This couldn't continue while other French towns returned to a safe and modern democracy. So de Gaulle appointed in October Gen. Edgard de Larminat to liberate the towns of the coastal pockets.

Larminat, a World War I veteran who'd fought in the horrific Battle of Verdun, had joined the Free French after an escape from a German POW camp, commanding divisions in North Africa and Italy, and trying to keep from public view the demons that shadowed him through two wars. Another Free French leader, the five-star general Georges Catroux, called Larminat unethical and mentally unstable. Nevertheless, de Gaulle tasked Larminat with the Atlantic job, enchanted by a glorious record that stretched back to 1916.

Larminat was to take the former *résistants* and organize them into groups of traditional soldiers, with a hierarchy of command that climbed back to him. Though he admired the rebels' bravery, he found their methods—the sabotages and attack-and-hide warfare—in poor taste. With veteran officers beneath him, he began to shape the underground fighters into a division of nearly twenty-four thousand soldiers. But, truth be told, the men shaped the division as much as it shaped them. La Rochefoucauld, for instance, landed in the Carnot Brigade, under the direction of Col. Jean de Milleret, a former Resistance leader who now led the Forces Françaises de la Point de Grave et Royan (FFGR). Milleret oversaw small groups of commando teams whose tactics were informed by their time in the underground. La Rochefoucauld's job was to helm one of those teams, a light cavalry unit, and teach his men all he himself had learned and done in the last three years.

His team was stationed not far from Saint-Vivien-de-Médoc, a small town near the southern mouth of the Gironde estuary, across the water from Royan, which would be a focal point in the fighting.

Robert heard that de Gaulle wanted to attack quickly, in November, but many soldiers were still joining up, some weren't properly trained, and reinforcements weren't ready. So the so-called Operation Independence was put off until Christmas Day 1944. On December 16, however, the Germans launched a counteroffensive hundreds of miles away, in northeastern France, a massive blitz with 250,000 German troops and five panzer tank divisions driving through the same Ardennes forest that the Nazis had traversed four years earlier, when taking the country the first time. And so the French armored vehicles and air support awaiting deployment in the Atlantic were ordered north and east, toward the Ardennes, to engage in what history would call the Battle of the Bulge.

Robert and the French troops around the Gironde estuary did not follow the tanks and planes. They had a mandate to stay where they were; their battle was coming, the French high command promised. For La Rochefoucauld, time stretched as daylight shortened. Soldiers in clogs and uniforms that thinned and ripped as the winter winds howled griped about the cold, the sicknesses that spread through the camp, and their inadequate rations. They drilled endlessly. La Rochefoucauld oversaw his troops' parachute training, instructing them on overcoming a fear of death that he himself still secretly battled. In their significant downtime, he and his men swapped stories, the twenty-one-year-old officer discussing his war and family, enlivening his audience. The commandos soon settled on a nom de guerre for him, Maxim. It was perfect, really, a suggestion of his *Three Musketeers*–esque service and his distant relative, the Duc de La Rochefoucauld, who'd written the aphoristic *Maxims*, which every French schoolboy had had to read. The troops respected La Rochefoucauld, but as with so many bands of warriors who had to live and fight together, they didn't want to openly revere him, and so the name acquired an ironic, even mocking tone on their lips. Maxim, they said, as if with air quotes.

The new year came and the fighters remained at their bases, and then watched on January 5 as something strange happened. Across the estuary, a fleet of 350 British planes dropped 800 tons of bombs on Royan. They fell primarily in the city center, and not on the Axis garrisons at its border, killing 442 civilians and only 35 Germans. Robert saw the fiery collapse of almost every building in Royan with a mix of confusion and horror. This episode would in part compel him to say, years later, "I'll tell you something very important: I do not have the least desire to hear or talk about the war." Allied officials offered no adequate explanation for the bombing—something about the fleet being scheduled to bomb a location in Germany but, due to inclement weather, rerouting to Royan, with orders to carry out a mission but without maps of German positions.

The destruction enraged de Gaulle. The loss of life was horrendous, and from a military perspective, the Brits had ignored his mandate that an aerial campaign be followed by one on the ground, led by French soldiers. The British aerial attack on Royan without any subsequent troop movement left de Gaulle, and the soldiers in the estuary, feeling ignored and abandoned. In the weeks ahead, some joked that they were the Forgotten French Forces.

The cruel irony for Royonnais was that the bombs didn't destroy the defensive line, the squat casemates that housed the Nazi artillery along the coast. This almost guaranteed a second attack, one that would feature more bombs and, the French high command insisted, the thousands of French troops stationed around the estuary.

In February, planning for this mission began in earnest. General de Larminat began inspecting the grounds and meeting with officers. On February 8, the general walked before aspirants like Maxim, and when he got to Robert, asked him to present himself. "So I stated my name: La Rochefoucauld."

Larminat was himself the son of an officer, educated at the Saint-Cyr academy and part of the military nobility. He knew of the La Rochefoucaulds. "I asked for your real name," Larminat said. "Not your nom de guerre."

But La Rochefoucauld said that was his name.

Larminat stared at him, seemingly surprised that someone with such lineage would want to lead a gauche commando team. But the confident gaze the young officer returned suggested he was very much at home here. "The general burst out laughing," La Rochefoucauld wrote.

The following month the reconnaissance began, small groups of men heading out by night in rubber boats to mark the enemy positions. The units finished the first part of their map by March 7 and had German-manned canals near Saint-Vivien-de-Médoc detailed by the twenty-second. "We badgered the enemy on its lines," La Rochefoucauld wrote. The men then grew bolder, and hid by day under bridges on the spits of territory the Germans oversaw near Saint-Vivien, bringing back "precious information on enemy terrain," the official record notes. By March 31, some of the roughly 850 men within the reconnaissance teams had begun the nerve-wracking work of demining the coasts. They found far too many bombs, so a pattern established itself. Night after night, crews bellied their way to German positions, and by the light of a fading moon dismantled the explosives, their anxiety compounded by the fear that Nazi sentries might see them. Morning after morning, though, the crews returned, the beaches a little safer, and the final battle for France that much closer.

Like many commandos, La Rochefoucauld's job in the newly named Operation Venerable was to help free two areas: Pointe de Grave, a spit of beach with heavy German fortresses on the southern mouth of the Gironde estuary, and Royan, which sat across the water from Pointe de Grave.

Over the weekend of April 14 and 15, the Allies at last launched
Operation Venerable. First came the twelve hundred B-26 bombers, "drenching" the Gironde, in the words of a front-page *New York
Times* story, with a unique weapon: "460,000 gallons of liquid fire
that bathed in flames the German positions and strong points." This
was a new bomb, napalm, that detonated on impact and then flung
everywhere a viscous fiery gel, which maintained its consistency
even as it burned. Robert peered out from his own fortified compound and saw the woods and the ruins of Royan alight in flames
that would not die out. A French admiral watched the scene from
the safety of Médis, northeast of Royan, with reverence and terror:
"Under a fantastic concentration of fire . . . The countryside and the
sky were thick with powder and yellow smoke. One could with
difficulty distinguish the mutilated silhouette of the clock tower of
Saint-Pierre, which burned like a torch."

Though Royan burned into the next day, some of the German
casemates, resembling squat low-slung houses, with thick cement
exteriors sheltering the artillery and men inside, made it through
the attack unharmed. The big guns kept blasting out their rounds
onto a torched and increasingly barren landscape. On the mouth
of the Gironde, La Rochefoucauld was amazed. "We were under
ceaseless fire," he wrote, "coming from a casemate that had weath-
ered the Allied air raid without too much damage."

A high-ranking French officer within La Rochefoucauld's regiment asked his subordinates to meet him in a safe house. There, he
told them that if they carried out their planned daytime attack on
that casemate, they would lose a lot of men and still fail to take the
Nazi position. So how could they accomplish their mission without
sacrificing all their soldiers?

La Rochefoucauld had asked himself the same question. Now
he spoke up, proposing "an unusual plan of action," he later wrote.
This casemate sat near the water's edge—so far out that some
water actually flowed behind the compound. La Rochefoucauld

proposed leading a team of men in a rubber boat—the sort that had been used for reconnaissance—and then paddling behind the casemate, sneaking ashore, planting some plastic bombs against the compound, and then watching from the estuary as the whole thing jumped to the stars.

"The captain was skeptical," La Rochefoucauld wrote. How could a handful of men succeed when twelve hundred bombers had not? The idea had the makings of a suicide mission. But La Rochefoucauld knew a pinpoint sabotage could be more effective than any number of bombers. That had been the case in Saint-Médard-en-Jalles. The commanding officer was aware of La Rochefoucauld's previous missions; the lore of Maxim had spread through the coastal towns, apparently. He eyed the twenty-one-year-old, and told him to find a rubber boat.

A round 10 p.m. that night he and three other men set off. On the bed of their vessel sat the necessary cords and explosives and submachine guns. There was no moon. A light rain fell. Perfect conditions for a stealth operation.

The paddles glided over the estuary, dipping and driving the boat ahead, lightly, rhythmically, the noise of wood against water almost inaudible. No one dared speak. It was a mile and a half to their landing spot.

The silence allowed reflection, and La Rochefoucauld no doubt felt self-assured. He had sabotaged utilities and rail lines, escaped Nazis in Auxerre and killed them in Bordeaux. He had dressed like a nun to avoid detection and placed bombs in bread to help free his country. The daring boy had become a daring man, and Robert could handle one more daring mission. But he also knew that if any of the events of the last three years had developed a little differently, going back to the Soissons postman, he would be dead now, or near death in a camp. And tonight, to press on? To attempt to succeed where nothing less than napalm had failed? That was

204 | PAUL KIX

Robert's courage, sure, and his deep desire to avenge his suffering, whatever the risk. But cleaved to this outward-facing élan was a private uncertainty influenced by too many close calls. La Rochefoucauld had been a poor student, but he was smart enough to know that luck and maybe even God's grace had brought him to this night as much as his sangfroid. He couldn't tell his men this, but he was not as brave as he wanted to be, which was the price paid for his previous heroic acts. Still, as the Duc de La Rochefoucauld had written in 1665, "Perfect bravery and sheer cowardice are two extremes rarely found. The space between them is vast, and embraces all other sorts of courage." Robert de La Rochefoucauld had come too far to turn around now.

It took two hours before they saw the darkened landing spot on the shore that would guide them to the casemate, a half mile inland. Slowly, they paddled to the beach and disembarked, taking their guns and supplies. The men fell into single file, La Rochefoucauld in the front, a flashlight guiding him. He hoped with each new step to avoid the mines that might still surround them. After an incremental advance, they saw rising in the night the outline of the casemate.

They saw a problem, too. Their target was protected by an outer wall, which ringed the grounds. Between that outer wall and the casemate itself was a courtyard of sorts, a walkway about eight feet across. It had camouflaged netting for a roof, which would repel any Allied parachutist daring enough to land there. The commando team assumed a guard patrolled this courtyard, and so La Rochefoucauld came up with a plan. Two of his men would position themselves on either side of the wall, commandos turned sentries. The third would climb the wall and crouch down on top of it, the explosives in hand. La Rochefoucauld himself would ascend to the top and then crawl out onto the netting, lying against it. If a guard walked beneath, he would cut a hole in the mesh, and then time his jump to land on the Nazi and end the man's life. The trick was to do it without firing a shot—because that would awaken the men inside the casemate. If he succeeded and silently executed the guard, his companion would toss the plastic explosives down to him. La Rochefoucauld would plant the bombs against the cement fortification, climb back out of the courtyard, and the four of them would take off.

A drizzle still fell, which would make the climb on the wall difficult, but also perhaps drown out any noise Robert made. He told his men to be ready. If a guard spotted him on the netting, they would need to fire on the Nazi. And if that were the case, whether Robert were dead or alive, they should run for cover. Otherwise they would die, too. The men nodded their heads.

They approached in battle crouches, half-running their way along the coastal grass slickened by rain, until they reached their positions. La Rochefoucauld scaled the wall with little noise or difficulty. He knelt on its precipice and peered down. There *was* a guard, walking back and forth through the courtyard. The German wore a hooded rain jacket. He didn't seem interested in what happened above him. Luck, even on this inclement night, shone once more on La Rochefoucauld.

He put one foot and then one hand on the camouflaged netting, wobbling his way into a steady position, and then moved his other leg and hand onto it. In a moment he hung in quiet suspension, perhaps a foot above the passing Nazi, who kept his head down with each turn, sheltering his face from the conditions.

La Rochefoucauld slowly took out his knife and began cutting the links of netting. Each gave way with little to no noise. He redistributed his weight as he cut a wider and wider hole, making sure it opened over the path the guard was walking—who still didn't glance up. Now La Rochefoucauld had a gap big enough to dive through. He looked around, and with hand signals told his team that the next time the guard passed, he'd jump.

The Nazi slung a rifle over his shoulder, walking close to the outer wall of the courtyard. La Rochefoucauld crouched near his hole, and the guard stepped under it.

Robert tackled the German, knocking him off his feet, the rifle splaying off his shoulder. Adrenaline and his training overtook La Rochefoucauld, and he pulled the Nazi close, the guard's back against Robert's chest. He sunk his dagger in the man's throat and swiped it across. The struggle ended almost as soon as it began.

La Rochefoucauld dragged the body against the wall, and let it lie there, slumped over. The only sound was the patter of rain.

His explosives man tossed the plastic bombs through the hole in the netting. La Rochefoucauld synced them up, timed them to burst in seven minutes, and then had his teammate help him out of the compound.

It was a slow scramble for the men, trying to distance themselves from the casemate while watching the ground for mines. "We hadn't covered five hundred yards when the enormous detonation rang out," La Rochefoucauld wrote. The team looked at one another, their eyes dancing. But they couldn't celebrate: The explosion would draw other Germans to the site. So they half ran and hopped their way back to the beach and then into the boat. They "set sail without losing a second," Robert wrote, paddling back down the Gironde, trying to move quickly but quietly. Hours later, they reached the safety of their camp.

Now, pure joy rushed through them, animating their limbs and speech and snorts of laughter. The skeptical captain came by, and asked what happened. His doubt turned to an exhilaration that matched the team's, and he promised La Rochefoucauld and his men that he would nominate them for the Croix de Guerre (War Cross), given for acts of heroism. La Rochefoucauld blushed, honored, and felt suddenly stunned, too, as he watched a new and wonderful day pinken the skies: He had survived his most dangerous night without even a splinter.

**B**ut he couldn't sleep well. A question worked in his mind: Had he actually succeeded? The boom of the sabotage echoed through the night, as loud as any of his other jobs, but this casemate was designed to sustain almost every blow. If the thing could make it through a napalm attack, shouldn't it withstand his plastic explosives, too? He got word that the regiment would advance again on the casemate, and onto Pointe de Grave, the following afternoon. Robert would have his answer soon enough.

At dawn the next morning, the Allies once again dropped bombs and fired artillery on the German positions, preparing the way for the ground assault. Around 4 p.m. La Rochefoucauld and his regiment moved out, Leclerc's tanks in front. They drew ever closer until at last Robert saw the casemate. It was disfigured, with gaping holes in its body. No shells shot out of the compound, no machine guns rattled. La Rochefoucauld's captain fell back in line until he found his commando.

"Bravo," he whispered.

**B**y evening the regiment reached the German lines closer to Pointe de Grave and the southern mouth of the Gironde. "It would still take two days," La Rochefoucauld wrote, "two extremely hard days of combat—the Germans were tenaciously resisting step by step." But the Allies, incrementally, unmistakably, gained ground. On April 20, French soldiers surrounded the German fortresses at Pointe de Grave, and the Nazis surrendered.

La Rochefoucauld, alas, didn't witness it. The previous day he'd stepped on a mine. "My knee was shattered," he wrote. The medics evacuated him first to Bordeaux for surgery and then to Rochefort-sur-Mer, north of Royan, to convalesce. "I made out with an arthrotomy and a silver kneecap," he wrote. And there, in a coastal town as sun-drenched as his childhood vacation spots, he heard on May 8, 1945, that the war in Europe was over.

His country was free.

# CHAPTER 22

I n that joyful and gratifying spring, however, darker clouds drifted in. From his hospital bed La Rochefoucauld learned that his older brother, Henri, fighting with the Second Armored Division in Alsace, had died in battle. He was twenty-three. Robert's grief took on beastly shapes, whole days "seized with rage," he wrote. Henri was dead, another man's potential stubbed out in the war's indiscriminate and "abominable slaughter."

The pain didn't prey upon Robert alone, of course, so many families in 1945 having their Henri. But in the coastal towns around him, as he convalesced, murmurs spread of a different sort of anguish: whether the battle for liberation had been worth it. In the weeks and months after May 8, in fact, many people La Rochefoucauld helped free, in particular those in Royan, began to view the fight for France as the scene of an Allied atrocity.

The attack on the Atlantic pockets came three weeks before V-E Day, while Hitler and Goebbels, deep in the führer's bunker, consoled themselves with horoscopes and even German radio stations carried news of the eastward-moving Americans and westward-moving Russians joining forces along the Elbe River, outside Berlin. Royannais challenged whether an attack on their town was needed. The war's end in Germany would free the Gironde waterways, too. "It would have been more logical," wrote a local commander after Royan's liberation, "to wait for the surrender of Germany and thus to avoid new human and material losses." The French high command, strangely, didn't refute the illogic of the operation, but argued its necessity because of *"l'aspect moral,"* in the words of Gen. André d'Anselme, who ordered the ground attack in

Royan. French troops wanted a victory, and to deny them that now, in 1945, would only frustrate them for the rest of their lives. So the battle was launched for its "ardent desire" of being won, d'Anselme said—not its military need, which other generals, including Leclerc, questioned.

In freeing the Atlantic pockets, the French military suffered nearly 1,400 casualties, the Germans 970. The government failed to provide an estimate of civilians killed or wounded.

The taking of Pointe de Grave and Royan demanded bravery from the men on the ground. Both sides were relentless; the Germans "wouldn't surrender unless they found themselves incapable of continuing the fight," La Rochefoucauld wrote. If the capture of Berlin made a mission in Royan pointless, then a terrible beauty revealed itself in the Gironde, too, the Germans defending ground for the sake of it, the French attacking positions for the honor in it, both sides aware they might be the last soldiers in the war to die, and both fighting anyway, for country or their brothers or themselves.

So when the burning glow of that notorious victory in Royan smoldered into white smoke, the French honored those who had fought admirably. Colonel de Milleret of the FFGR authored the citation for La Rochefoucauld's War Cross, one week after V-E Day. "Placed at the forefront of the squadron of Commandos," the short note read, "[La Rochefoucauld] showed the good qualities of composure, thus avoiding severe losses in his unit. [The] aspirant, full of energy and courage, proved worthy during the fighting of Pointe de Grave in the duty that had been entrusted to him."

The days turned hot on the Atlantic coast and La Rochefoucauld yearned to return home, to the chateau outside Soissons. In August, the same month that the Japanese surrendered and the war in the Pacific ended, doctors thought La Rochefoucauld's knee had fully recovered and released him from their care. He got a month's leave from the army and headed straight to the thirty-five acres of Villeneuve. He found a property "in fairly poor condition," he wrote, but his parents and surviving siblings focused his attention elsewhere. "The reunion was emotional," La Rochefoucauld said, the joy tinged with melancholy. "Henri's death had been trying on my mother and father." (They would keep for the rest of their lives more photos of Henri in the chateau than any other child.) Robert met his youngest sister during that leave, Olivier and Consuelo's tenth and final baby, born in February 1945, one month after Henri's death: Marie-Henriette, named after her fallen brother.

Though grief remained, the house also filled with a sense of simple serenity: La Rochefoucauld alive, his family with him at home.

"The month of leave went by quickly," he wrote. The army did not discharge him, and he would not have sought it anyway. The boy who'd dangled from the four-story roof of this chateau had grown into a man who still loved adventure. The army, even in peacetime, promised an alluring life. He left Villeneuve and, "I was soon called up as an aide-de-camp for General Noiret." This was Roger Noiret, who had led troops in North Africa and later joined the Free French Forces in Great Britain.

He and La Rochefoucauld stationed themselves in Berlin, watching the Russians and Americans carve up the spoils of the Third Reich. One night the Soviets held a reception in the city "to celebrate French-Russian friendship," La Rochefoucauld wrote. About thirty people attended, including the famed Marshal Georgy Zhukov, the most decorated officer in the history of Russia, who perhaps more than any other man contributed to the Allied success on the Eastern Front. When the French interpreter accompanying La Rochefoucauld introduced him to Zhukov, the Russian burst out laughing. "He'd heard my name rather quickly and thought I was called La Rochezhukov," Robert wrote. Zhukov announced that the Frenchman was a Gallic cousin and kissed him full on the mouth, the Russian custom. "From then on, all the Soviet officers would only call me La Rochezhukov," he wrote.

Everyone sat down for dinner. Robert saw a glass of vodka in front of him and servers standing behind and the boisterous Zhukov rising, at the head of the table, to give a speech. He toasted the Allies' health. He then began to list the countries that had contributed to success, pausing after each nation, the men at table expected to drink their whole glass. When they did, the servers refilled, and Zhukov would announce the next nation. La Rochefoucauld saw where this was headed and looked to Noiret, who motioned with his eyes that they couldn't refuse. Still, Noiret surreptitiously began dumping half of each glass on the carpet, before drinking the rest. La Rochefoucauld followed his general's lead. The Russians did not.

The night got away from the soldiers. When Zhukov made his good-byes he had to be accompanied down the front steps of the hall, and then out across the cobblestone street. He saw his car and chauffeur and dove into the backseat—and came crashing out the other side. Noiret and La Rochefoucauld chose to say nothing, only in slightly better states themselves.

The next morning was not kind to Robert, but when his mind cleared the day held its revelations, one of them even more amazing than Zhukov's drawn-out toast. A lifetime after the German blitz, here La Rochefoucauld was, a *résistant* the Nazis had spent three years trying to kill, free, and even feted, in the city of Berlin.

# EPILOGUE

**A**s had been the case with so many evenings in Robert's life, this one would be formal, and he stood before the mirror knotting his black tie. His fingers remained as dexterous as they'd been at ten, when he learned this nightly routine, but his cheeks had reddened and sagged with age, and his sweep of brown hair had turned white and begun to recede up his pate, collecting in shocks that with each new year bore a little less resemblance to the neatly parted look of his prime, when he'd gained the attention of every passing woman. He still had a noble bearing—all ironic gaze and straight-backed aplomb—and despite the evening's formal attire, he managed the easy poise of the carefree, walking from the mirror with a light smile on his lips.

He turned out of the master bedroom and onto the red carpet of the chateau's third-story hallway. He and Bernadette had moved here forty-two years ago, just after their marriage in 1955, and Robert still loved it. The sixty-six acres known as Pont Chevron featured a rolling lawn leading to the thirty-room chateau, and then another expanse falling from it, ending at the bank of the private lake that gave the estate its serenity. Situated just outside Ouzouer-sur-Trézée, a town in north-central France, the property had hosted Spanish kings and Portuguese queens before Robert and Bernadette moved in, but La Rochefoucauld liked it because it rivaled his own childhood home, Villeneuve. Both were pastoral idylls and great places to raise a family.

The guests began to arrive: his four adult children, seven grandchildren, and dozens of friends and acquaintances. He mingled with veterans and the local functionaries who'd helped him govern Ouzouer-sur-Trézée, in the thirty years he had been the town's mayor. Not just the energy of the room but its very color seemed to lighten when the former president of France entered, Valéry Giscard d'Estaing, a friend of the family's who would preside over tonight's ceremony. Robert looked across at Bernadette, still a striking blond, and smiled. She knew what this evening meant to him, even if there was so much about the war Robert still refused to discuss.

There had been the one morning just after their marriage, for instance, when she had woken up and begun padding for the door. She remembered Robert suddenly on her, throwing her to the ground.

"What's going on?" she'd screamed.

He had paused then, and seemed to gather himself in the moment, back in their bedroom. He'd told her that he was sure the Germans were coming.

She'd looked at him, numb and wanting to help, trying to see behind those darting eyes, but they were impenetrable. Robert didn't describe the images he saw that day. He never would.

At last, the ceremony began, the people squeezing into the salon, with its chandelier overhead, floor-to-ceiling windows showing the trace of the inky March night, and floral-patterned walls like something out of another century. President d'Estaing stood near the front, with La Rochefoucauld beside him. They moved in the same social spheres and had become hunting buddies. The former president said that, fifty-two years after the war, they had all convened in this beautiful home to celebrate a *résistant*. He had already been honored by the French state: He had received the War Cross; the Medal of the Resistance; a medal for escaping German imprisonment, as well as four other commendations. But tonight, Count Robert Jean-Marie de La Rochefoucauld would receive France's highest military distinction, the Legion of Honor, which had been awarded to the bravest of France's soldiers since Napoléon's reign.

The official government statement marking the occasion went on for a page, listing his accomplishments, and concluded by saying: "The honorary Major de La Rochefoucauld, Robert, *résistant* from the outset, decorated with three war awards, is a candidate worthy of being named chevalier of the Legion of Honor."

With that, d'Estaing pinned the star-shaped medal on the left breast pocket of La Rochefoucauld's jacket. Amid the applause and dabbed eyes, Robert's face flushed redder still. When the room quieted, he said in a humble half whisper that the *résistants* who died alongside him were more worthy of this distinction. He told the crowd he had these soldiers in his thoughts.

His family had never heard the full story of his fight; with the passage of time he'd only shared fragments. His oldest daughter, Astrid, then forty-two, had been hunting game with him in the Landes department as a teenager when Robert told her of the mini-Kommandantur not far from them, and the *résistants* who'd freed him by shooting up the place, nearly killing him in the process. Robert's other daughters, Constance and Hortense, pieced together the Saint-Médard sabotage from the war movies they watched with him, and the almost monosyllabic commentary he provided. His youngest, Jean, twenty-nine, who would inherit Robert's title of Count, had learned about the Occupation and his *papa's* place in it from the friends of his parents who gathered at the house for dinners and parties. *We thought for sure your father was dead so many times,* they'd said. The children swapped these anecdotes and remained fascinated by them even as they began having children of their own—but the narrative never satisfied them. Now, in the days after the Legion of Honor celebration, with the medal suspended in a case above the fireplace, the family's curiosity picqued. With enough prodding, Robert agreed to work with an audio-recording service, and over a series of interviews recorded and then edited and finally presented his full tale on two compact discs. "He didn't live to be a hero," Hortense said, years after receiving her own copy of the recording. "He was very humble." In fact, he seemed almost bashful on the CDs, a child of upper-class understatement, moving quickly and prosaically through the episodes of his war, as if everyone had dressed up as a nun or crawled onto suspended netting inches above a Nazi. Constance began to collect his military records, so the family might have a fuller portrayal of their father's service.

It should have ended there, the old man living his sunset years in the obscurity of his family's admiration. But a combat story as wily as Robert de La Rochefoucauld's found ways to keep twisting and unspooling, even a half century after the Germans fled.

In the fall of 1997, Maurice Papon's criminal trial began for deporting some of the sixteen hundred Jews who had been shuttled onto cattle cars in the Gironde department while he was the local prefecture's secretary general.

La Rochefoucauld had met Papon in the 1960s, at a party at the midpoint of Papon's political career. He was by then Paris' prefect of police; he would ultimately serve as President d'Estaing's budget minister from 1978 to 1981. After La Rochefoucauld and Papon were introduced at that party, they began discussing the war. Papon said he'd been the secretary general for the Gironde prefecture from 1942 to 1945. Though he worked for Vichy, Papon told Robert he'd secretly worked for the Resistance. Robert said in response that he remembered fighting alongside bands of Jewish resisters in the Gironde in 1944 and had asked one of the Jewish fighters why so many of them had joined. "There's no mystery to it," the rebel had said, as La Rochefoucauld recounted. "We have an excellent contact in the Gironde prefecture. He warns us as soon as the Germans start looking for one of us, or a raid is being organized." La Rochefoucauld studied Papon's face, and wondered aloud if Papon was that contact. Papon smiled and nodded. The two became friendly.

Thirty years later, as Robert read press accounts of the trial, he saw the prosecution describe Papon as a war criminal. Papon's signature, after all, allowed eight of the ten convoys of Jews to leave the Gironde. The news accounts also showed the defense shading the argument against Papon, demonstrating that he was a junior administrator in the Gironde who had literally been tasked with signing off on orders. Papon's lawyers scored a major point when they cross-examined the historian who first published the accusations against Papon. The historian said he had changed his mind. He no longer believed that the documents he'd found proved Papon's guilt.

But this, too, wasn't the whole story of Papon, and in a trial that would become the longest in French history, Robert's anecdote about the Jewish resisters reached the defense team. Robert met with the lawyers and agreed to testify. Over the protests of his family, Robert took the stand in Bordeaux one bleak February afternoon in 1998, four months into a trial that would last six.

"I left for England in 1942," the seventy-four-year-old said. "And I was parachuted into France several times together . . . with the English. After a lot of adventures, I was caught by the Germans. I escaped several times, including once from Fort du Hâ, and I ended up with a Maquis group . . . a Maquis called Charly, if I remember correctly.

"One of the few memories I have of being with this Maquis is that there was a Jewish community there and when I saw how many of them there were, I asked them what was the reason for being part of this Maquis. The commander's answer was very simple: . . . They had been warned by the prefecture that there would be a rounding up."

La Rochefoucauld continued. At that time, he said, "I did not know Mr. Papon from Adam, neither did I know anyone at the prefecture," but he later learned about Papon's significance when he met the man in the 1960s. "It was then that I told him about the

Jews of the Maquis," La Rochefoucauld testified. "He smiled and said: 'We were very well organized at the Prefecture.'"

Despite his own heroics, La Rochefoucauld felt it took "monstrous reserves of personal courage" to aid the Resistance from within Vichy. "I consider Mr. Papon one of those brave men."

After he testified, and after he encountered Papon's protesters on the streets, and the young man who spit on him, La Rochefoucauld thought about an eternal France that could nonetheless look and act in a manner so very different from the one he'd known. Robert had been granted fifteen minutes on the stand, but could any amount of time have properly relayed the nuance and fear and sadness of the Occupation, or the joy of liberation, or, most important, the bond that La Rochefoucauld still felt for the people who'd fought as he had? How to tell any of this to whole generations of people who had never seen a swastika flag above the Eiffel Tower? "I realize that [mine] was another era, and even the end of another era," La Rochefoucauld wrote.

But people began to learn the truth. As the evidence mounted and the trial staggered on, the affair became less about one man's actions than a country forced to reckon with its past. After the war, and for the better part of two decades, Charles de Gaulle had perpetuated the myth that every Frenchmen had resisted, that a military defeat in 1940 was not followed by a moral one. But slowly a counternarrative emerged, books and films and at last a criminal trial like Papon's, where the secrets of the dark years reached the consciousness of the nation. The trial repeated what the books and films established: Very few Frenchmen had taken up arms against the Germans, perhaps as little as 2 percent. This complacency in the face of German rule, if not complicity with the occupier (as many as 20 percent collaborated), ashamed people now. The press accounts from the trial brimmed with Frenchmen distancing themselves from ugly wartime realities, which produced something like a burning feeling among the populace that was worse than 1940, because seen in this light almost everyone had failed his country, or loved someone who had.

Papon's trial, then, as it neared its conclusion, attempted not only a collective condemnation but a public absolution. If Papon were found guilty, France could cleanse itself of the Occupation's disgrace. His trial sparked "an orgy of collective repentance for France's guilt," one historian noted. Among others, the Catholic Church and President Jacques Chirac issued apologies to the Resistance fighters and Jews who had died at the hands of their countrymen.

But Papon was not the monster France needed. Vichy's national police chief René Bousquet had issued the deportation papers, and Bousquet was dead. So too was Jean Leguay, Bousquet's second in command. "In fact," wrote the University of London historian Julian Jackson, "Papon would possibly never have been tried at all if either Bousquet or Leguay had still been alive; his trial acted as a kind of proxy for theirs." It seemed that not even the longest criminal proceeding in history could give weight to all the evidence.

In the end, the verdict reflected this. Papon was found guilty of "crimes against humanity," in the arrest of thirty-seven people and the illegal confinement of fifty-three more. But, parsing the judgment, the court acquitted Papon of the more serious charges of premeditated murder. He was sentenced to ten years in prison.

The resolution displeased La Rochefoucauld, who sensed that factors other than the ones pertinent to the case had influenced its outcome. So, unbeknownst to his family, Robert secretly gave Papon his passport as the old man's appeal was to be heard. Robert's loyalty to old résistants was greater, it seemed, than any verdict.

Papon fled the country. The police tracked him to a hotel in Gstaad, Switzerland, and television crews found the room registered under the name Robert Rochefoucauld. The case was now an international sensation. La Rochefoucauld himself agreed to two television interviews, where he freely admitted his role in the escape, and explained his rationale. "I lent him my passport . . . because I used to see him very often and he used to tell me: 'It's a real pain. Every time I go to a hotel to see my children, people are cross with me because of my name.' So I told him, 'Here's my passport so that you'll feel more at ease.' He used it maybe once or twice and then he must have used it to go to Switzerland." In the second interview, La Rochefoucauld said, "One of the reasons I helped him is that I was terribly scared. He might commit suicide."

Many members of La Rochefoucauld's family were furious with him, but they couldn't convince Robert of his gaffe. As he said in one of the TV interviews: "Whatever they say, [Papon] has been a great servant of the State." It was the old codes talking, of stoicism in battle and brotherhood for life.

Swiss authorities extradited Papon on October 21, 1999, and he served his sentence in Fresnes, outside Paris, the same prison where, during the war, German authorities had tortured and killed Jewish *résistants*. Papon's lawyers appealed his term to the European Court of Human Rights, in Switzerland. In 2002 that court overturned the French court's ruling. Papon, now ninety-two years old, was free.

La Rochefoucauld's own name had never been far from the old prefect's in the intervening years, and it had become just as sullied. Even Papon's freedom couldn't wash the dirt away. For the second time in his life, La Rochefoucauld felt he had to defend his honor, and the only way to do that was to discuss all he had done. With the help of a ghostwriter, and the support of his family, who had made a begrudging peace with his bullheaded act, he set about penning his memoir: *La Liberté, C'est Mon Plaisir*, a play on the family motto. It was published in late 2002, a slim book that relegated the Papon affair to a couple of pages and recounted in simple prose La Rochefoucauld's upbringing and the secret war that duty called him to fight.

It was an amazing tale. It was also ignored by the press and sold poorly.

C'est la vie. La Rochefoucauld turned eighty and had to deal with larger disappointments than a world that no longer understood him. His step slowed and his breath grew shallower; boyhood tuberculosis and a lifelong smoking habit had left him with lungs that functioned at one-fourth of their capacity. Then there was Bernadette's deteriorating state. Diagnosed with Alzheimer's, she struggled a bit more each day to remain with him in the present. In June 2011, Robert suffered a small stroke and Bernadette grew more confused visiting him at the hospital. A respiratory condition prolonged his stay, and by the time he was discharged Bernadette didn't know him. The family placed her in a retirement facility in November, and Robert roamed the chateau of Pont Chevron, hospice staff tending to his own fragile health.

His daughter Constance lived a couple miles away, and checked in often. Of his four children, she had been the most interested in his valiant young life, and now La Rochefoucauld began to share the secrets that even his memoir didn't recount. He'd worn dentures for years to replace the teeth the Germans in Auxerre had knocked out, he said. And he still thought about the war, almost every day.

By the spring of 2012, La Rochefoucauld had little energy and often didn't want to leave his bed. Constance asked him if he would make a final confession, and he said he would. There was something, in fact, he had never been able to say.

The daring that had brought him numerous medals, the highest honors in France—it all pained him, he told his daughter. "I have killed people," he said. He had killed them at close range, and sometimes with his own hands, and he had watched these soldiers die, soldiers who were in the end much like him, fighting for a cause. Their deaths may have been necessary, but he told Constance he had never quieted the daily, beastly whispers of culpability.

Constance tried to console him, but she also understood: Robert hadn't discussed his war because his own father had never discussed his. The old codes again. And the tradition that gave Robert de La Rochefoucauld courage and made him great and years later even bound him to men of ill repute had also shackled him to a ball of guilt that rolled behind him—one he dragged, painfully, quietly, his whole life. He had lived honorably, which is all he'd wanted as a boy, but he had never sought the guidance that would help him look past his deep valleys of regret. And if people were going to remember his bravery, he had finally told his daughter about its cost.

It was a small act, but in its way the most courageous of his life, to transcend those old mores demanding silence in the wake of suffering, and at long last to show a vulnerability as much a part of him as his valor.

He died a few days later, on May 8, V-E Day.

# ACKNOWLEDGMENTS

This book couldn't have happened without my beautiful and endlessly patient wife, Sonya. She not only tolerated the long hours I kept, but offered expert advice on the manuscript. I love you, sweetie.

I'd like to thank my agent, Larry Weissman, for believing in me and this undertaking. Larry and his wife, Sascha Alper, gave thoughtful notes on early drafts of the manuscript, long before it reached my editors at HarperCollins. They saved me from my worst tendencies. I'd like to thank Josie Freedman at ICM Partners. I'd also like to thank Claire Wachtel, Jonathan Jao, and Sofia Groopman at HarperCollins, for helping me shape the manuscript into its finished form. Every cut was a good one.

A very special thanks to Gabriella Kessler and Lilyana Yankova, my translators in Paris. One or the other accompanied me on interviews—my French remains far from fluent—and sat next to me amid high stacks of musty military reports, trying to parse almost illegible French handwriting. I literally couldn't have written this book without their help. There were other translators, too, who helped me when Gabriella or Lilyana couldn't. I'd like to thank Petra Krischok, who pulled files for me in Berlin and was a consummate pro; Almut Schoenfeld, who filled in when Petra was busy; Katia Martinez Garbaye, who found key information for me in Spain; Antoine Dain, who did the same in France; Jacques Clement, who dug up and then translated crucial testimony from the Maurice Papon trial; Sophie Detraz, who pulled some of La Rochefoucauld's military records; Allison Schein, who translated La Rochefoucauld's memoir at a time when my French wasn't as strong as I wanted; Yannick Demoustier, who accompanied me on my first trip to France; the various scholars of the French Resistance and SOE I contacted, in London, France, and Berlin; Claude Delasselle, the scholar who showed me around the Yonne department for two days and answered my (many) questions for the two years following that; my old professor, Tom Emmerson, who keeps a flat in London and kept asking me what other documents he could pick up for me long after I'd left London's beautiful National Archives; and his daughter Hilary and her husband, Marcus Thompson, who allowed me to stay at the aforementioned flat for a week.

I'd like to thank Jason Schwartz, Wright Thompson, and Eli Saslow, for their reads of the manuscript and the guidance they offered when I phoned or harassed them afterward.

I'd like to thank Chad Millman, at ESPN, who told me to "go for it" when I said I'd like to write this book.

Lastly, I'd like to thank the immediate and extended La Rochefoucauld family, for all the photos, letters, and multimedia sources they provided me, and the (I'm sure) seemingly endless follow-up questions they answered. I hope I've shown Robert for the man he was and the courage he embodied.

# NOTES

Before we get to the notes themselves, there are a few things to point out. Though I talked with many of Robert's living brothers and sisters, his cousins and nieces and nephews, two in particular deserve special attention, as their names will appear throughout the source material on the following pages. The first is Nicolas de Schonen, the family's unofficial historian and Robert's nephew, who during the course of my research lived in Robert's childhood estate, Villeneuve, and let me stay there for a few days. The second is Nicolas's mother, Robert's younger sister Yolaine, who recalled the privation's and milieu of the Occupation, and shared with me the attitudes of a teenaged Robert.

From France's Ministry of Defense I received La Rochefoucauld's military records, some three-hundred-plus pages in all, the majority of which were found in the Ministry's satellite campus in Pau. Unless he wanted to be killed by the Nazis, a *résistant* couldn't keep a paper trail of his handiwork during the Occupation, and these military records, compiled just after the war's end, from soldiers' memories, were invaluable. They offered me a close account of when Robert was where; and for that reason, I sometimes departed from the chronology of La Rochefoucauld's memoir in my narrative. It seems Robert—not exactly a fastidious student—didn't rely on all of his military files when he and a ghostwriter penned his memoir. At certain points, concerning certain dates and happenings, I went with what the military records stated, because they were written closer to the events themselves. The military files, however, sometimes offered conflicting views of specific details—memory is never perfect, after all—and so, on occasion, I interpreted what the facts in La Rochefoucauld's file suggested. This interpretation was nothing more than a triangulation of facts from multiple sources—Robert's military records with those of a Resistance group's, say—until a narrative emerged that I felt comfortable committing to the page.

When I was in London researching the book, I spoke with a few scholars of World War II and of Britain's Special Operations Executive, and some doubted whether Robert trained in England and became an SOE agent. After all, there is no case file for La Rochefoucauld in SOE's archives. While it's true that there is no conclusive evidence tying La Rochefoucauld to SOE, I believe he was an agent for the following reasons: 1) A bad fire after the war destroyed perhaps seven-eighths of SOE's records, according to its official historian, M. R. D. Foot. Furthermore, in the prologue to *The Secret History of SOE*, Foot writes that the British government itself destroyed still more records. "The weeding has been random; many important papers are gone." 2) Robert's French military records make note of his secret handlers in London, including one with the code-name "Henri." 3) In the fall of 1944, Robert's military records state how he taught other *résistants* to parachute. Now, if Robert were simply a French Resistance fighter, who never left French soil, he wouldn't have needed to learn to jump from a plane to reach a new Resistance cell. He could have simply biked or driven there. The fact that he not only learned to parachute but was asked to instruct French soldiers in their jumps strongly suggests he was first trained by an overseas band of fighters. 4) The SOE training Robert describes in his memoir, and in his recording and the family's DVD, is consistent with SOE training manuals and books about same. 5) In his memoir, Robert remembered the name of one British agent, Eric Piquet-Wicks. La Rochefoucauld said he was brought to the special operations world by Piquet-Wicks, who was the leader of the R/F Section, one of six French sections within SOE—another consistency between Robert's account and that of SOE. (The notes below carry a full accounting of source material.)

I wanted to be thorough with these endnotes, but also not over-whelm my publisher or readers; the sourcing, and the story of the sourcing, could take up as many pages as the book itself. Among many others, I'm indebted to the scholarship of Julian Jackson, Robert Paxton, Matthew Cobb, William Shirer, Jacques Delarue, M. R. D. Foot, the almost absurdly fun commando instructors of SOE, and Howard Zinn. I have made every effort to be as accurate as possible. Should a reader find an inconsistency, though, please blame me, and not any of the writers listed above or below.

## PROLOGUE

1     asking him *why*: This line, and paragraph, are informed by conver-sations with La Rochefoucauld's daughter Astrid Gaignault and his nephew, Nicolas de Schonen.

1     afternoon in 1998: A multivolume edition of the trial transcripts was later published. *Le Procès de Maurice Papon, Compte rendu sténographique*, Vol. 2 (Paris: Albin Michel, 1998).

1     longest in French history: Robert O. Paxton, "The Trial of Maurice Papon," *New York Review of Books*, December 16, 1999, http://www .nybooks.com/articles/1999/12/16/the-trial-of-maurice-papon/.

1     debonair: What Robert wore to the courtroom is based on a photo taken outside it. His daughter Constance Guillaumin said that the photo that appeared in his obituary in the *New York Times* was taken the day he testified in the Papon trial. Richard Goldstein, "Robert de La Roche-foucauld, Wartime Hero and Spy, Dies at 88," *New York Times*, July 9, 2012, http://www.nytimes.com/2012/07/10/world/europe/robert-de -la-rochefoucauld-noted-for-war-exploits-dies-at-88.html.

1     moved from one girl to the next: Guillaumin told me this while we looked at old photo albums of her father, which included many shots of his former girlfriends. Robert had placed captions beneath the photos

with the young women's names. There were pages upon pages of these photos, and sometimes he just placed a question mark in the caption.

2 Pont Chevron, his thirty-room chateau: Conversations with Jean de La Rochefoucauld.

2 nodded at the defendant: *Le Procès de Maurice Papon*.

2 bulletproof glass: John-Thor Dahlburg, "Ex-Official Accused of Aiding Nazis Begins Trial in France," *Los Angeles Times*, October 9, 1997, http://articles.latimes.com/1997/oct/09/news/mn-40871.

2 "and in North Africa": *Le Procès de Maurice Papon*.

2 He was sixteen then: Robert de La Rochefoucauld, *La Liberté, C'est Mon Plaisir: 1939–1946* (Paris: Perrin, 2002). La Rochefoucauld was born in September 1923.

2 re-enlisted in 1939: Olivier de La Rochefoucauld military records, Ministry of Defense, Paris.

2 five days after the Armistice: Ibid.

2 local chapter of the Red Cross: Conversations with Robert's nephew, Nicolas de Schonen, the La Rochefoucauld family's unofficial historian.

2 the Terrible Countess: Conversations with Yolaine de Schonen, Robert's sister, and the DVD the family produced, which was never meant for a distribution greater than successive generations of the clan but of which the family was kind enough to give me a copy.

2 four war medals and a knighthood: The medals were shown to me by his daughter Constance.

2 general secretary of the Gironde prefecture: Caroline Moorehead, *A Train in Winter* (New York: Harper Perennial, 2012).

3 223 of them children: Elaine Gainley, "Maurice Papon, 96; French Nazi Collaborator," *The Washington Post*, February 18, 2007, http://www.washingtonpost.com/wp-dyn/content/article/2007/02/17/AR2007021701355.html.

3 the final destination of the cattle cars: *Le Procès de Maurice Papon*.

3 René Bousquet: See Julian Jackson's magnificent account of the Occupation, *France: The Dark Years: 1940–1944* (London: Oxford University Press, 2003).

3   he no longer believed the documents proved Papon's guilt: Douglas Johnson, "Maurice Papon," *The Guardian,* February 18, 2007, https://www.theguardian.com/news/2007/feb/19/guardianobituaries.france.

3   "queasiness" about prosecuting the man: Paxton, "The Trial of Maurice Papon."

3   As he told the court: trial transcripts: Ibid.

4   Roger-Samuel Bloch: *Le Procès de Maurice Papon.* Also Richard Golsan, ed., *The Papon Affair: Memory and Justice on Trial* (New York and London: Routledge, 2012).

4   gated entryway of the courthouse: I found old CNN B-roll footage of the trial and what the courthouse looked like.

4   spit on him: Conversations with Constance Guillaumin.

4   shared loyalty: This paragraph is informed by the trial transcripts, multiple conversations with Constance Guillaumin, Nicolas de Schonen, and Astrid Gaignault, as well as the sentiments that emerge from *La Liberté,* and the recording Robert made of thoughts about the war and the subsequent peace.

5   they'd discussed them throughout their childhood: All four of Robert's children told me about his silence concerning the war and the snippets they pieced together.

5   Citroën: Conversations with Constance Guillaumin.

5   he told himself: His family told me how resistant he was to writing his story.

## CHAPTER 1

7   On May 16, 1940: For this, I relied on police and governmental reports from the Aisne department archives, which I accessed online at http://archives.aisne.fr/archive/salle-l-exode-8/n:103 and http://archives.aisne.fr/archive/panneau-l-exode-6/n:103.

7   menacing drone: Conversations with Yolaine de Schonen; I also relied on the files in the departmental archives to give me a sense of what Soissoinais said the blitzkrieg felt and sounded like.

7    German Stukas: Matthew Cobb, *The Resistance: The French Fight Against the Nazis* (London, Simon & Schuster, 2013). You can watch old clips on YouTube to get a sense of what the Stukas sounded and looked like.

7    ever closer to the chateau: Yolaine de Schonen described for me the bombing campaign, as did the diary Robert's mother Consuelo kept, which the La Rochefoucauld family was kind enough to give me. See also the Aisne department archives.

7    "we must go!": Conversations with Yolaine de Schonen.

8    The Allies had thought that terrain too treacherous: Brian Bond, *France and Belgium: 1939–1940* (London: Davis-Poynter, 1975).

8    stretching back for more than one hundred miles: William Shirer, *The Rise and Fall of the Third Reich* (New York: Simon & Schuster, 2011).

8    many of them reservists: Lt. Col. Thomas D. Morgan, United States Army (Ret.), "The Fall of France and the Summer of 1940," *The Institute of Land Warfare* (April 2006).

8    Britain's Royal Air Force had sent out seventy-one bombers: See the Battle for France timeline on the RAF's website: http://www.raf.mod.uk/history/rafhistorytimeline1940.cfm.

8    the greatest rate of loss: Ibid.

8    thirty miles wide and fifteen miles deep: Shirer, *Rise and Fall of the Third Reich.*

8    Soissons' factories: Consuelo de La Rochefoucauld diary and the Aisne department archives.

8    Consuelo told her eldest, Henri: Robert de La Rochefoucauld recording, and conversations with Yolaine de Schonen.

8    the Duchess of Maillé: La Rouchefoucauld, *La Liberté.*

8    Consuelo would stay behind: Conversations with Yolaine de Schonen.

9    serving as a liaison officer: Olivier de La Rochefoucauld's military files.

9    with only 25 percent stationed in country: Lt. Col. Faris R. Kirkland, United States Air Force (Ret.), "The French Air Force in 1940: Was It Defeated by the Luftwaffe or Politics?" *Air University Review* (October 1985).

9     The Germans bombed the train stations and many of the bridges: Consuelo de La Rochefoucauld diary.

9     screamed with each report: Conversations with Yolaine de Schonen.

9     "that interminable syrup": Antoine de Saint-Exupéry, *Flight to Arras* (New York: Harcourt Brace, 1969).

10    Local officials had sometimes been the first to flee: Jackson, *France: The Dark Years.*

10    Henri was serious and studious: La Rochefoucauld family DVD .

10    countenance that rounded itself into a slight pout: Constance Guillaumin sent me many photos of her father as a boy.

10    different boarding school nearly every year: La Rochefoucauld recording and *La Liberté,* and La Rochefoucauld family DVD.

10    to dangle from the parapet: Conversations with Yolaine de Schonen.

10    Grandmother La Rochefoucauld: Ibid.

10    Yolaine, twelve: I figured out the ages of the children at this time using the La Rochefoucauld family DVD. I also consulted the following website, which tracks the lineage of French nobility: http://gw .geneanet.org/frebault?lang=fr&pz=henri&nz=frebault&ocz=0&p =robert+guy+jean+marie&n=de+la+rochefoucauld. Yolaine de Schonen was also helpful in telling me who played with whom in the family, which cliques developed, and who protected whom.

11    he felt a sense of fraternity: La Rochefoucauld recording and *La Liberté.*

11    one thousand years of French history: The family's chateau, Chateau de La Rochefoucauld, traces its existence back one thousand years. http://www.reve-de-chateaux.com/en/residence/105-chateau-de -la-rochefoucauld. Also, Yolaine's son Nicolas de Schonen and I discussed the family's long history.

11    Grandmother La Rochefoucauld's private rail car: La Rochefoucauld recording.

11    become, he said, a committed Republican: Conversations with Nicolas de Schonen.

11    defend it, even if the military couldn't: La Rochefoucauld recording.

11    on the road for four days: Ibid.

11  As many as eight million people: Cobb, *The Resistance*.

11  bicycles were the best mode: Ibid.

12  Thousands of parents lost track: Jackson, *France: The Dark Years*.

12  taking hours just to cross the Loire River: Conversations with Yolaine de Schonen.

12  1.7 million Frenchmen: John Keegan, *The First World War* (New York: Vintage, 2000).

12  captured and recaptured seventeen times: Conversations with Nicolas de Schonen.

12  smoldered for seven years: Ibid.

12  hand grenade: Conversations with Nicolas de Schonen. He was in fact still digging hand grenades out when I visited him.

12  carried the indentations: The church still shows these scars.

13  an ankle wound incurred in 1915: Olivier's military records.

13  Consuelo carried the gun: Conversations with Yolaine and Nicolas de Schonen.

13  they didn't appear in public: Gabriel Chevallier, *Fear*, trans. Malcolm Imrie (New York: New York Review Books Classics, 2014).

13  "Throughout my childhood": La Rochefoucauld recording.

13  an officer whose job: Olivier de La Rochefoucauld military records.

13  the "meat" of dead comrades: Chevallier, *Fear*.

13  He was a distant father: La Rochefoucauld family DVD.

13  "must not cry—ever": Conversations with Yolaine de Schonen.

13  the dahlias he planted: La Rochefoucauld family DVD.

13  Consuelo, who'd lost two brothers to the trenches: Conversations with Nicolas de Schonen.

13  indelicate tongue: La Rouchfoucauld recording and conversations with Yolaine de Schonen.

13  upended by the war: Consuelo de La Rochefoucauld's diaries give a sense of her commitment to the Red Cross. Also conversations with Nicolas de Schonen.

14  France had one hundred divisions: This paragraph is informed by Shirer, *The Rise and Fall of the Third Reich*.

14    French Parliament voted 537 to 75: Jackson, *France: The Dark Years.*

14    "There is no glory in being French": Ibid.

14    "Rather servitude than war": Ibid.

14    "Queer kind of war": William Shirer, *Berlin Diary: The Journal of a For-eign Correspondent: 1934–1941* (New York: Rosetta Books, 2011).

15    "We were lucky": Conversations with Yolaine de Schonen.

15    a three-winged castle: Conversations with Nicolas de Schonen. With the help of a translator, I exchanged emails of documents, photos, and architectural blueprints of the castle with its current owner, Claude Charrier.

15    never tired of coming here: The La Rochefoucauld family DVD and La Rochefoucauld recording.

15    a hollowed-out exhaustion: La Rochefoucauld recording.

15    That very night: Shirer, *The Rise and Fall of the Third Reich.*

15    Consuelo rejoined the family a few nights later: Conversations with Yolaine and Nicolas de Schonen.

15    "No more windows, almost no more doors": Consuelo de La Roche-foucauld diary.

16    killing 254, 195 of them civilians: Cobb, *The Resistance.*

16    cows wandered some of its richest streets, mooing: Ibid.

16    departed without destination: Ibid.

16    bunched round the radio in their grandmother's salon that day: La Rochefoucauld recording and *La Liberté.*

16    two million people had fled and the city was silent: Cobb, *The Resis-tance.* The rest of the paragraph is informed by *The Resistance.* Twelve Parisians, that book noted, committed suicide that day.

16    rolled her own cigarettes from corn husks: Conversations with Yolaine and Nicolas de Schonen.

16    appeared anxious now before her children: La Rochefoucauld re-cording.

16    "It is with a heavy heart": Jackson, *France: The Dark Years.*

16    Robert drew back when he heard the words: La Rochefoucauld re-cording.

17    Hitler wanted this armistice signed on the same spot as the last: Shirer, *The Rise and Fall of the Third Reich*. The rest of this paragraph is informed by that book.

17    "I look for the expression in Hitler's face": Ibid.

17    humiliated the Frenchmen: Ibid.

17    The terms of the armistice were numerous and harsh: The Yale Law School's Avalon Project—a tremendous resource. http://avalon.law .yale.edu/wwii/frgearm.asp.

18    Hitler's brilliant political moves: Jackson, *France: The Dark Years*, and Cobb, *The Resistance*, offer good analyses of the political realities of the demarcation line.

18    "It was the first time I saw my mother cry": La Rochefoucauld, *La Liberté*.

18    "I was against it, absolutely against it": Ibid.

18    "Monstrous": Ibid.

19    even ghostwritten one of his books: Julian Jackson, *De Gaulle* (London: Haus Publishers Limited, 2005).

19    a pair of trousers, four clean shirts, and a family photo in his personal luggage: Cobb, *The Resistance*.

19    "I, General de Gaulle . . . call upon": Ibid.

19    listened to de Gaulle: La Rochefoucauld recording and *La Liberté*.

## CHAPTER 2

21    German soldiers had pillaged: Aisne department archives.

21    At last they saw the clearing: This paragraph is informed by the time I spent at Villeneuve.

21    the daughter of one of Napoléon's generals: Conversations with Nicolas de Schonen.

21    forty-seven rooms: Ibid.

21    German military vehicles: Conversations with Yolaine de Schonen.

21    armored cars and trucks: Ibid.

22    the same stone staircase: Descriptions of Villeneuve are based on my observations.

22 "There was absolutely nothing": La Rochefoucauld recording.

22 Consuelo told her children: Conversations with Yolaine de Schonen.

22 They soon redistributed themselves: Conversations with Nicolas and Yolaine de Schonen.

22 which seated twenty: Conversations with Nicolas and Yolaine de Schonen.

22 depicted a beautiful woman: A fable involves a La Rochefoucauld who married a woman who was actually a witch, and who bathed in a nearby castle once a week. One day, her husband spied on her as she bathed, and she kept saying, "It's my pleasure." The story, interpreted by successive generations, is an almost libertine allowance to enjoy what life gives you.

23 the staff of twelve: Conversations with Nicolas and Yolaine de Schonen. Yolaine told me the house was at times more like an embassy than a home.

23 But he couldn't stand: La Rochefoucauld recording. Robert makes plain how much he hated German intrusion.

23 a new dining room: Conversations with Yolaine and Nicolas de Schonen.

23 and the Germans only spoke: Ibid.

23 the Terrible Countess: La Rochefoucauld family DVD.

23 north-south: Conversations with Nicolas de Schonen.

23 parking up to seven bulky tanks: Conversations with Yolaine de Schonen.

23 *write on her walls*: Conversations with Nicolas and Yolaine de Schonen.

23 learned that a British bomb: Conversations with Nicolas de Schonen.

24 The Villeneuve staff: Ibid.

24 water still flowed down: Conversations with Yolaine and Nicolas de Schonen.

24 warm a brick over a wood-fired oven: Conversations with Nicolas de Schonen.

24 he had been arrested by German forces: Olivier de La Rochefoucauld military records.

24    Oflag XVII-A: La Rochefoucauld, *La Liberté*.

24    "little Siberia": Two French documentaries about the camp proved very helpful. *Oflag 17A: Sous le manteaux,* directed by Marcel Corre (1999), and *Oflag 17A: Tournage clandestin derrière les barbelés,* produced by Eclectic Presse and La France Télévision (2013).

24    two letters home every month: Ibid.

24    she slapped him across the face: Conversations with Nicolas de Schonen.

25    those *Boche*: La Rochefoucauld recording.

25    daily message: La Rochefoucauld, recording and *La Liberté*, also discusses how much Robert loved to listen to General de Gaulle.

25    Guy de Pennart: Conversations with Guy's son, Emmanuel de Pennart.

25    "I was convinced": Ibid.

25    graduated from high school: Ibid.

25    agricultural college in Paris: Robert de La Rochefoucauld military records, Ministry of Defense, Paris.

25    The Germans had disbanded: Avalon Project, Yale University.

25    snuffed out: Cobb, *The Resistance,* shows how early Resistance groups were brave but ill-equipped and naive.

25    despised the Germans: La Rochefoucauld recording and *La Liberté*.

25    a spa town: Jackson, *France: The Dark Years,* demonstrates the limitations of the Vichy regime.

26    "but honor—that's all": La Rochefoucauld recording.

26    replete with portraits and busts: I saw some of these myself when I stayed there.

26    dated back to 900 AD: Rebecca Lawn, "Chateau de La Rochefoucauld," *Living Poitou-Charentes* (February 2011), http://www.livingmagazine .fr/feature/entry/feature/categories/charente-attractions.html/visit -what-to-do-chateau-rochefoucauld-charente.html.

26    "It is a revolution": I first heard about this member of the family from Nicolas de Schonen. But this quote is ubiquitous in texts discussing the French Revolution.

26  Bernard Mandeville, Nietzsche, and Voltaire: Duc de La Rouche-foucauld, Preface, *Maxims* (1871).

26  the Society of the Friends of the Blacks: Tom Reiss, *The Black Count: Glory, Revolution, Betrayal and the Real Count of Monte Cristo* (New York: Broadway Books, 2012).

26  martyred during the Reign of Terror: James Andrew Corcoran et al., eds., "The French Clergy During the Reign of Terror," *American Catholic Quarterly Review* (January–October, 1907).

26  *directeur des Beaux Arts*: Jane Fulcher, *The Nation's Image: French Grand Opera as Politics and Politicized Art* (Cambridge: Cambridge University Press, 2002).

26  Others appeared in the pages: Marcel Proust, *In Search of Lost Time* (New York: Proust Complete, 2003). The website Proust Personnages lists ten references to the family in the masterpiece: http://proust-personnages.fr/?page_id=892. Proust drew on real-world encounters; there are many mentions of family members in Proust's letters. Also see William C. Carter, *Marcel Proust: A Life* (New Haven: Yale University Press, 2013), especially the index.

26  He was baptized: Conversations with Yolaine de Schonen.

26  father who'd received the Legion of Honor: Olivier de La Rochefoucauld military records.

27  "honor commanded us to continue the fight": La Rochefoucauld recording.

27  He felt cheated: Ibid., and La Rochefoucauld, *La Liberté*.

27  What galled him: La Rochefoucauld, *La Liberté*.

27  "intellectual and moral anesthesia": Michael Robert Marrus and Robert O. Paxton, *Vichy France and the Jews* (Palo Alto, CA: Stanford University Press, 1995).

27  passé scenery: La Rochefoucauld recording.

27  "assumed a rather abstract air": Jean-Paul Sartre, *The Aftermath of War*, trans. Chris Turner (Salt Lake City, UT: Seagull Books, 2008).

27  "wall of fire": Ibid.

28  German officer play the piano: Conversations with Yolaine de Schonen.

28    "He was playing very, very well": Ibid.

28    another Poland: Jacques Delarue, *The Gestapo: A History of Horror*, trans. Mervin Savill (New York: Skyhorse Publishing, 2008).

28    stiff disciplined courteousness: Richard Vinen, *The Unfree French: Life Under the Occupation* (New Haven: Yale University Press, 2006).

28    PUT YOUR TRUST: Timothy Parsons, *The Rule of Empires: Those Who Built Them, Those Who Endured Them, and Why They Always Fall* (Oxford: Oxford University Press, 2000).

28    The Nazis gave French communities: Jackson, *France: The Dark Years*.

28    French police: Ibid.

28    "exemplary, amiable and helpful": Ibid.

28    "aroused little sympathy": Ibid.

29    "to sting the Germans": Vinen, *The Unfree French*.

29    "the path of collaboration": Cobb, *The Resistance*.

29    "The Armistice . . . is not peace": A complete transcript of the broadcast may be found here: http://desinroc.free.fr/anglais/chrono3/message.html.

29    "the war's biggest catastrophe": La Rochefoucauld recording.

29    "There could be consequences": Ibid.

## CHAPTER 3

31    a collaborationist viewpoint: Jackson, *France: The Dark Years*. The rest of the paragraph is informed by Jackson's book, which is truly remarkable.

32    It was in the Bavarian Alps: La Rochefoucauld recording and *La Liberté*.

32    "Franzose": La Rochefoucauld, *La Liberté*.

33    couldn't help but feel giddy: La Rochefoucauld recording and *La Liberté*.

33    invaded the city of Graz: Shirer, *The Rise and Fall of the Third Reich*. Also: Albert Speer, *Inside the Third Reich* (New York: Simon & Schuster, 1997).

33    "Long live Hitler!": La Rochefoucauld recording.

33    simply for peering inside: La Rochefoucauld recording and *La Liberté*.

33    One exhibition defaming Freemasonry: Jackson, *France: The Dark Years*.

33    drew 635,000: Ibid.

33    flourished to the point: Ibid.

34    second coming of Joan of Arc: La Rochefoucauld recording.

34    were never actually a majority: Jackson, *France: The Dark Years*.

34    L'Oréal: Ibid., and Michael Bar-Zohar, *Bitter Scent: The Case of L'Oreal, Nazis and the Arab Boycott* (New York: Dutton, 1996).

34    "Heil Hitler": Jackson, *France: The Dark Years*.

34    One day he met in secret: Conversations with Emmanuel de Pennart.

34    The man stared hard: Ibid.

35    A resistance group in Soissons: For Vérité Française, see Soissons town archives and its digital extension: http://www.vallee-de-l-aisne.com /site/428/rueduquotreacuteseauveacuteriteacutefrancaisequot.html. On the Musée de l'Homme and its naiveté, see Cobb, *The Resistance*.

35    seven to death: Cobb, *The Resistance*.

35    six more died in concentration camps: See http://www.vallee-de-l-aisne .com/site/428/rueduquotreacuteseauveacuteriteacutefrancaisequot .html.

35    The Nazi agents who organized the Soissons raid: I saw this myself near the Soissons cathedral.

35    So their plan was foolish: Conversations with Emmanuel de Pennart.

35    400 million francs a day: Jackson, *France: The Dark Years*.

35    Soon, it was enough money to actually buy: Kim Oosternlinck and Eugene N. White, "How Occupied France Financed Its Own Exploitation in World War II, or Squeezing the Capital Markets for the Nazis," *National Bureau of Economic Research* (April 2006).

35    Oil grew scarce: Cobb, *The Resistance*.

35    biking everywhere: La Rochefoucauld recording and La Rochefoucauld family DVD.

35    imposed rations: Jackson, *France: The Dark Years*.

35    every bakery and grocery store: La Rochefoucauld recording.

35    a shifting curfew: Ronald C. Rosbottom, *When Paris Went Dark: The City of Light Under German Occupation, 1940–1944* (New York: Little Brown, 2014).

35    as early as 9 p.m.: Nicholas Foulkes, *Bernard Buffet: The Invention of the Modern Mega-Artist* (New York: Random House, 2016).

35    the patrolling secret police's boots: Sartre, *The Aftermath of War*.

36    assassinated two high-ranking Nazi officers: Robert Gildea, *Marianne in Chains: Daily Life in the Heart of France During the German Occupation* (New York: Picador, 2004).

36    "sown consternation everywhere": Ibid.

36    "Do not allow any more harm to be done": Ibid.

36    thirteen thousand Jews: The Vel' d'Hiv Roundup. See Jackson, *France: The Dark Years*.

36    overripened vegetables: Ibid., and Gildea, *Marianne in Chains*.

36    "bandits" or even "terrorists": Gildea, *Marianne in Chains*.

36    a show, *Répétez-le*: Sheila Fitzpatrick and Robert Gellately, eds., *Accusatory Practices: Denunciation in Modern European History, 1789–1989* (Chicago: University of Chicago Press, 1997).

36    three million denunciatory letters: Ibid.

37    "No more ingenious device": Henry Charles Lea, *A History of the Inquisition in Spain,* Vol. II (New York: Macmillan, 1922).

37    "I remember silence, silence, silence": Conversations with Yolaine de Schonen.

37    "Every time I met with friends": La Rochefoucauld recording.

37    for another destination: Conversations with Yolaine de Schonen.

37    "that Germans should be killed": Cobb, *The Resistance*.

37    Soissons postman: La Rochefoucauld recording and *La Liberté,* as well as the La Rochefoucauld family DVD.

## CHAPTER 4

39    He went first to Paris: La Rochefoucauld, *La Liberté*.

39    "Come back in fifteen days": Ibid.

39   head south, to Spain: Ibid.

39   But this in turn only raised more questions: La Rochefoucauld recording and La Rochefoucauld family DVD.

39   secretly worked for the Resistance: La Rochefoucauld, *La Liberté*.

40   needed two aliases: Robert de La Rochefoucauld military records.

40   "a nom de guerre I'd found who knows where": La Rochefoucauld, *La Liberté*.

40   The photo in his false identity card: Robert de La Rochefoucauld military records.

40   "the gray mice": Marie-Madeleine Fourcade, *Noah's Ark: A Memoir of Struggle and Resistance*, trans. Kenneth Morgan (New York: Ballantine Books, 1974).

40   epicenter of German collaboration: La Rochefoucauld recording and *La Liberté*.

40   "hostile": La Rochefoucauld, *La Liberté*.

40   "to be seen as little as possible": Ibid.

41   "I was wary of everything and everyone": Ibid.

41   "extremely nice": La Rochefoucauld recording.

41   "soak up this code of conduct": La Rochefoucauld, *La Liberté*.

41   "very pleasant": La Rochefoucauld recording.

42   stayed that night: Ibid. and La Rochefoucauld, *La Liberté*.

42   Germany produced annually: Cobb, *The Resistance*.

42   "of man or horse": Ibid.

42   That was what the man from Perpignan had: La Rochefoucauld recording, *La Liberté*.

42   They set off through the woods: La Rochefoucauld, *La Liberté*.

42   not particularly clean: Ibid.

43   called the VIC line: M. R. D. Foot, *SOE in France: An Account of the Work of the British Special Operations Executive in France, 1940–1944*, Government Official History Series (London, Routledge, Second Edition, 2004).

43   wasn't as demanding as in the high mountains: Ibid.

43   "honeycombed with German agents": Ibid.

43    childhood with English nannies suddenly came in handy: La Roche-
      foucauld recording and *La Liberté*.

43    seven left for Spain: Ibid.

43    "The hike was particularly difficult": La Rochefoucauld, *La Liberté*.

43    often misjudged distances: Hugh Dormer, *Hugh Dormer's Diaries*
      (Whitefish, MT: Kessinger Publishing, 2010).

44    Germans posted observation decks: La Rochefoucauld, *La Liberté*.

44    "Every two hours, we took a quarter of an hour's rest": Ibid.

44    "just as hard, and increasingly dangerous": La Rochefoucauld re-
      cording.

44    they redirected themselves: Ibid. and *La Liberté*.

44    Perthus Pass: La Rochefoucauld, *La Liberté*.

44    "The road is clear!": La Rochefoucauld recording.

44    Robert and the airmen laughed: Ibid. and *La Liberté*.

44    smugglers out after dawn risked imprisonment: La Rochefoucauld re-
      cording.

44    "This will take you to a town": Ibid.

45    a plan to get to the village: La Rochefoucauld, *La Liberté*.

45    "We looked more like highway robbers": Ibid.

45    two Spanish agents approached them: Ibid.

45    one of them spoke French: La Rochefoucauld recording, *La Liberté*,
      and La Rochefoucauld family DVD.

45    December 17, 1942: Archivo General Militar de Guadalajara, in Gua-
      dalajara, Spain. This is an important file because Robert's military
      records list *Renaud* as one of the pseudonyms he used during the war,
      and Robert himself said he often used portions of his real name with
      a pseudonym. Robert's middle name is Guy Jean. This doesn't prove
      conclusively that Robert de la Rochefoucauld was the Robert Jean Re-
      naud booked in 1942, but La Rochefoucauld's telling of the episode
      coincides with the Spanish records. Furthermore, Spanish scholars
      contend that many Frenchmen who fled their country and ended up
      at Miranda de Ebro used aliases—and Canadian aliases at that. (For
      instance, Matilde Eiroa, a lecturer in the School of Humanities and

Communication at the University Carlos III de Madrid, stated in her 2014 academic paper, "Uncertain Fates: Allied Soldiers at the Miranda de Ebro Concentration Camp," published in *The Historian,* that getting a French exit visa was "extremely difficult" in the Vichy regime, and that between thirty and forty thousand people hiked through the Pyrenees to get to Spain, and arrived under false names more times than not.)

46    Built in 1937: Matilde Eiroa, "Uncertain Fates: Allied Soldiers at the Miranda de Ebro Concentration Camp," *The Historian* (March 2014), http://onlinelibrary.wiley.com/doi/10.1111/hisn.12026/abstract.

46    Its watchtowers, barbed-wired fences: Alfredo Gonzalez-Ruibal, *The Archaeology of Internment,* Adrian Meyers and Gabriel Moshenka, editors. (New York, Springer Publishing, 2011).

46    Paul Winzer: Eiroa, "Uncertain Fates."

46    overly populated spaces: Gonzalez-Ruibal, *The Archaeology of Internment.*

46    held 18,406 prisoners: Ibid.

46    an estimated ten thousand people: David D. Nicolson, *Aristide: Warlord of the Resistance* (London: Leo Cooper, 1994).

46    baffled both the Allied and Axis powers: Eiroa, "Uncertain Fates."

46    "subjects": Ibid.

47    in the same cell: La Rochefoucauld, *La Liberté.*

47    "windowless huts": Paloma Diaz-Mas, *Sephardim: The Jews from Spain* (Chicago: University of Chicago Press, 1992).

47    holding 3,500 by the end of 1942: Eiroa, "Uncertain Fates."

47    began a hunger strike: Ibid.

47    begging for release: La Rochefoucauld, *La Liberté.*

47    food was scarce: Ibid.

47    airy barracks: Gonzalez-Ruibal, *Archaeology of Internment.*

47    to kill off the lice: E. Martinez Alonzo, *Adventures of a Doctor* (London: Robert Hale, 1962).

47    "mirandite": L. A. Héraut, "Miranda de Ebro: Medical Condition of the Concentration Camp in 1943, *Histoire des Sciences Médicales* (April–June 2008).

47   "necessitated a good deal of courage": George Langelaan, *Knights of the Floating Silk* (London: Anchor Press, 1959).

47   *Alerta!*: Nicolson, *Aristide*.

47   miniature grandstand: Langelaan, *Knights*. The rest of the paragraph is informed by this book.

48   trucks from the British embassy: Ibid.

48   Ambassador Hoare had a keen interest: Samuel Hoare, *Ambassador on a Special Mission* (London: Collins, 1946). Also: National Archives, London, in my research surrounding Hoare.

48   Allies increased their air missions: Nicolson, *The Resistance,* and William Mackenzie, *The Secret History of SOE* (London: St. Ermin's Press, 2000).

48   a man from His Majesty's Government: La Rochefoucauld recording and *La Liberté*.

48   Major Haslam: Madeleine Duke, *No Passport: The Story of Jan Felix* (London: Evan Brothers, 1957).

48   "for all you've done": La Rochefoucauld recording and *La Liberté*.

48   "grossly embellished": Ibid.

49   Hoare was aging and short: Ralph James Adams, *Oxford Dictionary of National Biography* (Oxford: Oxford University Press, 2004–16).

49   ambitious and competitive: Ibid.

49   Prime Minister Neville Chamberlain's cabinet: Hoare, *Ambassador*.

49   seemed to wear this rejection: J. A. Cross, *Sir Samuel Hoare: A Political Biography* (London: Jonathan Cape, 1977).

49   had done his job with aplomb: Eiroa, "Uncertain Fates."

49   his ease with the French language: Michael Alpert, *A New International History of the Spanish Civil War* (Basingstoke, UK: Palgrave Macmillan, 1994).

50   "perfect French": La Rochefoucauld, *La Liberté*.

50   originated a plot to kill Rasputin: See http://spartacus-educational.com/PRhoareS.htm, a great, fully sourced online biography of Hoare.

50   "that are beyond reproach": La Rochefoucauld recording and *La Liberté*.

## CHAPTER 5

53  London Reception Center: The website of the Royal Victoria Patriotic Building has a great page on its history: http://www.rvpb.com/history.htm.

53  to flush out German spies: Douglas Porch, *The French Secret Services: A History of French Intelligence from the Dreyfus Affair to the Gulf War* (London: Macmillan, 2003).

53  March 1943: National Archives, London.

53  stretched from one day to two: La Rochefoucauld recording and *La Liberté*.

54  good cop, bad cop: There are many sources on British interrogation techniques, but I found the fullest and most riveting account to be Andrew Miller's. He's a British historical novelist who keeps a website that brims with real-world primary sources on British interrogation during World War II: http://www.andrewwilliams.tv/books/the-interrogator/interrogation-tips/.

54  washing ashore in England: See Porch, *The French Secret Services*.

54  a school for orphans: Royal Patriotic Building website.

54  La Rochefoucauld was there for eight days: La Rochefoucauld, *La Liberté*.

54  like old friends: Ibid.

54  He had a boy's way: Photos from Eric Piquet-Wicks's SOE file in the National Archives, London.

54  all seafaring wanderlust: Piquet-Wicks's personality comes out in the book he wrote after the war. Eric Piquet-Wicks, *Four in the Shadows: A True Story of Espionage in Occupied France* (Peterborough, UK: Jarrold, 1957).

54  He wore a suit well: Photos in Piquet-Wicks's file, National Archives, London.

54  free of the paranoid thoughts: La Rochefoucauld recording.

55  Piquet-Wicks's mother: Picquet-Wicks, *Four in the Shadows*.

55  Borax: Ibid.

55    it had a report: Picket-Wicks's SOE file.

55    "in view of his indiscreet behavior": Ibid.

56    didn't have "enough guts to be an adventurer": Ibid.

56    "in a war of . . . consequence": Piquet-Wicks, *Four in the Shadows*. The following discussion is also informed by this book.

57    he would like Robert to work: La Richefoucauld recording.

57    "surprisingly close to each": Piquet-Wicks, *Four in the Shadows*.

57    liked the man with the goofy smile: La Rochefoucauld recording and *La Liberté*. (Though, in the memoir, Robert misremembers first meeting Piquet-Wicks in Spain.)

57    "If you get to meet him": La Rochefoucauld recording.

58    No. 4 Carlton Gardens: I saw this myself on my trip to London.

58    designed by architect John Nash: The history of the property and surrounding area can be found in London City Council, *Survey of London, Volume 20, St. Martin-in-the-Fields, Part III, Trafalgar Square and Neighborhood* (London: London City Council, 1940), 77–87, http://www.british -history.ac.uk/survey-london/vol20/pt3/pp77–87.

58    many a proper Londoner: "Historical Notes," Ibid.; also Charles Hibbert et al., *The London Encyclopedia* (London: Pan Macmillan, 2011).

58    The German embassy occupied 7–9 Carlton Gardens: Rob Humphreys and Judith Bamber, *The Rough Guide to London* (London: Rough Guides, 2003).

58    a bomb fell on No. 2 Carlton House Terrace: The Royal College of Pathologists is nearby, and its online official history notes what happened during the war: https://www.rcpath.org/Resources/RCPath /Migrated%20Resources/Documents/Other/2chtleafletweb.pdf.

58    A French soldier: Photos courtesy of *Établissement de Communication et de Production Audiovisuelle de la Défense*.

58    "which may have possibly facilitated things": La Rochefoucauld, *La Liberté*.

58    all dark wood and high Gothic ceilings: François Charles-Roux, "The Free French in London: Memories of Wartime London: 1942–1943," http://www.christopherlong.co.uk/pub/charles-roux.html. Charles-Roux was de Gaulle's aide-de-camp.

58  heart thrummed in his chest: La Rochefoucauld recording and *La Liberté*.

59  His presence filled the room: Ibid.

59  map of the world: For photos of de Gaulle's office see http://www
    .christopherlong.co.uk/pub/charles-roux.html.

59  "a head like a pineapple": Jackson, *France: The Dark Years*.

59  "never quite at ease": Gregor Dallas, *1945: The War That Never Ended*
    (New Haven: Yale University Press, 2006).

59  from 9 a.m. until evening: Charles-Roux's recollections, http://www
    .christopherlong.co.uk/pub/charles-roux.html.

59  a kind of moral absolutism: Dallas, *1945*.

60  "You are not France": Jackson, *France: The Dark Years*.

60  bully pulpit of the BBC: Ibid.

60  his initial Council of Defense: P. M. H. Bell, *A Certain Eventuality: Britain and the Fall of France* (London: Saxon House, 1974).

60  "authoritarian prelate": Jackson, *France: The Dark Years*.

60  "never on this scale": Ibid.

60  "simple" but also "cordial": La Rochefoucauld, *La Liberté*.

60  "To each his own de Gaulle": Dallas, *1945*.

60  "de Gaulle first complimented me": La Rochefoucauld, *La Liberté*.

61  "to prove to French eyes": Foot, *SOE in France*.

61  "the man of destiny": Ibid.

61  "gone off his head": Jackson, *De Gaulle*.

61  "monster": Jackson, *France: The Dark Years*.

61  kept "in chains": Ibid.

61  all of three hours' notice: Ibid.

61  "rival organization": Piquet-Wicks, *Four in the Shadows*.

61  Loyalties blurred: Ibid.

62  "allied with the Devil": La Rochefoucauld, *La Liberté*.

## CHAPTER 6

63  spring of 1938: Mackenzie, *The Secret History of SOE*.

63  Political Warfare Executive: Foot, *SOE in France*.

63    Section D: Ibid.

63    MI(R): Ibid.

63    "until that time unheard of": Ibid.

63    equally novel and just as fascinating: Ibid.

63    For as long as there had been war: Max Boot, *Invisible Armies: An Epic History of Guerrilla Warfare from Ancient Times to the Present* (New York: W. W. Norton, 2013). The rest of this paragraph is informed by *Invisible Armies*.

64    first counterinsurgency manual emerged in 600 AD: Ibid.

64    T. E. Lawrence's *The Seven Pillars of Wisdom*: Knoxville, TN: Wordsworth Classics, 1997.

64    "widespread revolt in [Germany's] conquered territories": Foot, *SOE in France*.

64    Hugh Dalton wrote a letter: Ibid.

65    a "most secret paper": Ibid.

65    SOE's founding charter: Ibid., and Mackenzie, *The Secret History of SOE*.

65    nothing like SOE: Boot, *Invisible Armies*.

66    often of his own devising: Ibid.

66    in 1895: David Stafford, *Churchill and Secret Service* (London: Thistle Publishing, 2013).

66    "everywhere and nowhere": Ibid.

66    Malakand Pass: Winston Churchill, *The Story of the Malakand Field Force* (London: Dover Publications, 1898).

66    gone to cover the Boer War: Stafford, *Churchill & Secret Service*, Ibid. The rest of the paragraph is informed by this book.

67    "And now, set Europe ablaze": Foot, *SOE in France*.

67    visiting SOE agents: Stafford, *Churchill & Secret Service*.

67    "order paper": Foot, *SOE in France*, Ibid.

67    Parliament had no control: Ibid.

67    "eccentrically English organization": Ibid.

67    the Ministry of Economic Warfare: Ibid.

68    bungled Section D mission: Stafford, *Churchill & Secret Service*.

68    which met twice: Ibid.

68   "SOE's in the shit": Ibid.

68   "My bombing offensive": Foot, *SOE in France.*

69   "funny operations": Stafford, *Churchill & Secret Service.*

## CHAPTER 7

71   his youthful arrogance: La Rochefoucauld recording.

71   he had a sense: La Rochefoucauld, *La Liberté.*

71   Reinhard Heydrich: Delarue, *The Gestapo,* and the Holocaust Research
     Project,   http://www.holocaustresearchproject.org/nazioccupation
     /heydrichkilling.htm. Also, for the assassination attempt: Czech Minis-
     try of Defense paper, "Assassination: Operation Anthropoid: 1941–1942,"
     http://www.army.cz/images/id_7001_8000/7419/assassination-en.pdf;
     Mario R. Dederichs, *Heydrich: The Face of Evil* (Philadelphia: Casemate
     Publishers, 2009).

71   Norsk Hydro: Thomas Gallagher, *Assault in Norway: Sabotaging the Nazi
     Nuclear Program* (Guillford, CT: Globe Pequot, 2002); Knut Haukeid,
     *Skis Against the Atom: The Exciting, First Hand Account of Heroism and
     Daring Sabotage During the Nazi Occupation of Norway* (Minot, ND:
     North American Heritage Press, 1989); and Paul Kendall, "A New Mis-
     sion for the Hero of Telemark," *The [London] Telegraph* (May 2, 2010),
     http://www.telegraph.co.uk/news/7664351/A-new-mission-for-the
     -hero-of-Telemark.html.

71   he said he wanted to join: La Rochefoucauld recording and *La Liberté.*

71   "from pimps to princesses": Foot, *SOE in France.*

72   France required six sections: Ibid.

72   were told it didn't exist: Ibid.

72   1 Dorset Square: Piquet-Wick, *Four in the Shadows.*

73   Even Piquet-Wicks had a hard time: Ibid.

73   "woefully small": Ibid.

73   convinced Churchill to provide: Stafford, *Churchill & Secret Service.*

73   four times the number: Foot, *SOE in France.*

73   Jean Moulin: Piquet-Wicks, *Four in the Shadows.*

73    Piquet-Wicks had developed tuberculosis: Piquet-Wicks's SOE files.

73    the "action" division: La Rochefoucauld, *La Liberté.* See also Foot, *SOE in France,* for more information on the action division and its close ties with the Free French.

## CHAPTER 8

75    The first thing they did: La Rouchefoucauld, *La Liberté.* One thing to note: SOE training was an ad hoc affair. "There was no book," wrote F Section boss Maurice Buckmaster in his memoir *They Fought Alone* (London: Biteback Publishing, 2014). But there were general phases or courses from which a trainee graduated, and on this Bernie Ross, "Training SOE Saboteurs in World War II," BBC (February 17, 2011), is a good guide. It pulls insights from a dozen books concerning SOE affairs, and can be found online at http://www.bbc.co.uk/history /worldwars/wwtwo/soe_training_01.shtml. Also see: Denis Ringden, introduction, *How to Be a Spy: The World War II SOE Training Manual* (New York: Crown, 2001). I organized the chronology of events in chapter 8 based on numerous accounts of people who either oversaw the training or participated in it directly. When events synced up—when a lieutenant colonel said *X* training regimen happened at the same time in the process as trainee *Y* said it did—I felt comfortable saying *X* training regimen happened, and then *Y* happened. Complicating matters were the specialty schools. SOE had a lot of them, and trainees would be sent there in fairly short order after arriving, which meant that the making of an agent was often as idiosyncratic as the agent himself. So in the end, I let Robert's memories guide the chapter. In a couple of spots, he seems to have confused the chronology of events. But on the whole, the order in which he said things happened aligned with the experiences of other agents, to the extent that such an experience can be generalized for the reader.

75    psychological and character assessments: Ringden, *How to Be a Spy.*

75    with full rucksacks: La Rochefoucauld recording.

75   Inchmery, near Southampton: Foot, *SOE in France*.

75   for security purposes: Ibid.

75   Manchester: La Rochefoucauld, *La Liberté*.

75   kept many secrets: Nicolson, *Aristide*; Foot, *SOE in France*; and Piquet-Wicks, *Four in the Shadows*.

75   Basic training lasted around three weeks: Accounts vary on the length. Foot, *SOE in France,* says basic training lasted two to four weeks, for example.

75   wild and stunning western coast: Ringden, *How to Be a Spy*.

75   "secure from inquisitive eyes": Foot, *SOE in France*.

76   "a most depressing place": Ibid.

76   the roughly thirty prospective agents: La Rochefoucauld recording.

76   how to jump from a train: Nicolson, *Aristide*.

76   how to crawl on their bellies: La Rochefoucauld, *La Liberté*.

76   to try escaping without getting caught: Foot, *SOE in France*, La Rochefoucauld recording and *La Liberté*.

76   learned to sabotage almost anything: Bernard O'Connor, *SOE Group B Sabotage Training Handbook* (Bernard O'Connor, 2014).

76   the safest explosives to practice on: Foot, *SOE in France*.

76   don of industrial sabotage: Ibid., and Ringden, *How to Be a Spy*.

76   Tall, somber, even forbidden-looking: Ringden, *How to Be a Spy*.

76   gained a supple understanding: O'Connor, *SOE Group B*, and Mark Seaman, *Special Operations Executive: A New Instrument of War* (London: Routledge, 2013).

77   "look at a factory with quite new eyes": Ringden, *How to Be a Spy*.

77   Rheam had personally instructed: Gary Kamiya, *Shadow Knights: The Secret War Against Hitler* (New York: Simon & Schuster, 2011).

77   stuffed rat carcasses: Ringden. *How to Be a Spy*.

77   left many workers afraid: Ibid.

77   adopted the teachings: W. E. Fairbairn and E. A. Sykes, *Shooting to Live* (Boulder, CO: Paladin-Press, 2013).

77   possibly the most dangerous: Frederic Wakeman, *Policing Shanghai: 1927–1937* (Berkeley: University of California Press, 1996).

77   French savate: On the styles of fighting taught, see Phil Matthews, "W. E. Fairbairn: The Legendary Instructor," *CQB Services* (August 6, 2015), http://combatives.forumotion.com/t3148-w-e-fairbairn-the -legendary-instructor-by-phil-matthews.

77   the best marksman anyone had seen: Ibid., and Fairbairn and Sykes, *Shooting to Live.*

77   a gun in one hand and a knife in the other: This anecdote comes from the SOE operative Henry Hall, "Personal Memories," BBC (January 2006), http://www.bbc.co.uk/history/ww2peopleswar/stories/70/a4 543670.shtml.

78   six hundred street fights: W. E. Fairbairn, *Scientific Self-Defense* (Boulder, CO: Paladin Press, 1981).

78   "Now, put your thumb in his eye": Hall, "Personal Memories."

78   retired bishop: Matthews, "W. E. Fairbairn: The Legendary Instructor."

78   webbing belt: Hall, "Personal Memories."

78   revised the course syllabus: Matthews, "W. E. Fairbairn: The Legendary Instructor."

78   special ops training ground in Canada: Ibid.

78   firing from the navel: Hall, "Personal Memories."

78   a quick shot was better: Fairbairn and Sykes, *Shooting to Live.*

78   how to kill up to four people: Phil Matthews, foreword, *Silent Killing: Nazi Counters to Fairbairn-Sykes Techniques* (Boulder, CO: Paladin Press, 2008).

78   "house of horrors": Matthews, "W. E. Fairbairn: The Legendary Instructor."

78   developed a knife: Ibid.

79   reach his organs: Richard Dunlop, *Behind Japanese Lines: With the OSS in Burma* (New York: Skyhorse Publishing, 2014).

79   began at the testicles: "Gutter Fighting," DVD, archives of the OSS. Found online at https://www.youtube.com/watch?v=feRX5rnS-i4.

79   a wooden chair: W. E. Fairbairn, *All-In Fighting.* (Uckfield, UK: Naval and Military Press, 2009).

79   "gutter fighting": Fairbairn created a system of fighting called Defendu based on the principle of gutter fighting. Fairbairn, *Scientific Self-Defense.*

79   come close to killing him: The examples in this paragraph come from Fairbairn, *All-In Fighting.*

80   Punching the enemy in the Adam's apple: The examples cited in this paragraph come from Fairbairn, *All-In Fighting,* and Matthews, *Silent Killing.*

80   "Your aim is to kill your opponent": Matthews, *Silent Killing.*

80   "The majority of these methods": Fairbairn, *All-In Fighting.*

80   which the Nazis called "savage": Matthews, *Silent Killing.*

80   some scholars contend: Ibid., and C. N. Truman, "The Commando Order," *The History Learning Site* (May 25, 2015), http://www.history learningsite.co.uk/world-war-two/special-forces-in-world-war-two /the-commando-order/.

80   captured Allied special operatives: Ibid.

80   "From captured orders": Eric Lee, *Operation Basalt: The British Raid on Sark and Hitler's Commando Order.* (Stroud, UK: The History Press, 2016).

80   violation of the Geneva Convention: Truman, "The Commando Order."

80   "In future, all terror and sabotage troops": Foot, *SOE in France.*

81   "I think the great advantage": Hall, "Personal Memories."

81   "superiority that few men ever acquire": Langelaan, *Knights of the Floating Silk.*

81   "The English were great coaches": La Rochefoucauld recording.

81   parachute drops: Ibid. and La Rochefoucauld, *La Liberté.*

81   "the bags thudded onto the ground": Foot, *SOE in France.*

82   A hot-air balloon: La Rochefoucauld, *La Liberté.*

82   "terrifying vertigo": Ibid.

82   "felt more and more afraid": Conversations with Astrid Gaignault.

82   broke his wrist: Robert de La Rochefoucauld's military files.

82   six fatalities from parachute drops: Foot, *SOE in France.*

82   were literally run by convicts: Ibid.

82   "They knew how to open the safes": La Rochefoucauld recording.

83   worked to catch them: La Rochefoucauld, *La Liberté*.

83   "like athletes in training": Ibid.

83   did not punish La Rochefoucauld: La Rochefoucauld, *La Liberté*.

83   "These rehearsals were grim affairs": Maurice Buckmaster, *They Fought Alone: The True Story of SOE's Agents in Wartime France* (London: Biteback Publishing, 2014).

83   "When you become angry": La Rouchefoucauld recording.

83   "all the intricate planning": Piquet-Wicks, *Four in the Shadows*.

84   "only four or five finally could be entrusted": Ibid.

84   "He that has a secret": Foot, *SOE in France*.

84   final redemption of the cyanide pill: Fredric Boyce et al., *SOE: The Scientific Secrets* (Stroud, UK: The History Press, 2011).

84   one of seven to become a saboteur: La Rochefoucauld, *La Liberté*.

## CHAPTER 9

85   one summer night in 1943: La Rochefoucauld, *La Liberté*, and Yonne department military records, Ministry of Defense, Paris.

85   French clothes, a French watch: La Rochefoucauld, *La Liberté*.

85   the colonel counted on seeing him: Ibid.

85   but quietly shook with fear: This paragraph is informed by ibid., and La Rochefoucauld recording.

86   Frenchmen who actively participated: James A. Warren, "The Real Story of the French Reisistance," *The Daily Beast* (December 10, 2015), and Cobb, *The Resistance*. This is "active" resistance. Some scholars believe that as much as 10 percent of the populace were "passive," meaning they contributed to underground newspapers or engaged in the misdirection, misinformation, and lies that protected Resistance fighters.

86   only six months in France: Fourcade, *Noah's Ark*.

86   650,000 Frenchmen: Jackson, *France: The Dark Years*.

86   42 percent of Germany's transport planes: Ibid.

86   "It was everywhere by June": Cobb, *The Resistance*.

87  "Sabotage their plans and hate their leaders": Ibid.

87  3,800 sabotages: Jackson, *France: The Dark Years*.

87  "spiritual resistance": Ibid.

87  "Kill the German to purify our territory": Cobb, *The Resistance*.

87  five million denunciatory letters: Fitzpatrick and Gellately, eds., *Accusatory Practices*.

87  "permanent, exhaustive, omnipresent surveillance": Ibid.

87  the Milice men were worse: Jackson, *France: The Dark Years*; Rod Kedward, "Life in Occupied France, 1940–1944: An Overview of Attitudes, Experiences and Choices;" and White Paper, *Post War Europe: Refugees, Exile and Resettlement, 1945 to 1950*, http://webfeetguides.com/pdf/whitepapers/gdc/LifeInOccupiedFrance.pdf. These sources inform the rest of the paragraph.

88  twenty-three different steps: Cobb, *The Resistance*.

88  S-Phone: Nicolson's *Aristide*.

88  La Rochefoucauld moved to its edge: La Rochefoucauld recording and *La Liberté*.

88  road near the woods and headed out: Ibid.

88  milky-skinned mother of two: Marie-Madeleine Fourcade, *Noah's Ark*. The rest of this paragraph is informed by the book.

89  blocked the light of the stars: In *La Liberté,* and in his recording, La Rochefoucauld named the towns in the Yonne where he fought. I visited those towns myself, with the aid of a local historian, Claude Delasselle, who showed me the Resistance hideouts. I also consulted Alliance records in the Yonne department and in Paris. All of these sources and experiences informed this chapter.

89  Quarré-les-Tombes: La Rochefoucauld, *La Liberté*.

89  tombstones near its church: Conversations with Claude Delasselle.

89  cigarettes and chocolates: La Rochefoucauld, *La Liberté*.

89  Father Bernard Ferrand: The descriptions of Ferrand come from Claude Delasselle et al., *Un Département dans la Guerre 1939–1945: Occupation, Collaboration, et Résistance dans l'Yonne*. (France, Tirésias, coll. Ces Oubliés de l'Histoire, 2007).

89   from other Resistance groups: Robert mentions fighting with the Alliance on his recording. However, he also makes plain in the recordings left behind, and in *La Liberté,* that he worked with many Resistance groups in the Yonne. His military records reflect this. One is Groupe Roche, which seems to have been a subset of another group, with him as the leader, if the *Roche* in the title is any indication. It is an inexact science, figuring out who led what group and where each was stationed, because keeping a paper trail during the Occupation meant inviting death from the Nazis or collaborating Frenchmen. So Robert's records, like all records from that period, were compiled after the war, from memory.

90   often lacked the technical skills: La Rochefoucauld recording and *La Liberté.*

90   "became a nightmare": Fourcade, *Noah's Ark.*

90   the apartment with the wireless transmitter: Foot, *SOE in France.*

90   "the first to sacrifice their lives": Fourcade, *Noah's Ark.*

90   southwest France called Scientist: Nicolson, *Aristide,* and Paddy Ashdown, *A Brilliant Little Operation: The Cockleshell Heroes and the Most Courageous Raid of WW2* (London: Arum Press, 2013).

90   Prosper, which crumbled: Foot, *SOE in France.*

90   June 1943: Ibid.

90   Klaus Barbie: Ibid, and Piquet-Wicks, *Four in the Shadows.*

90   "I was deeply afraid": Fourcade, *Noah's Ark.*

90   "total stagnation": Jackson, *France: The Dark Years.*

91   leading forty men: La Rochefoucauld recording. His military records also describe what he did in the Yonne.

91   Pius VII: La Rochefoucauld, *La Liberté.*

91   code-name Henri: Robert de La Rochefoucauld's military records.

91   July 22: As the language suggests, this paragraph is a triangulation of La Rochefoucauld's memories, as recorded on the CD and in his memoir; Claude Delasselle's histories, as recounted in his book, *Un Département dans la Guerre,* and in the journal he edits, *Yonne Memoire,* specifically the May 2007 issue, found online at http://www.arory

.com/fileadmin/images/Yonne_memoire/bulletin_18_n.b.pdf; and various military records of Resistance groups in the Yonne, Ministry of Defense, Paris. This is one of those spots where specific dates—and the actions taken on those dates—are tough to pin down, because everything relies on memories recalled years after the fact.

91    "personal messages": Cobb, *The Resistance*.

91    "The collaborators already have sad faces": Delasselle, *Un Département*.

91    to the moonlit horizon: I saw this myself.

92    Pierre Argoud: La Rochefoucauld's recording; Delasselle, *Un Département*; and military records.

92    "Everything we needed": La Rochefoucauld, *La Liberté*.

92    looked at Robert in awe: Ibid., and La Rochefoucauld recording.

92    "our main mission": La Rochefoucauld, *La Liberté*.

92    Prémery: Conversations with Claude Delasselle. La Rochefoucauld thought this sabotage took place in Avallon, and though there were sabotages in that town, the sort he described in his memoir, and in the time he said it took place, occurred in Prémery.

93    Groupe Roche: Robert de La Rochefoucauld's military records.

93    "Chance is the most extraordinary thing": La Rochefoucauld recording.

93    "Everything went perfectly well": La Rochefoucauld, *La Liberté*.

93    simply because they felt like it: Ibid. Though I should note that Delasselle does not describe any of La Rochefoucauld's sabotages in his historical works. That said, Delasselle, in *Un Département*, does note that more than sixty sabotages occurred in September 1943 in the Yonne. He doesn't list each one in the book.

93    wrote in September 1943: The words of the *sous-prefect* were dug up and published on the historical website http://www.lesormes89.fr/resistance.html.

94    reported nineteen injuries and twenty-seven deaths: Delasselle, *Un Département*.

94    "special brigade": Ibid.

94    Kurt Merck: Fourcade, *Noah's Ark*.

94    "Captain Kaiser": I found this nickname in Central Intelligence Agency archives, a working paper titled "An SD agent of Rare Importance." You can read the declassified account online at https://www .cia.gov/library/readingroom/docs/CIA%20AND%20NAZI%20 WARCRIM.%20AND%20COL.%20CHAP.%201–10,%20DRAFT%20 WORKING%20PAPER_0003.pdf.

94    who favored a silk scarf: This comes from more declassified CIA reports on Merck. You can read this one online at https://www.cia .gov/library/readingroom/docs/NEBEL,%20LUDWIG%20%20%20 VOL.%202_0111.pdf.

94    J. P. Lien: Fourcade, *Noah's Ark,* and Delasselle, *Yonne Memoire,* November 2003, online at http://arory.com/fileadmin/images/Yonne_memoire /bulletin_11.pdf.

94    Merck asked Lien to infiltrate: Fourcade, *Noah's Ark.*

94    Operation Gibet: Delasselle, *Yonne Memoire.*

95    the code-name Lanky: Fourcade, *Noah's Ark.*

95    "Do not try to contact any member": Ibid.

95    "Warning," Hedgehog said: Ibid.

96    In Sens, in the north: Delasselle, *Un Département* and *Yonne Memoire.* The following paragraphs are informed by these sources.

96    "Treachery": Fourcade, *Noah's Ark.*

96    private banquet in Dijon: Ibid.

96    "the Noah's Ark that we have been fighting": Ibid.

96    Groupe Roche was dismantled: La Rochefoucauld recording and military records.

97    gave up twenty: Delasselle, *Un Département.*

97    Why help these irregular fighters?: Foot, *SOE in France,* and Stafford, *Churchill & Secret Service.*

97    327 parachute drops: Mackenzie, *The Secret History of SOE.*

97    is a cold place to spend a winter: Conversations with Claude Delasselle. I was there in July 2014 and had to buy sweaters because the high for the day never exceeded 60-degrees Fahrenheit.

97    food grew scarce: Ibid.

97  Germans or their French collaborators: Ibid.

97  acreage outside Quarré-les-Tombes: La Rochefoucauld, *La Liberté*.

97  moved his remaining stores of weapons: La Rochefoucauld recording.

98  He could not shake the suspicion: Ibid., and La Rochefoucauld, *La Liberté*.

98  "the terrible year": Fourcade, *Noah's Ark*.

98  phoning his mother: La Rochefoucauld recording.

98  strictly forbade its fighters: Foot, *SOE in France,* and Nicolson, *Aristide*.

98  he never said why he phoned: La Rochefoucauld recording.

98  thought she was going mad: Fourcade, *Noah's Ark*.

98  Who would help him?: La Rochefoucauld recording and *La Liberté*.

99  "Crushed, oh, I was utterly crushed!": Cobb, *The Resistance*.

99  fast asleep on a bed of hay: La Rochefoucauld, *La Liberté*.

99  Then the blows fell: Ibid., and La Rochefoucauld recording.

99  "They tied me up like a sausage": La Rochefoucauld, *La Liberté*.

99  "I was sleeping here": La Rochefoucauld recording, and La Rochefoucauld family DVD.

## CHAPTER 10

101  beyond the forest: This paragraph is informed by my drive from Quarré-les-Tombes to Auxerre, and also by looking at old maps of the department.

101  took his shoelaces: The practices of what happens when an inmate enters Auxerre are summed up in a memoir, Jean Léger, *Petite Chronique de l'Horreur Ordinaire* (Yonne: ANACR, 1998).

101  December 7, 1943: Auxerre prison records.

101  no first name entered the rolls: Ibid.

102  a simple woodcutter: Ibid.

102  toward the B wing: The idea that this wing was reserved for political prisoners comes from Delasselle's scholarship of the prison, and the conversations I had with him.

102  many political prisoners did: Léger, *Petite Chronique,* and Delasselle, *Yonne Memoire*, and my conversations with Claude Delasselle.

102 The prison was constructed in 1853: A website tracking the history of the French criminal justice system, brimming with government documents and official sources, helped me here. http://criminocorpus.hypotheses.org/7243.

102 Stalag 150: http://www.ajpn.org/internement-Frontstalag-150-Auxerre-1031.html.

102 desperate for human interaction: Conversations with Claude Delasselle and Léger, *Petite Chronique*.

102 inmates who had short prison stays: Auxerre prison records.

102 narrow metal walkways: Léger, *Petite Chronique*.

102 doors themselves were wooden: André Daprey, *Traqués Par La Gestapo et La Police de Vichy: 1943–1944 dans l'Yonne* (self-published, 2003).

103 a low buzz of noise: Léger, *Petite Chronique*.

103 Roughly two thousand people: Website tracking the prison's history, http://criminocorpus.hypotheses.org/7243.

103 held between two and three hundred people: Conversations with Claude Delasselle.

103 thirteen-by-six-foot: Léger, *Petite Chronique*.

103 slop bucket in between: Ibid.

103 He was an epileptic: La Rochefoucauld, *La Liberté*.

103 "then went to find a doctor": Ibid.

103 He was a forty-six-year-old: Delasselle, *Un Département*.

103 as if to center his disproportionate, rotund appearance: Surviving photos of Haas.

103 and had a mouth full of gold teeth: Jorge Semprun was a Spanish-born novelist and memoirist who was imprisoned in Auxerre. Jorge Semprun, *Literature or Life* (New York, Penguin, 1998).

104 nothing in his personal file: Delasselle, *Un Département*.

104 Major developments in the Yonne: Ibid.

104 he might torture inmates: Ibid.

104 This baffled Robert: La Rochefoucauld, *La Liberté*.

104 "And I am neither!": Ibid.

105 These interrogations: Fourcade, *Noah's Ark*.

105  as they jarred Robert's teeth loose: Conversations with Constance Guillaumin. La Rochefoucauld told her after the war that he'd lost his teeth in Auxerre.

105  held weekly interrogations: Fourcade, *Noah's Ark*.

105  that Robert said little: There is next to no discussion of the pain he endured in *La Liberté*, in his recording, or in the La Rochefoucauld family DVD.

105  "the brutal return of past despair": Semprun, *Literature or Life*.

105  psychiatric hospital: I saw this for myself, on my sightseeing tour with Delasselle.

105  The French prisoners liked to joke: Ibid.

105  to kneel on a bench: Delarue, *The Gestapo*.

105  his arms tied behind his back: Ibid.

105  "torn apart for good": Semprun, *Literature or Life*.

106  a dry, flashing, almost electric pain: Jorge Semprun, *Exercices de Survie* (Paris: Gallimard, 2012).

106  ballasted the bat with lead: Ibid.

106  often needed guards to support him: Léger, *Petite Chronique*.

106  the halls suddenly silent: Ibid.

106  Haas enjoyed waterboarding inmates: Semprun, *Exercices de Survie*.

106  "I was helpless": This description of waterboarding comes from Forest Yeo-Thomas, an SOE officer of considerable renown in John Grehan and Martin Mace, *Unearthing Churchill's Secret Army: The Official List of SOE Casualties and Their Stories* (Barnsley, UK: Pen and Sword, 2012).

106  filling his tub with trash and feces: Semprun, *Exercices de Survie*.

106  "And indeed it was": Ibid.

106  pulling out one nail, and then another: Ibid.

107  Pius VII: La Rochefoucauld, *La Liberté*.

107  turned up the voltage: Conversations with Claude Delasselle.

107  beneath which starving rats swam: Darpey, *Traqués Par La Gestapo et La Police de Vichy*.

107  "Those who are overwhelmed": Semprun, *Exercices de Survie*.

107  "To win this contest with my body": Semprun, *Literature or Life*.

107 to ridicule the wounded man: "La cellule de tortures de l'hôpital psychiatrique d'Auxerre conservée telle quelle par le Dr Scherrer," Auxerre TV, November, 9. This local station aired a special on the hospital and what happened there. http://www.auxerretv.com/content/index.php?post/2011/11/09/La-cellule-de-tortures-de-l-h%C3%B4pital-psychiatrique-d-Auxerre-conserv%C3%A9e-telle-quelle-par-le-Dr-Scherrer#.

107 little better when a prisoner returned to his cell: La Rochefoucauld, *La Liberté*.

107 drying blood and sickness never left the wing: Léger, *Petite Chronique*.

108 could receive small parcels: La Rochefoucauld, *La Liberté*.

108 a small, black-haired Frenchman: Photos of André Bouy, provided to me when I visited his daughter, Françoise Millot Bouy, in Auxerre.

108 Auxerre's Hôtel de la Fontaine: La Rochefoucauld, *La Liberté*.

108 bunch his round cheeks into a warm smile: Photos of Bouy.

108 sometimes chocolates: Conversations with Françoise Millot Bouy.

108 why this man sent him anything: La Rochefoucauld recording and *La Liberté*.

108 to walk on salt: Delarue, *The Gestapo*.

108 and then light each piece: Ibid.

108 Punches to the face and body: Ibid.

109 it had been dumb enough: La Rochefoucauld recording and *La Liberté*.

109 gouged out his eyes: Fourcade, *Noah's Ark*.

109 from the skin of a Jewish man: Jackson, *France: The Dark Years*.

109 "so very human surrender": Semprun, *Exercices de Survie*.

109 "Who would dare to judge them?": Delarue, *The Gestapo*.

109 He jumped out the window: Jackson, *France: The Dark Years*.

110 "It is my pleasure . . . to serve the king": Conversations with Nicolas de Schonen and Constance Guillaumin.

110 here in Auxerre: La Rochefoucauld recording.

110 smell of roses: Semprun, *Exercices de Suvrie*.

110 He had been imprisoned for four months: Auxerre prison records.

110  most inmates didn't make it half that long: Conversations with Claude Delasselle.

110  His bushy beard: Conversations with Yolaine de Schonen, who saw him not long after his imprisonment.

110  "home in the world": Semprun, *Exercices de Suvrie*.

111  "an experience of brotherhood": Ibid.

111  transformed in the nineteenth century: *L'Horloge* magazine, http://www.lhorloge.fr/magazine/article.php?article=12.

111  Dr. Karl Haas: Delasselle, *Un Département*.

111  A man named Ribain: Ibid.

111  In a matter of a few minutes: La Rochefoucauld recording.

111  He was to be executed: Conversations with Claude Delasselle.

112  No one spoke until the evening: Léger, *Petite Chronique*.

112  March 20 at 8 a.m.: Auxerre prison records, which also note that La Rochefoucauld escaped.

112  didn't understand a word: La Rochefoucauld recording and *La Liberté*.

## CHAPTER 11

113  Just before 8 a.m.: Conversations with Claude Delasselle. He said that many executions took place early in the morning.

113  told him to sit on a coffin lying there: La Rochefoucauld, *La Liberté*.

113  here came a second prisoner: Ibid., and La Rochefoucauld recording.

113  closed behind La Rochefoucauld: I saw these for myself when I was in France.

113  listen to the birdsong: Claude Delasselle led me on the route from the prison to the execution range.

113  brown stone chapel: I saw this for myself.

113  *Why give in to the Nazis now?*: La Rochefoucauld recording and *La Liberté*.

114  There were no handcuffs: Ibid.

114  "I'm getting out!": La Rochefoucauld, *La Liberté*.

114  "You're crazy. It won't work!": Ibid.

114 The sudden stop: Ibid., and La Rochefoucauld recording and family DVD. Most of this chapter depends on these three sources.

114 Avenue Victor Hugo: Claude Delasselle told me this was where the SD had its local headquarters.

115 and sped right past it: La Rochefoucauld recording and *La Liberté*, and La Rochefoucauld family DVD.

116 He checked himself: Ibid.

117 He was back where he started: Ibid.

## CHAPTER 12

119 He walked into Auxerre: La Rochefoucauld recording *La Liberté*, and La Rochefoucauld family DVD. This chapter is heavily influenced by these sources.

119 an agrarian and somewhat antiquated department: Delasselle, *Un Département*.

120 "It was hard to explain": LA Rochefoucauld recording.

120 "one cannot answer for his courage": Duc de La Rochefoucauld, *Maxims* (1871).

120 entirely in someone else's: La Rochefoucauld recording and *La Liberté*.

121 "Of course I'm a good Frenchman": La Rochefoucauld, *La Liberté*. The rest of the dialogue in this anecdote comes from the book as well.

121 She "served me a meal big enough to choke on": Ibid.

121 "for several months": Ibid.

122 Would he talk to the hotelier?: Ibid and La Rochefoucauld recording.

122 and gave him a hearty embrace: Ibid.

122 Bouy was thirty-eight: Conversations with Françoise Millot Bouy.

122 and that warm smile: Photos of Bouy.

122 the family business was effectively his: Conversations with Françoise Millot Bouy.

123 sixty in one month in 1943: Delasselle, *Un Département*.

123 safety in transparency: Conversations with Françoise Millot Bouy.

124 René Lallier: La Rochefoucauld recording.

124 Bouy had been given an *Ausweis*: La Rochefoucauld, *La Liberté*, and conversations with Françoise Millot Bouy.

125 They could only hide him well: La Rochefoucauld, *La Liberté*, and conversations with Françoise Millot Bouy.

126 "Here you are, sir—my *Ausweis*": La Rochefoucauld recording and *La Liberté*.

126 told La Rochefoucauld they'd arrived: Ibid., and La Rouchefoucauld family DVD.

## CHAPTER 13

129 1,300-calorie diet: Jackson, *France: The Dark Years*, set it at 1,327 calories.

129 forage for acorns: Ibid.

129 meals of the countryside: Gildea, *Marianne in Chains*.

129 "Paris was arguably the safest place in Europe": Allan Mitchell, *Nazi Paris: The History of an Occupation, 1940–1944* (Oxford: Bergahn Books, 2013).

129 which were in fact bombed in 1943: Ibid.

129 central and southern France: Ian Ousby, *Occupation: The Ordeal of France, 1940–1944* (New York: Cooper Square Press, 2000).

129 but it looked more like 1938 here: Rosbottom, *When Paris Went Dark*.

130 an aunt and uncle of his: La Rochefoucauld recording and *La Liberté*.

130 "Robert!" she said: Ibid.

130 "For me, it was a marvelous moment": La Rochefoucauld, *La Liberté*.

130 "Well, we're very lucky": Ibid.

130 POW camp: La Rochefoucauld's recording mentions how they discussed family matters. Olivier de La Rochefould's military records note when he left the POW camp.

130 more than four children: Jackson, *France: The Dark Years*.

131 of another age, another life: La Rochefoucauld recording.

131 larger than he expected: Ibid.

131 at a post office: La Rochefoucauld, *La Liberté*.

131    He decided to call a friend: Ibid.

131    the king of Naples in 1808: Joachim Murat biographical information comes from a couple of online sources, http://www.arcdetriomphe .info/officers/murat/; and http://www.angelfire.com/realm/gotha /gotha/murat.html. The notion that Salomé was a stunning young woman comes from Getty Images I viewed of her subsequent wedding: http://www.gettyimages.com/detail/news-photo/princess-salome -murat-the-daughter-of-achille-napoleon-news-photo/104418991.

131    rue de Constantine: La Rochefoucauld, *La Liberté*.

131    "vying with each other": Ibid.

132    "I owe it to France": Cobb, *The Resistance*.

132    "declare their wish to set the motherland free": Ibid, and this educational website, which has a fuller transcript of the speech, https:// prezi.com/0oghl89ehjnk/annex-five/.

132    "We could feel victory coming": La Rochefoucauld recording.

132    "national insurrection and the German defeat": Foot, *SOE in France*.

132    now sent some men as old as sixty to Germany: Gildea, *Marianne in Chains*.

132    "or went into hiding": La Rochefoucauld, *La Liberté*.

133    back to the family chateau in Villeneuve: Conversations with Nicolas and Yolaine de Schonen.

133    and fight in Lorraine: La Rochefoucauld recording and *La Liberté*.

133    L'hôtel Wendel: Conversations with Yolaine de Schonen.

133    his mother's family built: Franck Beaumont, "L'hôtel Wendel en Photographies," *Evous*, December 12, 2011, http://www.evous.fr/La-saga-d -une-dynastie-industrielle-les-Wendel,1149214.html.

133    and began talking as if all this were normal: Conversations with Yolaine de Schonen.

133    Yolaine immediately noticed his beard and mustache: Ibid.

133    also announced he was no longer a boy: Ibid.

134    and thinking how surreal it was: La Rochefoucauld recording.

134    "such emotion": La Rochefoucauld, *La Liberté*.

134    He planned to contact his handlers: Ibid.

134    had even drawn up an itinerary: Ibid.

134   and left the room: Conversations with Yolaine de Schonen.

134   The doctor told Robert he had scabies: La Rochefoucauld, *La Liberté*.

134   where his parents came to see him: La Rochefoucauld recording and *La Liberté*.

135   thirty thousand borderline reprobates: Jackson, *France: The Dark Years*.

135   detained ten thousand Frenchmen: Delarue, *The Gestapo*.

135   Parisian Resistance group Prosper: Foot, *SOE in France*, has a good discussion of the destruction of that group.

135   Bernard de La Rochefoucauld: A good bio can be found on the website http://versainville.com/comte-versainville.html.

135   who was so hungry she tried to eat Yvonne: "France: The Aristocrats," *Time*, October 23, 1950.

135   The German heavyweight Max Schmeling: Mitchell, *Nazi Paris*.

136   the 10 p.m. curfew: Ibid. The curfew varied at times, but Mitchell writes that a 10 p.m. curfew was imposed in 1943 for Parisian theaters, concert halls, cinemas, restaurants, and nightclubs. There were occasional exceptions on the weekend.

136   "charming" but remote: La Rochefoucauld, *La Liberté*.

136   whom they all called, simply, "monsieur": Ibid.

136   trimming a few hedges: Ibid.

136   and headed out: Ibid.

136   "and France in particular": Nicolson, *Aristide*.

136   getting fast boats to safe beaches: Foot, *SOE in France*.

137   120 missions: Brooks Richards, *Secret Flotillas*, Vol. 1: *Clandestine Sea Operations to Brittany, 1940–1944* (London: Government Official History Series, 2004).

137   top-secret British records: Ibid., and Richards, *Secret Flotillas*, includes appendixes and notes from formerly classified documents. These proved far more helpful than even this wonderful book.

137   in April 1944: I also called the Royal Navy's press office and spoke with a representative who deals with historic facts. He confirmed this.

137   by motor gunboat: Ibid.

137   The fog of war was at its densest here: I say this because, in *La Liberté*,

Robert remembered taking off from Calais. But his French military records offer no point of debarkation for any return trip to England. Those military records were composed decades before La Rochefoucauld wrote his memoir, so I'm inclined to believe Robert was confused or didn't remember his date of departure or from where he departed.

137  "that of my passage into Spain": La Rochefoucauld, *La Liberté.*

137  according to British records: Richards, *Secret Flotillas.*

137  Atlantic Wall: Malise Ruthven, "Hitler's Monumental Miscalculation," *New York Review of Books* Daily Blog, June 5, 2014, http://www .nybooks.com/daily/2014/06/05/hitlers-mighty-miscalculation/.

137  The wall itself was a three-thousand-mile collection: "Nazi Megastructures," *National Geographic Channel,* http://www.natgeotv.com /uk/nazi-megastructures/facts.

137  Jean-Jacques: La Rochefoucauld, *La Liberté.*

138  about a half mile from the ocean: Ibid.

138  the operation was on: Ibid., and Richards, *Secret Flotillas.*

138  But they received no response: Ibid.

138  Motor Gun Boat 502: Richards, *Secret Flotillas.*

138  La Rochefoucauld and the other men: Ibid.

138  British records indicated roughly twenty people: Ibid.

138  "There was a brusque change": La Rochefoucauld, *La Liberté.*

139  mixed tea and whiskey: Ibid.

139  came under heavy German fire: Richards, *Secret Flotillas.*

139  "I'd never been so scared in my life": La Rochefoucauld, *La Liberté.*

139  the Brits never actually opened fire: Richards, *Secret Flotillas.*

139  a young sailor: Ibid.

## CHAPTER 14

141  The first thing they did: La Rochefoucauld, *La Liberté.*

141  "gave us a royal welcome": La Rochefoucauld recording.

141  no longer worked in London: Piquet-Wicks's SOE files, National Archives, London.

141  than his diagnosis of TB: Ibid.

141  relinquished his commission: Ibid.

141  doctors ordered him to work: Ibid.

141  "the worse for drink": Ibid.

142  75,000 French Resistance fighters: Foot, *SOE in France.*

142  "To them, I looked like a ghost": La Rochefoucauld, *La Liberté.*

142  "women fell into our arms!": Ibid.

142  "Hope was prevailing": Ibid.

142  "The hope of a victory": Ibid.

142  One day he was called to meet: Ibid.

143  5,500 laborers: Claude Courau, *Les Poudriers dans La Résistance: Saint-Médard-en-Jalles (1940–1944)* (Editions des régionalismes & PRNG éditions, 2013).

143  suburban Bordelais real estate: Ibid.

143  seventy-three British planes dropped 268 tons of bombs: RAF records, National Archives, London.

143  fires that burned: Ibid.

143  the Germans had large parts of the works: Hervé Pons, "Souvenirs de deux guerres," *Sudouest,* March 15, 2013, http://www.sudouest.fr /2013/03/15/souvenirs-de-deux-guerres-994938-3145.php. Courau, *Les Poudriers,* also shows how the works was operational a short time after the British bombing.

143  the Saint-Médard job: La Rochefoucauld's military records, Ministry of Defense, Paris and Pau.

143  reacquaint himself with the nuances: La Rochefoucauld recording.

## CHAPTER 15

145  On May 7: The chronology of La Rochefoucauld's military records differs from the narrative of his memoir. The records indicated he likely worked for the group Léon des Landes first in the Bordeaux region; La Rochefoucauld remembered, fifty years after the fact, aligning himself with Léon later in the summer of 1944. Because his military records

were composed somewhere between three to ten years after the end
of the war, I'm following the chronology that emerges there. On May
7, Léon received a massive air drop of ammo and men, according to its
records, found in the Ministry of Defense in Paris and in departmental
archives in Bordeaux.

145  take a nap: La Rochefoucauld, *La Liberté*. For personal recollections
about that spring and summer, I'm turning to the La Rochefoucauld
recording and family DVD. La Rochefoucauld's military records, like
almost all French military records, are incredibly terse and devoid of
personal anecdotes.

145  ninety miles south: Léon des Landes records.

145  "during those tense hours": La Rochefoucauld, *La Liberté*.

145  in Saint-Médard operating: Pons, "Souvenirs de deux guerres."

145  its output had armed the French: Courau, *Les Poudriers*.

145  a significant U-boat base: Nicolson, *Aristide*.

145  since August 1940: Delarue, *The Gestapo,* and Moorehead, *A Train in Winter.*

145  "a cemetery of the finest fighters": Moorehead, *A Train in Winter.*

145  for the Nazis across southwest France: Ashdown, *A Brilliant Little Operation.* Hans Luther was the nominal head of power in Bordeaux, but
as Ashdown makes clear, among others, Dohse was the real source of
power.

146  thirty-one in the spring of 1944: Moorehead, *A Train in Winter.*

146  Dohse spoke fluent French: Dominique Lormier, *Bordeaux Brûle-
t-il? ou, La Libération de la Gironde: 1940–1945* (Bordeaux: Les Dossiers
d'Aquitaine, 1998).

146  "He was an evil man": Around the time of the trial of Maurice Papon,
some of his defenders created a website that attempted to contextu-
alize what the Occupation was like. Hubert de Beaufort was one of
those defenders. His interview with people who knew Dohse directly
or knew of him can be found at http://livreblanc.maurice-papon.net
/saufr-terri.htm.

146  the reclaimed marshes: Nicolson, *Aristide*.

146  The surrounding hills scrambled: Ibid.

146  in a town called Mugron: Léon des Landes records.

146  He waited: La Rochefoucauld recording and *La Liberté*.

146  sprained his ankle: La Rochefoucauld, *La Liberte*. Robert seems to
not accurately recall the name of the group he worked with first in
the Aquitaine, because in the memoir he says it was Bayard, which is
wrong, while his military records suggest it was Léon des Landes. So
I have decided to blend these sources. I am attributing the thoughts
and on occasion the actions to Robert's memoir and recording, while
following his military records for the chronology of when he worked
for whom.

147  Léonce Dussarrat: Dussarrat military records, Léon des Landes
file, and the Bordeaux region's Museum of the Resistance, http://
museedelaresistanceenligne.org/media.php?media=4252&popin=true.

147  What followed is a bit unclear: http://museedelaresistanceenligne
.org/media.php?media=4252&popin=true.

148  growing to an estimated five thousand: The group's membership
over time is spelled out in its military records and also here, http://
histoiresocialedeslandes.fr/p5_liberation.asp.

148  Landes's fourth in three weeks: Léon des Landes records.

148  an underground cable: Ibid.

148  a second band of *résistants* about a sabotage: La Rochefoucauld recording and *La Liberté*.

148  75,000 men in country: Foot, *SOE in France*.

149  to 794 in the second: Mackenzie, *The Secret History of SOE*.

149  and 108 channels: Ibid.

149  which attempted to coordinate: Koenig's role is spelled out in many
books. Here I relied on Nicolson, *Aristide*.

149  disemboweled: Cobb, *The Resistance*.

149  "We fell upon some Germans": La Rochefoucauld recording.

149  a sort of mini-Kommandatur: La Rochefoucauld, *La Liberté*.

149  "I was convinced": Ibid.

149  and the French not wanting to answer: La Rochefoucauld recording
and *La Liberté*.

150  and 160,000 Allied soldiers: See U.S. Army, https://www.army.mil/d-day/.

151  at a command post outside Nanoose: Léon des Landes military records.

151  more than two hundred: Ibid.

151  the golden rule of irregular warfare: Foot, *SOE in France*.

151  up to a thousand sabotages on June 6 and the day after: Foot, *SOE in France*.

151  90 percent of the German army: Ibid.

151  It took two weeks: Ibid.

151  "final victory": Stephen E. Ambrose, *Ike's Spies: Eisenhower and the Espionage Establishment* (New York: Knopf Doubleday, 2012).

151  fifteen extra divisions: Thomas W. Zeller and Daniel M. DuBois, eds., *A Companion to World War II* (Hoboken, NJ: John Wiley & Sons, 2012).

## CHAPTER 16

153  Charly: Charly's military records, Ministry of Defense, Paris.

153  nearly 950 fighters: Ibid.

153  with a parent group, Groupe Georges: Resistance hierarchy records found at the Ministry of Defense, Paris. Here again I placed an emphasis on what the military records say. Robert in his memoir remembers fighting alongside a fighter named Bayard, who led a Resistance cell. But there was no Bayard in the Bordeaux area. I am assuming when he wrote Bayard fifty years after the war, he perhaps meant Bordes, for Alban Bordes. What is unequivocal is that La Rochefoucauld's military records show the groups that he fought among also partnered with Bordes's group, Groupe Georges, in the summer of 1944.

153  that "God himself cannot pardon": An associate of Bordes's, who recounted conversations after the war and published them online at http://www.cesgoysquidefendentisrael.com/fr/conflit-israelo-arabe/terrorisme-ou-resistance/.

153  This was in a group safe house: La Rochefoucauld recording and *La Liberté*. The following discussion is informed by these sources.

154 The munition works was massive: Carau, *Les Poudriers*.

154 The massive bombing campaign: RAF records, National Archives, London.

154 As the British sabotage instructors: This is largely a reflection of George T. Rheam's teachings, as found in Foot, *SOE in France*.

155 A man named Pierre: La Rochefoucauld recording and *La Liberté*. The following discussion is informed by these sources.

155 La Rochefoucauld arose early: Ibid.

156 The Nazis had hired a French firm: Courau, *Les Poudriers*.

157 Because of the Germans' lax oversight: La Rochefoucauld recording and *La Liberté*, and La Rochefoucauld family DVD. These sources inform the following discussion.

159 22,000 feet per second: To get a sense of the sabotage materiel used during World War II, I spoke with an explosives expert at the CIA. To better understand how quickly those explosives might burn, I spoke with Col. Christopher Benson, an engineering and explosives expert in the U.S. Army. I am deeply appreciative of the time they gave me.

159 When he had cased everything: La Rochefoucauld recording and *La Liberté*. The rest of the chapter is informed by these sources.

## CHAPTER 17

161 the dusty throbbing particular to the overserved: La Rochefoucauld recording and *La Liberté*.

161 water mains and conduits leveled: Nicolson, *Aristide*, appendix, and confidential report by former SOE member Maj. R. A. Bourne-Patterson, "The 'British' Circuits in France 1941–1944," Imperial War Museum, London. The attack at Saint-Médard carried out by Groupe Georges is included within this report.

161 According to two subsequent British reports: Ibid.

161 British bombing campaign: Pons, "Souvenirs de deux guerres."

161 found the limbs of their livestock: See RAF records of the April bombing campaign. Also Carau, *Les Poudriers*.

161 Everyone assumed the streets: La Rochefoucauld recording and *La Liberté*. The following discussion is informed by these sources.

162 the worst civilian massacre: Cobb, *The Resistance*.

162 their makeshift hospital: Ibid.

162 dismembering men: Conversations with Constance Guillaumin.

162 the seminarian he'd once been: Moorehead, *A Train in Winter*.

162 in reprisal: Ibid., and Gildea, *Marianne in Chains*.

163 "massacred": Moorehead, *A Train in Winter*.

163 member 192: Ibid.

163 and had executed 285 people: Michael Curtis, *Verdict on Vichy: Power and Prejudice in the Vichy France Regime* (New York: Arcade, 2002).

163 fewer than twenty men under him: Hubert de Beaufort interviews.

163 Brigade of Killers: Moorehead, *A Train in Winter*.

163 he saw no one: La Rochefoucauld recording and *La Liberté*. These sources and the family DVD inform the rest of the chapter.

## CHAPTER 18

165 in 1453: Nicolas Faucherre, "Le château Trompette et le fort du Hâ, citadelles de Charles VII contre Bordeaux," *Revue archéologique de Bordeaux*, No. XCII (2001). Also "Un mystérieux édifice bordelais, Le fort du Hâ, palais devenu prison . . ." *Bordeaux Gazette* (May 29, 2015), http://www.bordeaux-gazette.com/Un-mysterieux-edifice-bordelais -Le.html.

165 three-story towers: Jean-Jacques Déogracias, *Le Fort du Hâ de Bordeaux: Un palais, une prison, un fabuleux destin* (Bordeaux: Les Dossiers d'Aquitaine, 2006).

165 penal infrastructures in Pennsylvania: http://www.restaurantadmin istratifduha.info/cuisine/0453459aa00c3c904/index.php.

165 but separated into small cells: Historical Society of Pennsylvania, *Pennsylvania Prison Society Records*, Collection 1946 (2006), and found online at http://hsp.org/sites/default/files/legacy_files/migrated/findingaid 1946prisonsociety.pdf.

165 Fort du Hâ's reputation: La Rochefoucauld recording and his testimony during the Papon trial.

165 in French, German, and Spanish: M.-R. Bordes, *Quartier Allemand: La Vie au Fort du Hâ sous l'occupation* (Bordeaux: Éditions Bière, 1945).

166 he was there by mistake: La Rochefoucauld recording.

166 no more romantic than the soldiers: Ibid., and *La Liberté*.

166 They then counted the money: Bordes's *Quartier Allemand*, Ibid. Bordes said every prisoner went through this protocol, and though Robert doesn't describe it, I assigned these actions to the guards that greeted him because Bordes says that's how they treated every new arrival.

166 or the French Forces of the Interior: Ibid.

166 La Rochefoucauld's military records made clear: Robert de La Rochefoucauld's military records.

166 save his pleas: La Rochefoucauld recording.

166 He was born in 1913: Lormier, *Bordeaux Brûle-t-il?*

166 Dohse questioned *résistants*: Hubert de Beaufort interviews. This one in particular is helpful: http://livreblanc.maurice-papon.net/chap1 -suite.htm.

166 taught French: Ibid., and Moorehead, *A Train in Winter*.

167 a slight frame and easy smile: Resistance blog, *La Loupe*, http://la-loupe .over-blog.net/article-dohse-friedrich-122136595.html.

167 Though he dressed well: Ashdown, *A Brilliant Little Operation*.

167 a bulbous forehead: *La Loupe*.

167 Schutzstaffel, or SS: Ibid.

167 for career advancement: Hubert de Beaufort interviews.

167 Internationale kriminalpolizeiliche Kommission: Steven Lehrer, *Wartime Spies in Paris: 1939–1945* (New York: SF Tafel, 2013).

167 he saw a kindred soul: Lormier, *Bordeaux Brûle-t-il?*

168 who lived on a yacht: Moorehead, *A Train in Winter*.

168 Dohse's encroachment: Ibid.

168 "loved me like his son": Lormier, *Bordeaux Brûle-t-il?*

168 Hans Luther: Moorehead, *A Train in Winter*.

168 the real head of power: Moorehead, *A Train in Winter*; Ashdown, *A Brilliant Little Operation*; Lormier, *Bordeaux Brûle-t-il?*

168 Luther far outranked him: Ashdown, *A Brilliant Little Operation*.

168 he wasn't even an officer: Ibid.

168 though he was later promoted: Ibid.

168 Luther was a captain: Hubert de Beaufort's interviews, and this one specifically: http://www.maurice-papon.net/documents/dohse.htm.

168 "terrorists" to be grilled by Dohse: Ashdown, *A Brilliant Little Operation*.

168 This annoyed Luther: Hubert de Beaufort's interviews.

169 forty thousand fighters at the ready: Nicolson, *Aristide*, and Lormier, *Bordeaux Brûle-t-il?*

169 134 British air drops: Nicolson, *Aristide*.

169 Resistance group, Prosper: Ibid., and Cobb, *The Resistance*.

169 address in Bordeaux: Ashdown, *A Brilliant Little Operation*, and Lormier, *Bordeaux Brûle-t-il?*

169 members' names and their addresses: Ibid., and Nicolson, *Aristide*.

169 Lucette Grandclément: Lormier's *Bordeaux Brûle-t-il?* She was André's second wife, and her arrest is what some scholars believed convinced André to work with Dohse.

169 the son of a French admiral: Ibid.

169 entering the army as a soldier: René Terisse, *Grandclément: Traître ou bouc-émissaire?* (Paris: Aubéron, 1996).

170 conservative ideology: Lormier, *Bordeaux Brûle-t-il?*

170 but the Communists, too: Ibid.

170 if Grandclément agreed to drop the fight: Ibid.; Terisse, *Grandclément*; Nicolson, *Aristide*.

171 and drew his automatic pistol: Nicolson, *Aristide*.

171 He did the deal with Dohse: Ibid., and Ashdown, *A Brilliant Little Operation*.

171 show two German officers *résistant* compounds: Lormier, *Bordeaux Brûle-t-il?*

172 even more effective than anyone: Ashdown, *A Brilliant Little Operation*.

172 Roger Landes: Nicolson, *Aristide*, and Lormier, *Bordeaux Brûle-t-il?*

172   Dohse began to arrest more French agents: Ashdown, *A Brilliant Little Operation*.

172   roughly 250 fighters: Ibid.

172   Landes had to leave the country: Nicolson, *Aristide*.

172   single-handedly wiped out the Resistance: Ibid., and Ashdown, *A Brilliant Little Operation*.

172   almost never wore a uniform: Ibid.

172   with his mistress: Lormier, *Bordeaux Brûle-t-il?*

172   secretly thought Hitler and the Nazis: Hubert de Beaufort interviews.

173   champagne and cognac: Ibid.

173   not as terrorists to be tortured: Ashdown, *A Brilliant Little Operation*, and Lormier, *Bordeaux Brûle-t-il?*

173   the humanity that was their right: Ashdown, *A Brilliant Little Operation*.

173   "a dangerous adversary": Ibid.

173   his careful interrogation: Nicolson, *Aristide*.

173   he brought in the brutes: Ashdown, *A Brilliant Little Operation*.

173   a new Resistance group, Actor: Nicolson, *Aristide*.

173   comprised two thousand men: Foot, *SOE in France*.

174   Dohse wanted to nab Landes: Ashdown, *A Brilliant Little Operation*.

174   were so small and secretive: Foot, *SOE in France*.

174   one of three colored cards: Bordes, *Quartier Allemand*.

174   no crime was more serious: Ibid.

174   its twelve holding chambers: Ibid.

174   "reception centers": Ibid.

174   "letting off a vile odor": Ibid.

175   light automatically shut off: Ibid.

175   French, Czech, Polish, Spanish, Portuguese: Ibid.

175   Could he endure more?: La Rochefoucauld recording and *La Liberté*.

175   "feeling at home in the world afterwards": Semprun, *Exercices de Survie*.

175   even if he couldn't verbalize it: La Rochefoucauld, *La Liberté*. This idea is borne out by how little he says of Auxerre and how he freely admits to wanting to kill himself in Bordeaux, because of what he'd endured under Dr. Haas.

175 *What a fool*, Robert thought: La Rochefoucauld recording. The following discussion is informed by the recording as well as La Rochefoucauld, *La Liberté*, and the family DVD.

178 five sectors that led to the infirmary: Bordes, *Quartier Allemand*.

178 passing cell doors with peepholes: Ibid.

179 The guards' quarters?: La Rochefoucauld recording, *La Liberté*, and the family DVD informed the rest of this chapter.

**CHAPTER 19**

181 needed to find the fighter: La Rochefoucauld recording, *La Liberté*, and the family DVD.

182 SOE heavy Roger Landes: Nicolson, *Aristide*.

182 "First, I'll go see him": La Rochefoucauld, *La Liberté*. The following discussion is informed by La Rochefoucauld recording, *La Liberté*, and the family DVD.

184 This was likely Ginette Corbin: Nicolson, *Aristide*.

184 Landes's Resistance group: Lormier, *Bordeaux Brûle-t-il?*

184 the woman coyly said: La Rochefoucauld recording and *La Liberté*. These sources, and the family DVD, informed the following discussion.

185 his Basque beret: Nicolson, *Aristide*, and Lormier, *Bordeaux Brûle-t-il?*

185 accidentally dropped a suitcase: Nicolson, *Aristide*.

185 too many loose-lipped friends: Ibid.

185 thought he was stationed in the Middle East: Ibid.

185 "Can I help you Sister?": La Rochefoucauld, *La Liberté*. The following discussion is informed by La Rochefoucauld recording and *La Liberté*.

186 twenty-hour days that summer: Nicolson, *Aristide*.

186 the order to execute André Grandclément: Ibid., and Ashdown, *A Brilliant Little Operation*.

186 Landes was highly decorated: Nicolson, *Aristide*.

186 Robert said good-bye: La Rochefoucauld recording and *La Liberté*. The rest of the chapter is informed by these sources and the family DVD.

## CHAPTER 20

189   one hundred to the railways alone: Léon des Landes military records, and Phillippe Souleau, *La Ligne de Démarcation en Gironde: Occupation, Résistance et Société, 1940–1944* (Périgueux: Éditions Fanlac, 2003). The following discussion is informed by these sources.

190   nearly one thousand men: Charly's military records, Ministry of Defense, Paris.

190   fifteen years of hard labor: Charly's fate is spelled out in Courau, *Les Poudriers*.

190   seventy *résistants* raided: Charly's military records.

190   oversaw a small group of men: Robert de La Rochefoucauld's military records.

190   secretly warned them of a roundup: La Rochefoucauld's testimony at the Maurice Papon trial.

190   "simultaneously intense and limited": La Rochefoucauld, *La Liberté*. The rest of this section is informed by La Rouchefoucauld recording and *La Liberté*.

191   refused their patrols: Cobb, *The Resistance,* notes how the French police state in Paris was virtually nonexistent.

191   35,000 FFI fighters: Foot, *SOE in France.*

191   Gen. Jacques Leclerc's Second Armored Division: Many books recount the fight for Paris. Cobb, *The Resistance,* offers a good synopsis.

191   Hitler's order to blow up the Eiffel Tower: Ibid.

192   Ernest Hemingway: Foot, *SOE in France,* gives the heroic portrayal of Papa returning enemy fire. But many news sources have since laid out another scenario: That Hemingway drank the afternoon away in the Ritz bar, because the Germans had already left. The Paris website *The Local* gives a good account of what actually happened. http://www .thelocal.fr/20140822/whcn-hemingway-took-back-the-ritz-bar.

192   "Paris!": Cobb, *The Resistance.* De Gaulle's speech has been widely reprinted.

192   "whose destiny does not seem likely to be a nunnery": Peter Mat-

thews, *House of Spies: St. Ermin's Hotel, the London Base of British Espionage* (Stroud, UK: The History Press, 2016).

192 Western armies had lost 500,000 men: Shirer, *The Rise and Fall of the Third Reich*.

192 made a bonfire on the streets: The liberation of Bordeaux and photos from that day can be found on the website of the Musée d'Aquitaine: http://www.musee-aquitaine-bordeaux.fr/fr/evenement/exposition -la-liberation-de-bordeaux.

192 "and crossed the same squares": La Rochefoucauld, *La Liberté*.

193 *Napthalenes*: Nicolson, *Aristide*.

193 the people of Maillé: Cobb, *The Resistance*.

193 124 people in all: Ibid.

193 "A punishment for terrorists": Lizzy Davies, "64 Years after Massacre, Villagers of Maillé May Get Some Answers at Last," *The Guardian*, July 15, 2008, https://www.theguardian.com/world/2008/jul/16/second worldwar.france.

193 felt only savagery and oppression: Cobb, *The Resistance*.

193 guerrillas became de facto mayors: Ibid., and Jackson, *France: The Dark Years*.

194 miniature coffins: Jackson, *France: The Dark Years*.

194 "like feudal lords": Ibid. Cobb, *The Resistance,* is also fantastic on the purges.

194 French killed in the purges: Cobb, *The Resistance*.

194 had their heads shaved: Ibid.

194 "proud when you compare them": Ibid.

194 "lofty coldness": Jackson, *France: The Dark Years*.

194 the role the Resistance played: Ibid.

194 de Gaulle told the SOE boss Roger Landes: Foot, *SOE in France*.

195 reserve officers' school in Bordeaux: Robert La Rochefoucauld military records.

195 "natural sense of command": Ibid.

195 "Will be an excellent reserve officer": Ibid.

195 "very 'cavalier'": Ibid.

195 "combat that I'd acquired myself": La Rochefoucauld, *La Liberté.*

## CHAPTER 21

197 as many as nine thousand soldiers: *France Histoire,* chronicled the local fight in the fall of 1944 through 1945: http://www.france-histoire
-esperance.com/poche-de-royan-et-pointe-de-grave/.

197 no fewer than 218 casemates: Ibid.

197 280-millimeter guns: Ibid.

197 "pockets": Ashdown, *A Brilliant Little Operation.*

197 long lines of nasty fortifications: Malise Ruthven, "Hitler's Monumental Miscalculation," *NYR Daily,* June 5, 2014, http://www.nybooks
.com/daily/2014/06/05/hitlers-mighty-miscalculation/.

197 210,000 mines in Royan alone: http://www.france-histoire-esperance
.com/poche-de-royan-et-pointe-de-grave/.

197 an impressive defense for its submarine bases: Ashdown, *A Brilliant
Little Operation.* The Germans called it impregnable, in fact.

197 These nine thousand Germans: Some accounts placed it higher: at ten
thousand or as high as sixteen thousand troops. Ashdown, *A Brilliant
Little Operation,* has the higher figure.

198 forced eight thousand: Royan's municipal website has a good page ded-
icated to what happened toward the end of the war: http://www.ville
-royan.fr/index.php?option=com_content&view=article&id=219&Itemid
=562.

198 Edgard de Larminat: http://www.france-histoire-esperance.com
/poche-de-royan-et-pointe-de-grave/.

198 with a hierarchy of command: Royan and FFGR military records,
Ministry of Defense, Paris.

198 nearly twenty-four thousand soldiers: Ibid.

198 Col. Jean de Milleret: Robert de La Rochefoucauld and FFGR's military records.

198 not far from Saint-Vivien-de-Médoc: La Rochefoucauld, *La Liberté*.

199 Christmas Day 1944: http://www.france-histoire-esperance.com /poche-de-royan-et-pointe-de-grave/.

199 250,000 German troops: http://www.history.com/this-day-in -history/battle-of-the-bulge.

199 Soldiers in clogs: http://www.ville-royan.fr/index.php?option=com _content&view=article&id=219&Itemid=562.

199 oversaw his troops' parachute training: Robert de La Rochefoucauld's military records.

199 a nom de guerre for him, Maxim: La Rochefoucauld, *La Liberté*.

200 a fleet of 350 British planes: Howard Zinn, *The Zinn Reader: Writings on Disobedience and Democracy* (New York: Seven Stories Press, 1997).

200 killing 442 civilians: Ibid.

200 "I do not have the least desire": La Rochefoucauld recording.

200 no adequate explanation: Zinn, *The Zinn Reader*. Zinn gets somewhat angry recounting all this.

200 Forgotten French Forces: http://www.ville-royan.fr/index.php ?option=com_content&view=article&id=219&Itemid=562.

200 planning for this mission began: FFGR military records.

200 "So I stated my name": La Rochefoucauld, *La Liberté*.

201 "burst out laughing": Ibid.

201 detailed by the twenty-second: FFGR and Point de Grave military records, Ministry of Defense, Paris.

201 "badgered the enemy on its lines": La Rochefoucauld, *La Liberté*.

201 "precious information on enemy terrain": FFGR military records.

201 Operation Venerable: http://www.ville-royan.fr/index.php?option =com_content&view=article&id=219&Itemid=562.

202 "460,000 gallons of liquid fire": Zinn, *The Zinn Reader*.

202 a viscous fiery gel: Robert M. Neer, *Napalm: An American Biography* (Cambridge: Belknap Press, 2015).

202 "a fantastic concentration of fire": Zinn, *The Zinn Reader*.

202  "under ceaseless fire": La Rochefoucauld, *La Liberté*. The rest of the chapter is informed by *La Liberté*, La Rochefoucauld recording and family DVD, and La Rochefoucauld's military records.

## CHAPTER 22

209  "seized with rage": La Rochefoucauld, *La Liberté*. This paragraph is also informed by the La Rochefoucauld recording.

209  the battle for liberation: Zinn, *The Zinn Reader*.

209  consoled themselves with horoscopes: Shirer, *The Rise and Fall of the Third Reich*.

209  "would have been more logical": Zinn, *The Zinn Reader*.

209  "l'aspect moral": Ibid.

210  an estimate of civilians killed or wounded: Ibid.

210  "of continuing the fight": La Rochefoucauld, *La Liberté*.

210  "at the forefront of the squadron": Robert de La Rochefoucauld's military records.

210  released him from their care: La Rochefoucauld recording. The rest of the chapter is influenced by the recording, *La Liberté*, the family DVD, and Robert's military records.

## EPILOGUE

213  so many evenings in Robert's life: Conversations with La Rochefoucauld children, in particular Constance Guillaumin.

213  just after their marriage in 1955: Constance Guillaumin directed me to her parents' marriage certificate.

213  Pont Chevron: Constance Guillaumin gave me a tour of the house, and I also spoke with Jean de La Rochefoucauld, Robert's son, who rents out some of the rooms.

213  four adult children, seven grandchildren: Conversations with Constance Guillaumin.

214    still a striking blond: Robert's children shared with me many photos of their parents.

214    "What's going on?": La Rochefoucauld recording.

214    didn't describe the images: Ibid. His children said Robert never spoke about what he endured and how it troubled him—not until his last confession with Constance Guillaumin.

214    like something out of another century: Photos of the Legion of Honor event, which the family shared with me.

214    in the same social spheres: La Rochefoucauld recording, and conversations with La Rochefoucauld children.

214    four other commendations: La Rochefoucauld military records. The medals are kept by La Rochefoucauld's daughter Constance Guillaumin.

215    official government statement: Grande Chancellerie de la Légion d'Honneur, Paris.

215    left breast pocket of La Rochefoucauld's jacket: Photos of the event, courtesy of the family.

215    *résistants* who died alongside him: Conversations with Constance Guillaumin.

215    he'd only shared fragments: Conversations with La Rochefoucauld children.

216    met Papon in the 1960s: La Rochefoucauld testimony, Papon trial. Also conversations with the La Rochefoucauld family.

216    he would ultimately serve: Douglas Johnson, "Maurice Papon," *The Guardian*, February 18, 2007, https://www.theguardian.com/news/2007/feb/19/guardianobituaries.france.

216    began discussing the war: La Rochefoucauld testimony, Papon trial.

216    "There's no mystery to it": Ibid.

217    no longer believed that the documents he'd found: Johnson, "Maurice Papon."

217    Robert met with the lawyers: Conversations with François Vuillemin, Papon's lawyer.

217    in 1998: La Rochefoucauld testimony, Papon trial.

217 "I left for England in 1942": Ibid. The following discussion is informed by La Rochefoucauld's testimony.

218 the young man who spit on him: Conversations with Constance Guillaumin.

218 an eternal France: La Rochefoucauld, *La Liberté*.

218 "and even the end of another era": Ibid.

218 Charles de Gaulle had perpetuated the myth: Jackson, *France: The Dark Years;* conversations with scholars like Claude Delasselle, and other Resistance scholars in Paris; Papon trial coverage, in English and French; and *The Sorrow and The Pity* (1969), which changed perceptions of the Occupation in France.

219 "an orgy of collective repentance": Jackson, *France: The Dark Years.*

219 "his trial acted as a kind of proxy": Ibid.

219 sentenced to ten years: Craig R. Whitney, "Ex-Vichy Aide Is Convicted and Reaction Ranges Wide," *New York Times*, April 3, 1998, http://www.nytimes.com/1998/04/03/world/ex-vichy-aide-is-convicted-and-reaction-ranges-wide.html.

219 Robert secretly gave Papon his passport: La Rochefoucauld recording and *La Liberté* say surprisingly little about this, perhaps because with the passage of time La Rochefoucauld grew contrite. In the moment, however, during two television interviews, he was far more bullish. TF1 broadcast, October 25, 1999; and Third Channel France broadcast, October 24, 1999.

220 "I lent him my passport": TF1 broadcast.

220 "I was terribly scared": Third Channel France broadcast.

220 "Whatever they say": Ibid.

220 Swiss authorities extradited Papon: Jon Henley and Peter Capella, "Swiss Extradite Nazi Collaborator Papon," October 22, 1999, *The Guardian*, https://www.theguardian.com/world/1999/oct/23/jonhenley.

220 served his sentence in Fresnes: Robert O. Paxton, "The Trial of Maurice Papon," *New York Review of Books*, December 16, 1999, http://www.nybooks.com/articles/1999/12/16/the-trial-of-maurice-papon/.

220 overturned the French court's ruling: Whitney, "Maurice Papon, Convicted Vichy Official, Dies at 96."

220 ignored by the press: Conversations with La Rochefoucauld family members.

221 Diagnosed with Alzheimer's: Conversations with Constance Guillaumin.

# ABOUT THE AUTHOR

**PAUL KIX** is a deputy editor at *ESPN The Magazine*. His work has appeared in the *New Yorker*, *GQ*, *New York Magazine*, *Men's Journal*, and the *Wall Street Journal*. He lives in Connecticut, with his wife and children.